UNDERSTANDING
U.S. HUMAN
RIGHTS POLICY

UNDERSTANDING U.S. HUMAN RIGHTS POLICY

A Paradoxical Legacy

Clair Apodaca

R Routledge
Taylor & Francis Group
New York   London

Routledge is an imprint of the
Taylor & Francis Group, an informa business

Published in 2006 by
Routledge
Taylor & Francis Group
270 Madison Avenue
New York, NY 10016

Published in Great Britain by
Routledge
Taylor & Francis Group
2 Park Square
Milton Park, Abingdon
Oxon OX14 4RN

Printed in the United States of America on acid-free paper
10 9 8 7 6 5 4 3 2 1

International Standard Book Number-10: 0-415-95423-1 (Softcover)
International Standard Book Number-13: 978-0-415-95423-5 (Softcover)
Library of Congress Card Number 2006008695

Library of Congress Cataloging-in-Publication Data

Apodaca, Clair, 1956-
    Understanding U.S. human rights policy : a paradoxical legacy / Clair Apodaca.
        p. cm.
    Includes bibliographical references and index.
    ISBN 0-415-95422-3 (hardcover : alk. paper) -- ISBN 0-415-95423-1 (pbk. : alk. paper)
    1. Human rights--United States--History. 2. United States--Foreign relations--20th century. 3. United States--Foreign relations--2001- 4. United States--Politics and government--20th century. 5. United States--Politics and government--2001- I. Title: Understanding US Human rights policy. II. Title.

JC599.U5A75 2006
323.0973--dc22
                                           2006008695

This book is dedicated to my husband and colleague,
François Debrix, the man who has diligently read every
word I have ever put to paper and loves me nonetheless.

CONTENTS

ACKNOWLEDGMENTS

There are several people to whom I owe a debt of thanks for their support, suggestions, and advice when I took up this project. First, and foremost, I would like to thank François Debrix for his constant encouragement and, when needed, prodding in the writing of *Understanding U.S. Human Rights Policy: A Paradoxical Legacy*. I would also like to thank Michael Stohl for igniting my intellectual interest and guiding my study in human rights policy. A thank you goes to Nick Onuf, Patricia Price, and Cindy Weber for their sage advice. And among my colleagues in the profession who provided direction throughout my career are David Cingranelli, Mark Gibney, T. David Mason, Julie Mertus, Eric Neumayer, and Steven Poe. I would also like to acknowledge Robert Tempio, my editor, for his tireless support of my work.

INTRODUCTION

The Paradoxes of U.S. Human Rights Policy

The history of U.S. human rights policy is a series of different paradoxes that change depending on the presidential administration. Far from paralyzing the development of U.S. human rights policy, these paradoxes move the policy forward and give it its meaning and importance. U.S. human rights policy is the outcome of the intricate power struggle, inconsistencies, and contradictions between the major actors in the foreign policy decision-making process. Understanding *U.S. Human Rights Policy: A Paradoxical Legacy* examines the erratic evolution of U.S. human rights policy, often the product of the conflict and cooperation among the major foreign policy makers, with particular attention being paid to the tensions between presidential preferences and unfolding political events, and to the allocation of U.S. economic and military foreign aid. The allocation of foreign aid is influenced by the evolving, continuing, and paradoxical values, ideals, and beliefs of the various policy makers.

The U.S. Constitution protects the integrity of the American political system with a system of checks and balances. Congress and the Executive share powers in the making of U.S. foreign policy. This ostensibly prudent allocation of power conceals the power struggle that takes place between the executive and the legislative branches of the U.S. government in the making of foreign policy. The constitutional grant of overlapping powers between the Executive and Congress has been called "an invitation to struggle for the privilege of directing American foreign policy" (Corwin 1957, 171). This constitutionally imposed struggle in foreign policy making is made more convoluted by the significant role played by other organized interests, such as the governmental bureaucracy, advocates, and nongovernmental interest groups (nongovernmental organizations, or NGOs).

The formulation and realization of American foreign policy involve many different actors. The four primary participants in the creation of U.S. human rights policy are the president, the U.S. Congress, the government bureaucracy, and the American public. Understanding the conceptual and practical debates in international relations theory, which underlie the foreign policy process in the American context, including the cooperative, conflictual, and often unpredictable methods of decision making, is a crucial point of departure. To this extent, the first chapter of this study, "The U.S. System of Foreign Policy Making," is dedicated to this matter. The United States' style of foreign policy combines notions of realism, idealism, and a unique sense of destiny.[1] America's practice of foreign policy is based on the opposition between idealist principles and the realist balance of power. The idealist segment of the United States' foreign policy making structure has always been concerned with the moral content of U.S. foreign policy. For proponents of idealism, the question of foreign policy ought not to be one of power and domination, but instead one of social justice and equality. By contrast, for the realists, foreign policy is dominated by the state's international struggle for power. In this view, foreign policy makers are rational actors and, under international conditions of anarchy and self-help, must be power maximizers to ensure national survival. Foreign aid, one of the many tools available to foreign policy decision makers, is an important instrument through which U.S. human rights policy is supposed to be established. Foreign aid fulfills both ideological needs: it promotes moral principles while preserving the national security of the United States. Foreign aid is a particularly powerful method of congressional control over the Executive's foreign policy behavior since the president is dependent on Congress to appropriate the funds. Congress can modify or terminate foreign aid programs by attaching rigid conditions, exhaustive stipulations, and meticulous specifications to the foreign assistance legislation. Thus, the inclusion of human rights into the Foreign Assistance Act of 1961 was a crucial procedure in Congress' effort to restrain presidential powers while acting as a salve to heal the conscience of the American public for the perceived immorality of U.S. foreign policy.

The policy process directly impacts the policy outcome. There is often a disparity between what Congress legislates or the president negotiates and the actual policy implementation. The bureaucracy has the ability to resist, reform, or remake unpopular legislation. Bureaucratic politics—the jostling and even rivalries among various agencies—has long characterized policy making and often frustrated the successful performance of U.S. foreign policy.

Understanding U.S. Human Rights Policy is intended to ground the international relations student and foreign policy practitioner in an understanding of the historical and political conflict and cooperation involved in the making and implementing of American human rights policy. Moreover, an understanding of the complex and convoluted historical record, along with an analysis of the formation of human rights policy, is vital to any reader interested in contemporary human rights issues. An interested and newly awakened American public concerned with the reports and accusations of U.S. violations will find the paradoxical nature of U.S. human rights policy revealing. The chronological approach of this book will provide the reader with the historical, social, and cultural context of the development and implementation of U.S. human rights policy.

After reviewing the theories and bureaucratic politics that affect much of U.S. human rights policy, the book then turns to an evaluation of the different paradoxes that can be associated with each presidential administration. Overall, as a concept and a practice, U.S. human rights policy represents one of the greatest paradoxes in the analysis of foreign policy. In chapter 2, "A Matter of Unintended Consequences: The Nixon and Ford Administrations," I show how the Nixon Administration had nothing but utter contempt for the concept of human rights. And yet, during Richard Nixon's tenure in office, human rights issues made great advances. In reaction to Nixon's "imperial presidency," Congress made sweeping reforms, legislating a reduction in presidential power. Congress passed human rights legislation in an attempt to regain its constitutionally authorized powers in the realm of foreign policy and to restrain the expanded power, and many would say immoral policies, of the Nixon presidency.

The first real changes in U.S. foreign policy during the Cold War era came during the Nixon Administration in the form of a détente with the communist bloc,[2] but also and more importantly with the U.S. Congress' imposition of human rights considerations in the allocation of foreign aid. The dissatisfaction of Congress with the executive branch's blatant disregard for human rights prompted congressional hearings in 1974, chaired by Representative Donald Fraser (D-MN), to examine and make recommendations for increasing the priority given to human rights by the United States. At the time, Congress enacted legislation linking foreign aid and trade benefits to the status of human rights in foreign countries.

The United States' human rights policy was undeniably shaped at this time, during the heat of political battle between President Nixon and Congress. U.S. human rights policy was not an intentionally planned strategy. The formation of U.S. human rights policy under Nixon was the unintended and paradoxical consequence of the conflict between Congress and the executive branch.

On the other hand, as will be demonstrated in chapter 3, "U.S. Human Rights Policy, the Unintended Victim: The Carter Administration," although Jimmy Carter was supposed to be the champion of human rights, due to the internal strife within the White House and the State Department during his term in office, the United States' human rights policy became the unintended victim of the disunity and power politics of the executive branch. The Carter Administration pledged to implement a foreign policy based on moral considerations. Yet, Carter's words of goodwill and moral conduct failed to be realized. President Carter's failed foreign policy was, in part, an outcome of the divisions and conflicts between the idealism of Secretary of State Cyrus Vance and the realism of National Security Advisor Zbigniew Brzezinski. The struggle for power between the secretary of state and the national security advisor, along with the organizational competition between the Department of State and the National Security Council staff over control of U.S. foreign policy, resulted in a human rights policy that was fragmented, inconsistent, and even contradictory. In addition, Carter's human rights policy was complicated by the bureaucratic infighting in the State Department and between the Bureau of Human Rights and Humanitarian Affairs and other agencies. Thus, during the Carter Administration, the U.S. human rights policy became the unintended victim of power politics and bureaucratic infighting.

Still, the concern for human rights did not come to an end when Carter left office, as is demonstrated in chapter 4, "The Contradictions of U.S. Human Rights Policy: The Reagan Administration." Upon inauguration, Ronald Reagan did endeavor to abandon what he believed was the idealistic, irrelevant, and impractical human rights policy of his predecessor. But human rights actually remained a core moral value which, at least in the abstract, the American public was still highly committed to. Consequently, despite the president's personal agenda, the issue of human rights in foreign policy had to be dealt with by the Reagan Administration. Subsequently, though, the Reagan Administration strategically planned to usurp the concept of human rights. The Reagan Administration redefined human rights very narrowly to exclusively mean democracy and anticommunism. Furthermore, Reagan appointed an ardent anticommunist (Elliot Abrams), not a human rights advocate, as the chief spokesman for U.S. human rights policy. The Bureau of Human Rights and Humanitarian Affairs was more a propagandist for anticommunism than a promoter of human rights. Human rights were to be put to the service of condemning the Soviet Union, and nothing more. The foreign policy process conflict, which during the Nixon Administration was situated between Congress and the Executive, and during the Carter Administration was within the executive branch itself, once again shifted back to the level of intractable tension between Congress and the Executive under Reagan. But the Reagan Administration, for the most part, simply ignored Congress' efforts to rein in the president's foreign policy adventures. However, Congress countered presidential maneuvers by earmarking entire foreign aid programs and legislating for itself veto power for reprogramming arrangements.

Interestingly, during the Reagan years, "human rights actually became more and more institutionalized in U.S. foreign policy" (Donnelly 1995, 239). Congress was committed to human rights or, at least, committed to maintaining congressional initiatives constraining executive prerogatives in foreign policy. The 1980s were also associated with a rise in pressure groups and NGOs concerned with human rights. Moreover, the State Department bureaucracy became more professional, developing exacting procedures and meticulous routines in collecting and reporting on country-specific human rights. Paradoxically, and contrary to Reagan's attempt to first abandon and then disingenuously redefine "human rights," human rights would become institutionalized in U.S. foreign policy making under his tenure.

Despite the end of the Cold War, the paradoxes of U.S. human rights policy would continue with the George Bush Sr. Administration. The next chapter, "Human Rights in the New World Order: The George H. W. Bush Administration," examines the continuation of U.S. human rights paradoxes under Bush Sr. With the collapse of the Soviet Union, and the United States' apparent victory over communism, human rights and democracy seemed assured. The end of the Cold War brought a new hope for peace and prosperity. Expectations were high. The erratic and vacillating progress in U.S. human rights policy in the previous administrations, advanced through different yet all equally defining paradoxes, led human rights activists, scholars, and policy makers to believe that human rights would now be put at the center of U.S. foreign policy initiatives. The paradoxes that were present in previous administrations, and that appeared to have been able to shape a tangible human rights policy, were now in a position to bear fruit. But this sense of euphoria was short-lived. Despite the unprecedented historical opportunity, the Bush Sr. Administration would bring a reversal of fortune in the recognition of the importance of human rights in U.S. foreign policy. For the hungry and violated, the "new world order" was similar to the Cold War era. George H. W. Bush actually put the United States on a path toward more human rights violations. And, the Bush Sr. Administration refused to recognize the growing humanitarian crises around the world. In the overly cautious words of the president, surrendering U.S. foreign policy to human rights considerations "wouldn't be prudent."

The defining paradox of the Clinton Administration, as will be established in chapter 6, "Selling Off Human Rights: The Clinton Administration," centered on Bill Clinton's use of idealist rhetoric and on his appointment of human rights advocates, which gave the impression that the president was willing to revive Carter's call for a moralistic foreign policy agenda. Indeed, Bill Clinton's initial foreign policy actions raised expectations that human rights would have a central place in the new administration's guiding principles. Campaigning for the presidency, Clinton reproached George Bush Sr. for his indifference to democracy and human rights in foreign policy considerations. Yet, it was Clinton who, while in office, failed to act during the Rwandan genocide and during the ethnic cleansing of Bosnia. Clinton's subsequent foreign policy decisions and his overall privileging of domestic economic issues, often to the detriment of human rights, soon dampened the rising expectations of the human rights community. Clinton's foreign policy was one that stressed trade expansion and the opening of foreign markets at the expense of human rights. Thus, the Clinton Administration exchanged human rights protections for American corporate donations. Furthermore, Congress, the primary source of human rights initiatives in previous decades, would now be a serious impediment to the implementation of U.S. human rights policy. The traditional foreign policy conflict between Congress and the president resumed with a vengeance during the Clinton tenure. The Republican majority of the 104th Congress confronted Clinton on nearly every foreign policy decision. Congress not only cut foreign aid but also passed legislation restricting Clinton's foreign policy options.

It would take the arrival to power of George W. Bush to resolve the paradoxes that had determined previous administrations' human rights policies. Chapter 7, "U.S. Human Rights Policy, the Calculated Victim:

The George W. Bush Administration," shows how the defiant and rebellious Congress, as well as the media, during the Clinton Administration quickly transformed into a group of deferent, timid lackeys during President George W. Bush's Administration. In the aftermath of the terrorist attacks of September 11, and with the acquiescence of Congress, President Bush issued a series of executive orders, introduced several pieces of legislation, and issued exemptions that, in effect, overtly victimized human rights guarantees, both domestically and internationally. Under Bush's leadership, with Congress now fully behind him, and with the media and many NGOs effectively silenced, human rights would become blatantly ignored, if not brazenly violated, by U.S. policy. The paradoxes that had helped to create a U.S. human rights policy under previous administrations were now not allowed to progress. Instead, no conflict, contradiction, or paradox was permitted in the era of a war against terror, and U.S. human rights policy became the calculated victim of Bush's campaign against evil. Bush's war on terror absolutely and violently eradicated U.S. human rights policy. Any progress in the evolution of U.S. human rights policy, often inconsistently and sometimes inadvertently, that had taken place toward making foreign policy actions more in line with morality and basic humanitarian considerations was turned back.

The use and abuse of U.S. foreign aid have been central to the Bush Administration's attempt to further the security interests of the United States. Bush has significantly increased U.S. military aid, and continues to contribute funding to an even greater number of states, many of which are known to be egregiously undemocratic and repressive. Since September 11, antiterrorism has replaced anticommunism or economic engagement as the primary rationale for granting U.S. bilateral foreign aid. In order to secure U.S. national interests in an increasingly unstable world, human rights critics and foreign policy realists argue that the United States has to temporarily abandon human rights considerations to pursue more urgent goals. However, abusive governments, in the long run, are thought to be unstable and dangerous because they lack popular support. When the United States sides with an abusive leader, the vileness of the tyrant's acts stains the United States' image. When the victims of human rights abuses overthrow the repressive regime, they may not be willing to deal with the United States if it supported the former regime. Or, more perilously for the United States, they may seek revenge for the abuses they suffered under the U.S.-backed tyrant.

Yet, there may be still one more paradox looming in the near future. Chapter 8, "Conclusion: Paradox Lost?" surveys contemporary world events to determine if the seeds for a final paradox, the global acceptance of international human rights standards, are present. In reaction to the United States' present foreign policy practice of unilateralism and rejection of international law and internationally recognized protections of human rights, human rights norms have in fact spread widely. Foreign governments, NGOs, and civil society now acknowledge human rights standards. There are signs of a global acceptance of human rights norms.

However, a domestic understanding among U.S. government leadership and the American public of the importance of human rights norms is still underdeveloped. U.S. political leaders have routinely dismissed, deferred, or rejected human rights issues, and the public is willing to sacrifice its liberties and ignore the human rights violations of strangers for the delusion of security. As this book shows, an effective and successful human rights policy depends, in large part, on conflict between Congress and the executive branch, and support by NGOs and the American public. Reestablishing human rights and morality in U.S. foreign policy may require the courage and tenacity of the 94th Congress (the Congress that reined in the imperial presidency of the Nixon Administration).

CHAPTER 1

The U.S. System of Foreign Policy Making

The struggle between Congress and the president over foreign policy will continue so long as the Constitution lasts.

Stephen Ambrose (1991)

The United States' foreign policy can be defined as the United States' behavior with regard to other states in the international arena to achieve its goals. The United States' approach to foreign policy is an unusual combination of realism, idealism, and a unique sense of destiny. Consequently, America's style of foreign policy is based on the tension between idealism's moral principles and the realist balance of power. Many Americans believe that the United States has a divine mission to spread liberty, democracy, and freedom across the globe. Because of the superiority of American culture and values, many Americans think, the United States is unparalleled among the world's nations. During the United States' isolationist periods, its Manifest Destiny was to lead by example. By establishing a democratic and just system, the United States would serve as a model to the rest of the world. During an era of active and energetic international engagement, the United States would lead through intervention, exerting, by force if necessary, its benign and benevolent influence on other nations. Woodrow Wilson summed up America's foreign policy spirit when he said, "God created the United States to show the way to the nations of the world how they shall walk in the paths of liberty" (as quoted in Murchland 2002). But, not satisfied to demonstrate by example, President Wilson sent American troops to occupy Haiti in 1915, the Dominican Republic in 1916, and Mexico periodically from 1914 to 1917.

THEORIES OF FOREIGN POLICY

Often in foreign policy, particularly foreign policy relating to human rights, political ideology seems to be a compelling determinant of government behavior. As stated earlier, the American style of foreign policy incorporates a curious mixture of realism and idealism. American cultural values shape United States' political institutions that ultimately influence foreign policy behavior. This is not simply a matter of ideological dispute between the American Left and the American Right. Obviously, the idealist segment of the United States has always been concerned with the moral content of U.S. foreign policy. For these people, the rationale of foreign policy ought not to be one of power and dominance, but rather of peace and cooperation. Interestingly, the religious right, or neoconservatives, are also concerned with balancing power politics with moral issues. For these right-wing conservatives, communism posed the greatest of evils and stood in direct contrast to America's moral values of democracy and liberty. Thus, the United States had a moral duty to combat Soviet communist expansion.

Idealism and Foreign Policy

Idealism is a theoretical perspective that assumes that states are capable of mutual aid and collaboration. Self-determination and democratic governments would assure international peace, social justice, and human rights. All people, idealists argue, hold a common interest in these values, and their representative governments will reflect these principles. By submitting states to the power of an international organization and the prudence of public will, security could be ensured, war averted, and a moral rational order would prevail. Foreign policy, for idealists, is generally one of cooperation and humanitarian concern. Morality and human rights according to idealist foreign policy are important not only because they represent the right thing to do, but also because these values reflect the true character of the nation and its people. From this theoretical perspective, foreign policy, in the case of the United States, must mirror the moral principles enshrined in the nation's political institutions and culture: freedom, justice, liberty, and equality.

From the beginning of the American Republic, the new nation believed that America had a special destiny; since it was the first democracy, America was morally superior to other nations. Therefore, the United States had a responsibility, perhaps a divine mission, to lead the world by example and inspiration toward freedom, liberty, and justice. Thomas

Jefferson described this noble inspiration of the United States for the world in the following words:

> [T]he solitary republic of the world, the only monument of human rights . . . the sole depositary of the sacred fire of freedom and self-government, from hence it is to be lighted up in other regions of the earth, if other regions shall ever become susceptible of its benign influence. (As quoted in Tucker and Hendrickson 1990, 136)

The United States was to be a living ideal, the "shining city on the hill," "holding the beacon of liberty" to cheer the hearts of the downtrodden and repressed all over the world. When the country was young, this sense of destiny and American exceptionalism initially manifested itself in the rejection of the dirty politics and secret diplomatic maneuvers of the European powers. If the United States was to be the shining city on the hill holding up the torch of liberty, it would have to remain isolated from the affairs of Europe. Although the United States sought commercial exchange with Europe, the United States refused to become embroiled in the politics and conflicts of the old continent. Indeed, the United States' desire for isolationism would impede the impulse to become involved in world conflict. However, this desire for isolationism would later evolve into a perceived duty to provide global leadership. The United States, true to its idealistic character, would also feel the need to emancipate the weak and oppressed from tyranny. In periods of active and energetic international engagement, and given the United States' sense of destiny, U.S. foreign policy has often run the risk of becoming an ideological crusade between good versus evil, right versus wrong, freedom versus repression, and liberty versus subjugation. The idealist foreign policy of President Jimmy Carter, for example, attempted to incorporate moral principles, ethics, and human rights into U.S. foreign policy. These values, in the opinion of Carter, reflected the true character of the United States and the American people. Carter promised to return America's foreign policy to the path of righteousness, vowing never to do anything that would dishonor America's moral nature and Wilsonian past. President Bill Clinton, a liberal internationalist, moved the ethereal principles of idealism into a more tangible paradigm of democratic enlargement and open markets through the use of international institutions and multilateral action.

Another idealist legacy of foreign policy is the idea of foreign aid. From an idealist perspective, the granting of foreign aid serves basic humanitarian purposes: to eradicate poverty and hunger, to save the lives of children, and to improve the health of the poor. In idealist terms, foreign aid is not only the right thing to do but also our moral obligation. When President John F. Kennedy signed into law the Foreign Assistance Act (FAA) of 1961, he declared,

> The answer is that there is no escaping our obligations: our moral obligations as a wise leader and good neighbor in the interdependent community of free nations—our economic obligations as the wealthiest people in a world of largely poor people, as a nation no longer dependent upon the loans from abroad that once helped us develop our own economy—and our political obligations as the single largest counter to the adversaries of freedom. (Kennedy 1961)

Despite these altruistic motivations, idealists, like their realist counterparts, rely on the concept of self-interest when tying human rights to foreign policy. William Schulz (2001) argues that it is in the United States' own best interest to support and defend human rights around the world. Human rights are the foundation of not only economic prosperity but also true democracy and world peace. The statistical evidence on this issue is clear. Countries that respect human rights and protect democratic freedoms are less likely to become embroiled in violent civil conflict. They also tend to be more economically viable and politically stable, the very characteristics needed to attract direct foreign investment and trade (Apodaca 2001).

A moral foreign policy can prevent the United States from becoming allied with repressive governments that, in the long run, are unstable and dangerous because of their lack of popular support. President Kennedy was well aware of the fact that foreign assistance was in the best interest of the United States when he signed the FAA into law. Kennedy further stated,

> To fail to meet those obligations now would be disastrous; and, in the long run, more expensive. For widespread poverty and chaos lead to a collapse of existing political and social structures, which would inevitably invite the advance of totalitarianism into every weak and unstable area. Thus our own security would be endangered and our prosperity imperiled. A program of assistance to the underdeveloped nations must continue because the Nation's interest and the cause of political freedom require it. (1961)

Previous studies have supported this view that idealists represent a mixture of humanitarian concerns and self-interest in their beliefs about foreign policy issues. David Lumsdaine (1993), for example, found that humanitarian concerns were a primary motivation in the allocation of multilateral foreign aid. But the United States' rationale for contributing aid was a mix of humanitarian and strategic concerns.

Realism and Realpolitik

Although the United States' sense of destiny has held a sacrosanct position in international affairs since the birth of the nation, the Founding Fathers also understood the role of power politics and need for self-interest in foreign policy behavior.[1] Realism is a dominant theory of foreign policy. The principal assumption of realism is that the international system is characterized by anarchy. Because there is an absence of a strong governmental authority to maintain international order, a state must rely on its own resources and power to promote and protect its national interests. International relations is a struggle for power. The acquisition of power means the survival of the state. Self-interest, defined as power, must be a state's main goal. Nothing else, and particularly not morality, should stand in the way of power. Thus, universal moral principles cannot and must not guide state behavior (instead, power guides state behavior).

Often, though, the state may act morally, but only if it is in its national interest to do so. Sometimes, selfish acts may have moral implications too. Nevertheless, states are not moral agents. When states do claim to be acting on behalf of universal moral principles—human rights, democracy, and equality—they are in reality projecting their particular cultural views and codes on the rest of the world (Morgenthau 1949). Foreign policy is based on power and national interests, not on ideological or moral crusades. Morality, if it is to exist in foreign policy, is the product of power (Carr 1939). What is right, what is wrong, what is just, and what is unjust are determined by the values, beliefs, and, more importantly, the interests of the powerful. Common notions of justice and morality cannot be applied to states and their foreign relations. Therefore, leaders are permitted to undertake illegal or immoral acts if such acts enhance the power of the state.

George Kennan clearly believed, "Government is an agent, not a principal. Its primary obligation is to the interests of the national society it represents, not to the moral impulses that individual elements of that society may experience" (1985/1986, 206). Standards of moral conduct for the state at the international level are substantially different from those of an individual in society. Any attempt to formulate a foreign policy based on abstract principles of morality, human rights, and global justice is not simply misguided but also downright dangerous.

Consequently, for the realist, foreign policy is the state's international struggle for power among states.

Within the Cold War scenario, there were two extreme realist positions in U.S. foreign policy: a traditional realist approach, and a conservative realist attitude. A traditional realist viewed the Soviet Union as a threat but one that could be contained with time-honored power politics, such as deterrence, the balance of power, and patient containment. During the Nixon Administration, Secretary of State Henry Kissinger brought the assumptions of realism into diplomatic relations. In what is referred to as "realpolitik," based on practical politics and expediency in addition to the realist sense of power politics, Kissinger forged a foreign policy devoid of any moral or ideological component. The United States, under Kissinger, sought to contain communism, not because it is an evil ideology that needs to be crushed (the conservative realist view), but because it was a direct threat to U.S. economic and strategic interests (the traditional realist perspective). Thus, détente was merely a strategy used to secure U.S. interests at lower costs and with a lower level of tension. Interests remained constant, and alliances were transitory and used for purposes of expediency.

On the other hand, a Reaganite conservative espoused a conservative realist attitude and viewed the Soviet Union as a malicious menace (or, as President Ronald Reagan would say, an evil empire) and the source of all international threats. A conservative realist believed that any attempt to cooperate or collaborate with the USSR was a dangerous and immoral miscalculation. The Soviet Union only understood military might and confrontation. America's moral duty, according to the Reagan-styled conservatives, was to conquer communism for the benefit of humanity. A middle position between the extremes of realist thought is the pragmatic realism, or pragmatic conservatism, of President George Bush Sr. President Bush Sr.'s foreign policy style is characterized by the practical utility of what works, a no-nonsense approach to problem solving that rejects ideological crusades for power politics.

Under the theory of realism, foreign aid is to be used for geopolitical and strategic purposes—the furtherance of U.S. national security interests. During the Cold War, foreign aid was a tool used to contain the spread of communism and to keep the power of the Soviet Union in check. In the post-Cold War era, foreign assistance is now viewed as an important instrument in preventing terrorist attacks. Foreign aid is an additional mechanism to further U.S. national interests. First, foreign aid can be used to maintain nations as U.S. allies. By economically or militarily supporting a pro-American foreign government, the United States can prevent the recipient state from falling into the enemy's camp. Second, foreign assistance may be granted in an attempt to gain foreign allies. Many countries that are ideologically neutral can be brought into the United States' sphere of influence with promises of economic aid or military equipment. Finally, by building an economically strong and dependent state, the United States can ensure its trade advantage. The United States is not motivated to help foreign states develop because of humanitarian concerns, but rather is interested in guaranteeing future customers for its goods and services. By gaining or maintaining allies, the United States strengthens its international security, while development aid reinforces its economic hegemony.

FOREIGN POLICY ACTORS

The creation and implementation of U.S. foreign policy involves many different participants, each with their own interests, values, and perspectives. The four key actors in the making of U.S. foreign policy are the president and his advisors, the U.S. Congress, the bureaucracy (notably, the State Department and the U.S. Agency for International Development, or USAID), and nongovernmental organizations (NGOs) representing the organized interests of the American public. The Founding Fathers created a foreign policy system based on shared responsibility. Their recent experience with King George III emphasized the need to control executive power. Yet, international events often require quick, decisive, or even clandestine decisions. A president who is hampered by the need to consult Congress during a crisis, an invasion, or an assault against U.S. personnel cannot act in the best interest of the country. On the other hand, a strong congressional role is basic to democratic government. Only an active and assertive Congress can hold the Executive accountable and ensure that policy is subject to evaluation and review. Therefore, the U.S. Constitution grants shared and overlapping powers between Congress and the Executive. This seemingly rational delegation of power hides the struggle that actually takes place between the executive and the legislative branches of the U.S government in the making of foreign policy. The sharing of power and responsibility in foreign policy making, built into the U.S. Constitution, requires a delicate balancing act between Congress and the president. When the executive role in foreign policy expands, the congressional role tends to contract, and vice versa. The separate and overlapping powers of the Executive-Congress relationship have been called "an invitation to struggle for the privilege of directing American foreign policy" (Corwin 1957, 171). This constitutionally imposed mêlée in foreign policy making is further complicated by the prominent roles played by other vested interests, such as the governmental bureaucracy, and the organized interests of the American public as advocated by NGOs.

The Supremacy of the President

Most presidential scholars hold the view that the president is the primary actor in U.S. foreign policy. According to Phillip Trimble, "The president dominates American foreign policy and is the principal force shaping the constitutional law governing foreign relations" (2002, 10). The presidency's dominance is guaranteed by constitutional grants of power, the need for a strong centralized authority in times of crisis, and the expectations of the general public. The Constitution specifies the powers of the Executive to make foreign policy. The president is the commander in chief of the armed forces. He has the power to negotiate treaties as the chief executive of the diplomatic and policy bureaucracies. He is the head of state and can nominate and remove officeholders. Additionally, the president has the power to veto congressional legislation.

Trimble (2002) believes that the expansive power of the president in the realm of foreign policy and foreign aid allocations, which has evolved and expanded over time, is not found in the text of the Constitution but in the Vesting Clause (Article II), which states that "the Executive Power shall be vested in a President of the United States." The Vesting Clause is quite broad and undefined, and, therefore, any power not specifically granted to the other branches of government in conducting foreign relations has been claimed by the president. The president's increasing dominance in the foreign policy realm is largely due to an increase of the president's "inherent or recognized" powers. The recognized powers of the president are those powers assumed but not officially granted by the Constitution. As a consequence of the Vesting Clause, Dan Wood and Jeffrey Peake believe that "there can be little doubt that the presidency has evolved through time as the primary actor responsible for U.S. foreign policy" (1998, 173).

The president's domination of the foreign policy making process, which many claim is based on the writings of the framers of the Constitution and clarified through the *Federalist Papers*,[2] is, according to noted constitutional historian Leonard Levy, a matter of "words and actions [that] have been wrenched out of context and twisted in meaning" (1997, 275). Arthur Schlesinger (1973) believes that the rank of commander in chief did not confer the president with an independent base of authority. The Founding Fathers merely made the president the highest-level officer in the command chain of the military with the power to issue orders when and if Congress declares war. When U.S. Representative John Marshall (Federalist-VA) claimed, in 1800, that "the President is the sole organ of the nation in its external relations, and its sole representative with foreign nations," he was referring only to presidential powers with respect to diplomatic representation and negotiation (Nathan and Oliver 1994, 94). The framers of the Constitution may have intended the president to have predominance in foreign policy matters, but they certainly did not intend an omnipotent presidency.

The Powers of Congress

Although the president is central in the foreign policy decision-making process, the U.S. Congress is far from powerless in the making of U.S. foreign policy. Presidential power is limited by congressional prerogative. The Constitution endows Congress with the power to legislate the foreign policy behavior of the Executive, to allocate or terminate funds, to tax, to approve treaties negotiated by the Executive, to confirm presidential appointments, and, furthermore, to declare war. Thus, Congress has several important tools to regulate foreign policy and control presidential authority. In order to control presidential power or foreign policy behavior, Congress often attaches conditions to expenditures that will determine how and when the money can be spent. Congress acts through its power of legislation by denying foreign aid or restricting the use of the aid, for example, and by appropriating funding in the first place. The ability to tax is important for human rights, since Congress has the power to grant or deny Most Favored Nation (MFN)[3] trading status.

Congress, through its power of the purse, can expressly deny funds for a particular purpose or to a specific country. The decision to appropriate funding is crucial for foreign policy actions. In order to protect its control over the budget, Congress passed the Anti-Deficiency Act (1870). The Anti-Deficiency Act (31 U.S.C. 1341.A.1) makes it a crime to spend money unless Congress has appropriated it. No money can be spent by the U.S. government unless Congress has acquiesced to it. Despite Congress' tight grip on its constitutional control over the budget, the president has found an ambiguity in the law. The president can transfer funds from one account or agency to another, and in this manner the Executive is able to reprogram appropriated funds.

As will be seen later on, the congressional prerogative to restrict or fund programs will be particularly important in the defense of human rights in U.S. foreign affairs. The U.S. Congress has placed several human rights restrictions on foreign aid allocations. In protecting and promoting human rights, Congress has on occasion refused to provide aid to those countries that violate the human rights of their citizens. Equally important for foreign aid allocations, Congress must appropriate funding for the establishment, maintenance, and salaries of the foreign policy bureaucracy, for example, the Department of State and USAID. In so doing, Congress defines the missions and goals of these two departments. Congress can deny them funding, thus in effect terminating any activity that Congress does not approve.

A very successful prerogative not specifically granted by the Constitution but in fact assumed by the First Congress was the power of investigation and oversight. Congress can investigate anything it wants at anytime it so desires. Congress can also compel testimony, call for the production of documents, and conduct international inspections and interviews. Congress holds hearings to investigate particular issues, and calls witnesses to testify and determines what can be done to solve problems. Congressional hearings are powerful tools to publicize incidents, formalize congressional opinion, and shape foreign policy objectives. Moreover, congressional committee hearings always attract media attention.

Another key method of congressional oversight is the reporting requirement placed on the executive branch. For example, the State Department has been responsible for compiling the annual public reports on the human rights conditions of every state that receives U.S. foreign assistance (and now compiles reports on all United Nations [UN] members). These detailed reports are then to be forwarded to Congress for review in February of every year, prior to the determination of foreign aid allocations. Overall, authorization and appropriation of funding, in addition to extensive congressional oversight, make Congress a compelling force in the foreign policy decision making process.[4]

The ability of Congress to legislate has become an important tool in influencing U.S. foreign policy. Congress has used its legislative powers to constrain presidential initiatives or regulate executive actions. The ability to legislate the foreign policy behavior of the executive branch is important for human rights in that Congress has required the Executive to report on and take into account the human rights conditions in countries when requesting foreign assistance.

During the 1970s, Congress enacted legislation linking foreign aid and trade benefits to the status of human rights in foreign countries. The U.S. Congress wrote into law, over Nixon's presidential veto, formal requirements for the restriction or denial of military and economic aid to countries that consistently violated the human rights of their citizens. The three key human rights amendments on this matter are the Harkin Amendment (1975) and the Humphrey-Cranston Amendment (1976) of the Foreign Assistance Act, and Section 701 of the International Financial Assistance Act (1977). The Harkin Amendment prohibits economic assistance to any country that commits gross human rights violations, unless it can be shown that the aid will directly benefit the poor and the needy within the recipient country. The Humphrey-Cranston Amendment directs that the president will be legally obligated to deny or restrict military aid to countries violating human rights, unless extraordinary circumstances can be proven. Section 701 of the International Financial Assistance Act instructs U.S. representatives to the international financial institutions, such as the International Monetary Fund (IMF) and the World Bank, to oppose loans, extensions, or technical assistance to any country described in the above provisions, unless the aid is directed to programs that will fulfill the basic human needs of the country's citizens.

The Foreign Policy Bureaucracy

The institutional competition between the president and Congress is further complicated by the bureaucratic politics of the large executive branch bureaucracies of the Department of State, the Department of Defense, the Department of the Treasury, and USAID. It has been said that the United States does not have a single foreign policy but several policies based on the number of bureaucratic agencies involved. The foreign policy bureaucracies manage and implement the foreign policy initiatives formulated by the Executive and Congress.

While Congress and the president operate under election cycles, the bureaucracy's tenure is potentially endless. The foreign policy bureaucracy is expected to implement current policy until a new administration institutes a new mandate. The foreign policy bureaucracies are populated by career bureaucrats who were in place before the elected official came to power. Most of these bureaucrats also know that they will remain in their post when the current administration leaves office. As civil servants, these governmental employees cannot be fired or replaced by presidential whim or political patronage, thus allowing the executive branch bureaucracy some level of independence. To further complicate matters, bureaucrats understand that it is Congress, not the president, that approves programs and authorizes the funding of the governmental organization for which they work. While these bureaucracies are officially under presidential authority, the ability to fund or withhold funding gives Congress considerable influence on the kind of policies the bureaucrats will implement.

Although the president may initiate foreign policy, he necessarily has to rely on a vast bureaucracy to implement it. While the bureaucrats are only in charge of implementing the policy, they often do so in a manner that increases their authority and furthers their institutional interests. Howard Wiarda writes that "agencies such as the State Department, the Department of Defense, the Central Intelligence Agency, and others have independent bureaucratic interests (budgets, power, prestige, access to the White House) that they seek to enhance and protect" (2000, 175). Thus, bureaucratic politics—the jostling and even rivalries among agencies—has long characterized and often frustrated the successful carrying out of U.S. foreign policy.

The bureaucratic politics model, also referred to as the governmental politics model, portrays the policy decision-making process as one where "power is diffused and the process revolves around political competition and compromise" (Rosati 1993a, 255). Participants involved in the bureaucracy often choose options or interpret policy requirements that favor their position or organization. Foreign aid allocations are therefore often the result of behind-the-scenes compromises made by the representatives of the different agencies attempting to protect and promote their own parochial interests. Policies detrimental to a particular agency are often delayed or simply ignored by that agency. The State Department's Bureau for Human Rights is a case in point. The State Department, under Kissinger, obstructed a congressional dictate to collect and publish the human rights conditions of foreign countries because the State Department thought that doing so would interfere with the diplomatic purposes of their embassies. The State Department sees its primary duty as building cordial relations with foreign leaders, and reporting on a country's shortcomings often runs counter to this principal responsibility. In addition, the State Department has traditionally viewed foreign aid as an important tool in maintaining friendly relations. The denial of aid could be a serious threat to those good relations, particularly if the denial is predicated on a condemnation of a country's human rights record.

The Department of State

The first and foremost bureaucracy in charge of diplomacy and foreign policy implementation is the U.S. Department of State. The Secretary of State is the highest-ranking cabinet officer under the authority of the president of the United States. The State Department identifies its role as being

> the lead U.S. foreign affairs agency, and the Secretary of State is the President's principal foreign policy adviser. The Department advances U.S. objectives and interests in shaping a freer, more secure, and more prosperous world through its primary role in developing and implementing the President's foreign policy. (United States, Department of State 2006)

The Department of State is a massive bureaucracy made up of geographical and functional bureaus, each headed by an assistant secretary of state. The regional bureaus are assigned the day-to-day implementation of U.S. foreign policy and answer to the undersecretary for political affairs. As such, the regional bureaus, in the bureaucratic hierarchy of the State Department, are at the pinnacle.

Among the many bureaus is the Bureau of Democracy, Human Rights, and Labor (DRL; previously known, and still often referred to, as the Bureau of Human Rights and Humanitarian Affairs, or HA). The DRL is headed by an assistant secretary of state who is nominated by the president subject to congressional approval. The function of the DRL is to gather information on human rights situations around the world, prepare the State Department's *Country Reports on Human Rights*, globally advocate human rights, and keep human rights issues in the forefront of foreign policy considerations. The DRL's mandate to impose human rights in diplomacy and foreign policy has been a source of irritation between the DRL and the rest of the State Department. However, unlike the State Department or USAID, the DRL has the support of Congress and of a powerful domestic constituency. At least at a theoretical level, the concept of human rights is popularly supported by the American public and many members in Congress.

The Department of State is the principal agency in the foreign aid decision-making process. Although the State Department is the primary organization responsible for the overall conduct of foreign affairs, in the realm of foreign aid, other agencies share authority.[5] The State Department has primary responsibility for the Economic Support Fund (ESF), voluntary contributions to United Nations specialized agencies (for example, the United Nations Development Fund for Women and the United Nations Children's Fund, or UNICEF), and, recently, for the funding of the transitional economies of Eastern Europe and the former Soviet Union. The State Department is also actively involved in the determination of aid allocation for country-specific development assistance (the major program directed and managed by USAID).

Critics of the State Department charge the State Department with clientism. "Clientism" here refers to the tendency of the State Department, particularly its regional bureaus, to see foreign governments as their clients, and thus identify with the foreign governments' interests and represent those interests within the U.S. government. Consequently, pleasing a foreign government can easily become confused with U.S. national interest. Laurence Silberman writes,

> Inevitably a Foreign Service officer has a tendency toward what is referred to in the State Department as "clientism," a term which suggests overemphasizing the interests of a foreign country (as defined by the governing elite) vis-à-vis the broader interest of the United States. "Good relations" between the host country and the United States (often at our expense) become an end in themselves without sufficient regard to U.S. geopolitical and geostrategic interests. (1979, 882)

The goals and objectives of U.S. foreign policy, particularly U.S. human rights policy, can be hampered, if not distorted, by an overemphasis on "good relations."

U.S. Agency for International Development

The largest development aid agency is the U.S. Agency for International Development, or USAID. Under the direction of the Department of State, USAID is the bureaucracy that directly administers U.S. bilateral economic, development, and humanitarian assistance around the world in support of U.S. foreign policy objectives. USAID is led by an administrator and deputy administrator, both of whom are appointed by the president and confirmed by the Senate, and report to and serve under the secretary of state. The director of USAID is the secretary of state's main advisor on international development activities. USAID was created by executive order in November 1961, when President John F. Kennedy signed the Foreign Assistance Act into law. USAID is a semi-autonomous federal government agency within the Department of State superstructure. USAID is headquartered in Washington, D.C., with field offices around the world. USAID, like the State Department, has both geographic bureaus (responsible for regional branches in sub-Saharan Africa, Asia and the Near East, Latin America and the Caribbean, and Europe and Eurasia) and functional bureaus (responsible for agency programs—Global Health, Economic Growth, Agriculture and Trade, and Democracy, Conflict and Humanitarian Assistance).

USAID has been in charge of policy leadership in the administration, management, and delivery of bilateral development assistance, food aid, and emergency assistance. USAID has a minor partnership role in the allocation of the ESF and must coordinate its work with the State Department in country allocations. The majority of the United States' bilateral economic assistance, even the ESF, is channeled through USAID managed activities.

The Department of Defense

The Department of Defense (DOD) has primary responsibility for the distribution and supervision of foreign aid in the form of military education and training, foreign military loans, sales of military equipment, and antiterrorism programs. Military assistance is administered by the Department of Defense's Defense Security Cooperation Agency,[6] in coordination with the State Department's Politico-Military Affairs bureau. The Defense Security Cooperation Agency recommends the appropriate level of country funding, determines what military equipment is suitable and available, procures the equipment, provides overall policy guidance, and implements the United States' security assistance programs.

The Department of the Treasury

The Department of the Treasury manages multilateral development bank funding and debt relief. The president of the United States, through the Treasury Department, serves as the U.S. executive director of the World Bank, and votes in the positive or in the negative for countries requesting loans from the World Bank or one of the regional multilateral development banks. U.S. votes in multilateral lending institutions are governed by Section 701 of the International Financial Institutions Act of 1977, which prohibits U.S. support for loans to governments that engage in a systematic pattern of gross violations of internationally recognized human rights, unless the loan addresses basic human needs. However, the Treasury Department claims that a strict financial orientation is the best route for development and poverty reduction. In general, the Treasury Department believes that human rights requirements may prevent the primary objective of multilateral lending, that is, the promotion of economic development. Thus, it has actively resisted the imposition of Section 701 or political considerations into its work. In 2001, U.S. multilateral aid via international financial institutions was only 14 percent of the total of U.S. foreign aid.[7]

The Influence of Nongovernmental Organizations

Traditionally, foreign policy is conducted by an elite group of congressional leaders, the Executive and his advisors, and the bureaucracy, with little public input. With the emergence of nongovernmental organizations, however, this framework for foreign policy making has been altered. NGOs, interest groups, and public opinion now also play an important role in foreign policy decision making. These private groups pressure the Executive and Congress through lobbying, voting, and funding in order to attain their objectives. Special interest groups and NGOs tend to be better informed, better connected, and better funded than the general public, and therefore have enhanced access to the foreign policy elites that the general public does not have. In addition, NGOs and interest groups advocate a single issue or topic, which gives them the ability to collect in-depth statistics, documentation, and reports to provide to sympathetic congressional members. An NGO's influence on human rights policies depends on its "visibility, constituency, and reputation for accuracy; the legitimacy of its interest in human rights; and its access to decision makers" (Weissbrodt 1981, 241). NGOs tend to focus their influence on congressional members and their staff since the State Department has historically proven inhospitable to the counsel and recommendations of "outsiders." Nongovernmental organizations, armed with reliable and reputable information, are often able to challenge the *Country Reports on Human Rights Practices* issued by the State Department.

The more democratic and open the government, the greater the influence of the public in the decision making process. The general public, often at the instigation of organized NGOs, can "vote the rascals out of office" if the elected members of the government do not curry the favor of the voter or do not support voters' preferences. However, the public ordinarily has a limited access to information and often shows a lack of interest in foreign affairs. Nevertheless, it has been proven that when the public is aroused by the media or interest groups, it can change foreign policy. The Vietnam War is a notable example.

One human rights writer, William Korey (2001), has reviewed the historical influence of NGOs on the attainment of human rights. NGOs, Korey indicates, were instrumental in the development of the United Nations and the drafting of the UN Charter and, later, the Universal Declaration of Human Rights. Other scholars have also given credit to the human rights lobby for the passage of the United States' human rights legislation by petitioning Congress and providing Congress with factual information about human rights violations around the world. Initially, human rights NGOs worked toward establishing "international norms by which the conduct of states can be measured or judged" and toward fact-finding (Korey 2001, 3). Subsequently, NGOs became "actively involved in the creation of various types of implementing agencies or institutions" (2001, 3). For example, recently, USAID has created a formal advisory council on bilateral foreign aid where NGOs can provide guidance on the objectives and management of foreign assistance.

TOOLS OF U.S. HUMAN RIGHTS FOREIGN POLICY

The United States government has several tools it can use to further its human rights policy. Chief among these options are quiet diplomacy, public condemnation that includes human rights reporting, and the use of foreign aid. Each method has its benefits and drawbacks. Quiet diplomacy can be used when the goal is to maintain friendly relations with allies by not publicly embarrassing the foreign government. For this reason, quiet diplomacy is the method of choice among diplomats and political leaders alike. Regrettably, quiet diplomacy can easily be ignored with few if any negative consequences. Also, while the use of quiet diplomacy has the advantage of not embarrassing the offending country, it is difficult to quantify and often conceals the administration's apathy and neglect of human rights issues. For example, Secretary of State Henry Kissinger claimed that public denunciations of human rights-violating states were counterproductive and, therefore, advocated the use of quiet diplomacy. When asked by Senator Claiborne Pell (D-RI) to provide examples of his use of quiet diplomacy on behalf of human rights, it took eight months for the State Department to produce a mere handful of cases (Crabb and Holt 1980).

Public diplomacy, the U.S. government's open criticism of a foreign country's human rights practices, can bring the matter to the attention of the media, the American public, and the international community. But it is often little more than mere words—often politically motivated words. Undoubtedly, public diplomacy can be successful in individual cases when prominent political dissidents or other public figures have been jailed. There are numerous examples where diplomacy has resulted in the release or improved treatment of well-known persons. Unfortunately, the majority of human rights victims are unknown to the international media, the American public, or even human rights NGOs. These nameless victims of human rights abuses, known only to their families and friends, rarely benefit from either public or quiet diplomacy.

However, public diplomacy does have some advantages. Public diplomacy has the ability to strengthen the target country's local NGOs and human rights activists. No longer can the abusing government claim that the accusations of human rights abuses are simply the ranting of politically motivated or fanatic enemies of the state. Moreover, public pronouncements may provide some minor comfort to the victims, who know that the outside world recognizes their suffering.

Among the most important U.S. public diplomacy instruments are the congressionally mandated *Country Reports on Human Rights Practices*. In these reports, the State Department carefully documents the human rights conditions in countries around the world. Although initially weak and biased, the *Country Reports* are now considered accurate, balanced, and truthful reflections of a country's human rights conditions. Furthermore, public diplomacy efforts, particularly the *Country Reports*, are used by the U.S. Congress to determine the level of foreign aid to be granted or whether to impose sanctions upon an abusing country.

United States human rights policy, however, assumes its most tangible consequence with the granting or restricting of economic and military foreign assistance. Human Rights Watch argues, in regard to Latin America, that "experience has shown that quiet diplomacy means no diplomacy as long as the armed forces feel assured of an uninterrupted stream of military aid" (1993, 138). Studies indicate that the most effective human rights tool is the denial of foreign aid (Liang-Fenton 2004). Not only do target countries respond to the threat of the restriction of bilateral or multilateral aid, but also the threat of aid termination can "prod the White House into action on issues that it may be reluctant to address and send a strong signal to foreign governments about the seriousness with which the United States regards particular human rights issues" (Liang-Fenton 2004, 441). The case of El Salvador provides a clear example. In 1983, Vice President George Bush explained to the Salvadoran civilian and military command that its egregious human rights practices were complicating Reagan's attempts to persuade Congress to allocate military funding to El Salvador. In order to continue funding, the paramilitary death squads would have to be controlled. Bush provided the names of several military officers connected to the death squads who ought to be assigned overseas before Congress reconvened. The reassignment of these military officers greatly reduced the number of death squad victims. "The Salvadoran armed forces' dependence on U.S. financing and training was so great," Susan Burgermann reports, "that the threat of losing that aid was a principal factor leading to their eventual subordination to civilian authorities" (2004, 273). The denial or restriction of U.S. foreign assistance can be a valuable mechanism designed to encourage adherence to international standards of human rights. Moreover, Burgermann argues that civilian governments often cannot restrain or control the human rights violations of the military if the armed forces receive continuous unrestricted security aid from the United States. Therefore, because of its importance in securing human rights protections, foreign aid will be one of the central focuses of this book.

WHAT IS FOREIGN AID?

The declared purpose of foreign aid is to facilitate the development and security of underdeveloped countries, to alleviate poverty, and to protect the interests of the United States. Foreign aid amounts to resources given to a foreign government, on concessional terms (with at least a 25 percent grant element),[8] for broadly defined economic development or for the improvement of social and political conditions. USAID reports that the purpose of U.S. economic aid is to promote democracy and assist the poor: "U.S. foreign assistance has always had the twofold purpose of furthering America's foreign policy interests in expanding democracy and free markets while improving the lives of the citizens of the developing world" (USAID 2006a).

Economic aid includes cash or credits, food, medicine, commodities, funding projects for democracy building, emergency relief activities, debt relief, and technical advice and training. There are three major categories of U.S. economic aid.[9] The first and largest category of economic assistance is the Economic Support Fund (ESF),[10] originally called the Economic Support of Defense program and later renamed the Security Supporting Assistance program. The ESF program is categorized as economic development assistance, not military aid, even though its primary purpose is to support U.S. political and security interests. ESF is intended to promote political stability in countries deemed important to U.S. economic, political, or military interests. On average, ESF loans account for more than half of all U.S. economic assistance. The ESF program is financial assistance for budget support that allows recipient countries to use their own resources to build up their defense infrastructures.[11] Yet, its security component is evidenced by the fact that the State Department, not USAID, controls its allocation and disbursement.[12] USAID states, "The Economic Support Fund is the point at which the development and security programs 'meet', so that the Secretary [of State] is empowered to determine what countries receive ESF assistance and the amounts, [while] the USAID Administrator implements the ESF programs" (USAID 2006b). ESF resources are often allocated in lieu of military aid in order to avoid a congressional debate on the ethical, moral, or political consequences of providing military aid to certain countries or groups (Ruttan 1996).

The second category of economic aid is development assistance (DA), which presently encompasses several functional programs such as the Child Survival and Health Programs (previously known as the Child Survival and Disease Programs), the Development Assistance Fund (DAF), the Development Fund of Africa (DFA), Assistance to Eastern Europe and Baltic States (AEEB), and Assistance for the Independent States of the former Soviet Union (FSA). Development assistance is administered by USAID. The purpose of DA is to sponsor advances in health, education, and agriculture development. DA can be in the form of either loans or grants provided to the recipient country.

The third category of economic aid is the Food for Peace program. The Food for Peace program was established by the Agricultural Trade Development and Assistance Act of 1954 and is also known as PL 480. The food aid program is made up of three titles. Title I of PL 480 is administered by the U.S. Department of Agriculture for sales of agricultural commodities to Third World countries under concessional credit terms. Titles II and III are administered by USAID. Title II involves the donation of U.S. agricultural commodities to meet humanitarian food needs in foreign countries. Title III entails grants to support long-term economic development in the least developed countries. Title III is currently not funded.

Security assistance consists of military aid, military support equipment, military education and training, and antiterrorist assistance. Security assistance is intended to strengthen U.S. allies' legitimate self-defense capabilities while enabling them to participate in multinational military missions. Proponents of military aid claim that this aid is critical for U.S. national security as it promotes internal, regional, and international security. The Foreign Military Financing (FMF) program is the oldest and largest category of military assistance.[13] Its proponents claim that FMF increases bilateral relations, encourages coalition building, and facilitates military operation coordination between the United States and its allies' military forces. The FMF is administered by the Department of Defense after the Department of State determines the level of allocated funds. Initially this program was a direct transfer of excess U.S. military equipment to recipient countries at no cost. Presently, the FMF provides outright grants (gifts provided at U.S. taxpayers' expense) to "friendly nations" in the developing world. In an FMF arrangement, the U.S. government either buys the requested military equipment from U.S. manufacturers at market price and gives the equipment to the recipient government, or simply loans the funds at lower than market rates to the recipient country so that it can purchase the arms directly.

Under the rubric of security assistance, one also finds the International Military Education and Training (IMET) program. IMET trains foreign soldiers in the use of U.S. supplied military equipment, advanced military tactics, and the rules of war. Under intense public pressure, the IMET was forced to include training of basic human rights. DOD manages the program, and the State Department determines the political advisability of its recipients. The first mission of IMET is to provide professional military training to U.S. friends and allies. The second mission is to expose military officers to democratic values, human rights, and the rule of law. IMET, its defenders claim, exposes foreign military officers to professional, civilized, and military organizations and procedures, which emphasize codes of conduct and support of democratic governments. IMET is directly financed by U.S. taxpayers.

The Transfers of Excess Defense Articles (EDA) program is administered by the Department of Defense. When defense articles are deemed excess by the U.S. military, they are offered to allied foreign governments supporting American security objectives. Surplus military equipment and supplies are given at no cost to the allied government.

"Drawdown" is yet another type of security assistance. In the event of an unforeseen emergency, such as a military crisis, a humanitarian disaster, a peacekeeping mission, or a counternarcotics operation, the U.S. Congress can authorize the president to transfer defense articles and services, on a grant basis, from the Department of Defense's on-hand inventory. In these urgent situations, the president can draw down military equipment, shift budgets, and reallocate security assistance to meet the needs of the particular crisis. There is a $300 million limit per year, of which $100 million can be taken from the Department of

Defense. The limitation is to protect U.S. defense operations since draw-downs can present a significant drain on the Department of Defense's resources. Over the years, drawdowns have tended to be mostly used for antidrug operations in Latin America.

FOREIGN AID AND HUMAN RIGHTS

The United States provides foreign assistance to help economies prosper and to raise the living standard of the poor. The promotion of democracy and the protection of human rights remain core objectives of U.S. foreign aid strategy. U.S. aid contributes to global security by tackling threats to human security, such as human rights violations, disease, population growth, environmental degradation, and the growing gap between the rich and the poor. Political instability is frequently a function of human rights abuses and the tensions generated by extreme inequalities. Thus, many believe, poverty and repression are often causes of social instability and civil unrest, which in turn can produce flows of refugees and acts of terrorism, potentially making the United States less secure. Thus, aid helps build a safer, more peaceful world, while it also helps bolster the United States' national interest.

However, foreign aid is often provided for interests other than humanitarian reasons. Foreign aid can also be used to further economic interests, for instance to open foreign markets, subsidize domestic firms, and provide employment for American workers. Foreign aid can be used to promote strategic interests, for the right to build and maintain foreign bases, to strengthen alliances, or to keep pro-American regimes in power. Foreign aid is also used to maintain friendly relations with foreign governments. Foreign aid facilitates cooperation, and it builds strong alliances. Aid can be withdrawn to create economic hardship and destabilize an unfriendly or ideologically antagonistic regime. It can be used to directly support an authoritarian regime too. Foreign aid can also be used for political purposes, as a reward for backing the United States, as was the case with the United States forgiving Egypt's military debts when it backed the United States in the first Gulf War. Finally, foreign aid can be mobilized to encourage governmental adherence to internationally recognized human rights standards. Clearly, the United States' goals and objectives of aid are mixed, and often contradictory.

As indicated above, realist scholars and politicians believe that U.S. foreign policy needs to be realistic, pragmatic, but also generally flexible in order to pursue U.S. national interests. These scholars further reason that Congress' mandate of giving human rights consideration priority in the allocation of aid or loans, notwithstanding the existing loopholes of the system, is unwise or even dangerous. In 1977, Ernest Lefever, Reagan's first nominee for the position of assistant secretary of state for the Bureau of Human Rights and Humanitarian Affairs, believed that human rights had no place in the making of U.S. foreign policy. To invoke human rights would serve neither American interests nor the cause of freedom and liberty (Heaps 1984).

In order to maintain friendly relations with a strategically important country, many in the U.S. government believe that the United States may have to abandon human rights considerations to pursue more crucial goals. For example, in the recent fight against global terrorism, the United States has partnered with states with dubious human rights practices and records. The United States provided Pakistan with $814 million in economic aid and an additional $306 million in military aid in 2002 alone, despite Pakistan's horrendous human rights abuses.[14] Yet, in this allegedly perilous world, the U.S. government believes that U.S. economic, military, and strategic support should not be hampered by what many government officials see as idealistic concerns for human rights: regrettably, the United States' overall national interest in its fight against terrorism may best be served by supporting autocrats and despots.

A second argument that has been advanced for ignoring human rights is that by requiring a standard of human rights achievement in the allocation of aid, the United States might in effect be imposing its own values on other countries with different cultures and moral codes. Cultural relativists claim that human rights are not universal but culturally and regionally specific.[15] From this perspective, the community-based value systems of a state determine what is or is not a human right. The Western idea of human rights focuses primarily on political and civil rights. Therefore, by requiring a foreign government to fulfill the U.S. style of human rights, the United States is violating the cultural integrity of the aid recipient state.

A third argument against the linkage between foreign aid and human rights is that foreign aid is one strategy the United States uses to influence foreign governments on a broad range of issues. Military aid and economic aid are sometimes simply viewed as political tools that allow the United States access and influence in the domestic and foreign affairs of other states. State Department foreign service officers may support foreign aid even to repressive governments since "the diplomat without an aid program has to work much harder to advance U.S. objectives" (Zimmerman 1993, 14). Foreign aid is an expedient tool for the diplomat in smoothing the way for mutual cooperation on a wide range of issues. The denial of aid would break the bonds of friendship and would jeopardize U.S. security. Thus, bringing human rights into the picture can be detrimental since the United States could lose its ability to influence another country if it tried to punish or threaten that foreign government. An offending government could revolt against any attitude that suggests paternalism. The United States, many foreign leaders believe, ought to lead by example, a low-key, muffled, and quiet example.

A fourth argument suggests that denying economic and military aid merely hurts U.S. business and may end up threatening U.S. jobs. If the United States does not sell foreign governments the weapons it manufactures, then other countries will. For instance, in Guatemala, as a result of the Carter Administration's restriction on the allocation of security assistance that was imposed because of Guatemala's consistent pattern of gross violations of human rights, the Guatemalan military simply found other suppliers of armaments in Taiwan and Israel (Burgermann 2004). In this case, the United States not only lost lucrative business opportunities, but also lost the potential political leverage that security aid had in controlling offensive military behavior.

Finally, military aid, to the surprise of no one, can be used by iniquitous tyrants to suppress dissent and defend their own power position. Repressive governments, whose domestic control is maintained by violence and brutality, are abusive because of their political and territorial insecurity. For this reason, ironically, the United States may actually be contributing to the improvement of human rights in a state by providing that state with the necessary means to protect itself from outside forces or internal opposition. Once a state is safe and secure, it will no longer fear normal, moderate, and popular challenges to its policies, and thus it will no longer feel the need to repress dissension. This argument is believed to be particularly pertinent for military regimes. Once a military government has secured its authority, it will be amenable to the idea of human rights and democracy. Therefore, large outlays of military aid are sometimes seen by realist scholars as the best way to assure democracy and respect for fundamental freedoms.

Despite the frequent attempt by the U.S. government and some scholars to delink foreign aid and human rights, there are many compelling reasons why human rights should underlie U.S. foreign policy. William Schultz believes that protecting human rights "is in our own best interest" (2001). Identification with repressive regimes, through economic and military support, will hurt the United States and its citizens. As early as the 1970s, there were clear warnings by human rights activists and scholars of the connection between U.S. support or perceived support of human rights violators and the rise of terrorism (Vogelgesang 1980, 80). When the United States sides with an abusive leader, the vileness of the tyrant's acts stains the United States' image. Tyrants abuse the human rights of their citizens because they believe it is in their interests to do so. Jailing opponents, terrorizing citizens, and disappearing dissidents are methods that keep oppressive leaders in power without the expense of having to meet the political, social, and material needs of the citizens.

A case in point was the U.S. support of the Shah of Iran, Mohammed Reza Pahlavi, a particularly brutal U.S. ally. In 1953, the shah was briefly deposed by street rioters supporting Prime Minister Mohammed Mossadegh's plan to nationalize the oil industry. The shah fled to Rome in disgrace. The Central Intelligence Agency (CIA) went into action, arrested Mossadegh, and returned the shah to power. The free flow of oil resumed in only three days. The U.S. government knew that the shah's secret police, the Savak, engaged in reprehensible abuses of human rights. The Savak was accused of murder, torture, and false imprisonment of thousands of Iranians. While the majority of the population remained poor and illiterate, the Iranian government used its oil wealth to purchase military equipment. The shah then became one of the largest recipients of U.S. produced weaponry. One-third of all U.S. arms sales went to Iran during the shah's reign of terror. History has shown that when these abusive leaders are toppled their foreign supporters also pay the consequences. The taking of U.S. hostages in Iran after the fall of the shah is an unambiguous example. When the victims of human rights abuses overthrow the repressive regime, they may not be willing to deal with the United States if the United States was believed to support the former regime. Or, more perilously, the victims may seek revenge for the abuses they suffered under the U.S.-backed tyranny.

Additionally, there is ample evidence that human rights violations often lead to internal conflict that may result in refugee flows, ethnic wars, and a general disruption of international peace. Human rights violations often increase political dissatisfaction. Respect for human rights and recognition of democratic expression act as "safety valves for equitable, nonviolent conflict resolution" (Schulz 2001, 60). Countries that respect human rights and democratic freedoms are less likely to become embroiled in violent civil conflict. Schulz reports that regimes that rely on human rights violations to control minority populations are more likely to disintegrate. As UN High Commissioner for Refugees Sadako

Ogata has stated, "[T]oday's human rights abuses are tomorrow's refugee movements" (1995, 57). It is important to note that the majority of the world's refugees are people who would not have chosen to leave their homes if they had not been faced with human rights violations, genocide, or political disempowerment. As the case of the Democratic Republic of the Congo illustrates, a foreign country's human rights violations also threatens regional stability. Within the flow of innocent refugees hides the presence of militia groups bent on continuing the fight across international borders. As a direct consequence of the genocide in Rwanda, and the resultant refugee movement, the government of Zaire was destabilized and ultimately overthrown.

Another reason to encourage human rights in foreign policy is that politically unstable countries are a risk to trade and investment. Liberal economic theory maintains that the liberalization of markets strengthens human rights by promoting economic development. Trade and investment have long been considered the engines of economic growth for developing countries. Not only does trade increase the amount of capital available to entrepreneurs and government officials (taxes), but it also enlarges employment opportunities while reducing the cost of goods (comparative advantage). Analysts for *The Economist* have concluded,

> Morality is not the only reason for putting human rights on the West's foreign-policy agenda. Self-interest also plays a part. Political freedom tends to go hand in hand with economic freedom, which in turn tends to bring international trade and prosperity. And governments that treat their own people with tolerance and respect tend to treat their neighbours in the same way. ("Human Rights" 1997, 16)

Countries experiencing social and political unrest cannot lure private investment. Hooshang Amirahmadi and Weiping Wu argue that political instability increases the risk to investors in several ways: "the potential loss of funds resulting from a political breakup; possible government confiscation; uncertain rate of return; and disruptions in the supply of goods, services and work force" (1994, 183). Governments that suffer chronic political and social instability end up losing foreign investment. Political instability is often a function of human rights abuses and of the tensions generated by extreme inequalities. Sylvia Maxfield points out another way that foreign investment increases the prospects of democracy and equity in developing countries. Foreign capital may reduce the political power of traditional monopoly or oligopoly businesses by spreading the economic benefits to more people while reducing the potential of corruption. The reduction in governmental involvement would also decrease the opportunity "for politically-motivated distribution of resources" (Maxfield, 1998, 1216). Therefore, it is in the United States' best interest to encourage respect for human rights and fundamental freedoms.

Finally, the United States has assumed international obligations under international law. The United States is a founding member of the United Nations and a leader in the development of human rights standards. The standards set by the Universal Declaration of Human Rights are in large part due to the efforts of the U.S. delegation led at the time by former First Lady Eleanor Roosevelt. Mrs. Roosevelt is credited as the driving force behind the adoption of the Universal Declaration and the preparatory work on the International Covenant on Civil and Political Rights and the International Covenant on Economic, Social and Cultural Rights. Indeed, the development of human rights as an international norm, requiring global consensus building, diplomatic initiatives, and political policies, was initially an American project. Another noted human rights scholar has remarked that "the American role is critical. No forward movement is possible without Washington's support and leadership" (Meyer 1999, 45). Thus, human rights issues are elevated internationally when the United States shows an interest in them. The United States' interest in human rights issues creates interest in human rights elsewhere in the world.

CONCLUSION

United States foreign policy is the outcome of a complicated power struggle between the major actors in the foreign policy decision-making process. The U.S. Constitution instigated the foreign policy struggle between Congress and the Executive by granting a system of checks and balances, shared and overlapping powers. Furthermore, foreign policy, particularly foreign aid policy, is shaped by a battle of ideological positions. Realists believe that foreign assistance is simply an instrument of U.S. power to further U.S. interests abroad. Idealists, on the other hand, believe that the granting of foreign aid serves a basic moral rationale: to save lives and to help the poor. The administration of foreign policy is made more problematic by the bureaucratic politics of the large executive branch bureaucracies. An inordinate number of U.S. bureaucratic agencies have authority over U.S. foreign policy. The management of foreign aid requires the collaboration and cooperation of several disparate bureaucratic departments (for example, the Department of State and the Defense Department) and subunits (for example, the Defense Security Cooperation Agency [DSCA] or the Bureau of Democracy, Human Rights, and Labor). As Wiarda laments,

> Congress and the White House play politics with foreign policy-making, doling out whole programs to different agencies on political and bureaucratic grounds. Then each agency conducts its own foreign policy with little or no attachment to a central core of principles and interests. (2000)

U.S. foreign aid policy is the outcome of the pulling and hauling of the American political system. The allocation of foreign aid is particularly illustrative of the political and bureaucratic interplay between the key actors in the making of U.S. foreign policy. Foreign aid allocations are the result of political negotiation and compromise made by the president, Congress, and representatives of the different agencies attempting to protect their interests, promote their own agendas, and satisfy a particular constituency. Foreign assistance is also a crucial component in the implementation of U.S. human rights policy. The arduous examination of a country's eligibility for foreign aid, and the impending threat of aid termination, can "prod the White House into action on issues that it may be reluctant to address and send a strong signal to foreign governments about the seriousness with which the United States regards particular human rights issues" (Liang-Fenton 2004, 441). Either the president modifies his foreign policy agenda and uses his authority to influence the behavior of recipient regimes, or Congress can do it for him.

CHAPTER 2

A Matter of Unintended Consequences:
The Nixon and Ford Administrations

There is a worldwide growing abuse of human rights, with violations of international standards so widespread that we are, indeed,
facing a global human rights crisis.

Congressman Donald Fraser (1977)

U.S. human rights policy was not an intentionally planned strategy. Congress saddled presidential foreign and domestic policy initiatives with
human rights mandates in order to restrain the immoral, if not illegal,
behavior of an imperial president.[1] Contemporary congressional interest in human rights was originally spurred by the American civil rights
movement, the backlash against American involvement in Vietnam, and
a reaction to President Richard Nixon's Administration's unscrupulous
foreign policy behavior. Kate Doyle credits U.S. concern with human
rights to the fact that the

> reports of CIA [Central Intelligence Agency] assassination pro-
> grams in Vietnam, the use of torture by agents trained by U.S.
> police advisors in Latin America and Southeast Asia, and the
> American role in the overthrow of Chile's President [Salvador]
> Allende fed a growing sense of outrage about the conduct of U.S.
> foreign policy in the early 1970s. (2003)

The imperial presidency of Richard Nixon was shattered by the reasser-
tion of congressional power limiting the expanded power of the presidency. With the erosion of presidential powers, due to the revelation
of President Nixon's "dirty tricks" and secret wars and of the Watergate scandal, Congress moved to reinstate its constitutional authority in

the foreign policy realm. Congress would finally restore the balance of power in foreign policy between the legislative and executive branches. Congress imposed its will in the spheres of foreign policy, human rights, and budget policies when it passed the War Powers Act over presidential veto in 1973, a series of human rights legislations in the late 1970s, the Case Act of 1972, and the Budget Reform Act of 1974.[2]

It was during the Nixon Administration that the U.S. Congress wrote into law formal requirements for the restriction or denial of foreign aid to countries that consistently violated the human rights of their citizens. U.S. human rights policy was shaped during the heat of political battle between President Nixon and Congress. Congress laid the foundation for the United States' human rights policy in an attempt to rein in a renegade president and restore morality to U.S. foreign policy. Thus, it can be said that the United States' human rights policy was a matter of unintended consequences. Against the Executive's wishes, Congress pushed human rights considerations on a reluctant State Department, Treasury Department, Department of Defense, and the United States Agency for International Development (USAID).

As was demonstrated in the previous chapter, the provision or denial of foreign assistance, a valuable tool of U.S. foreign policy, is the direct result of the conflict and cooperation among the major foreign policy makers, based on their ideological worldviews, policy agendas, and political wherewithal. Unquestionably, Nixon and his bureaucracy actively opposed congressional efforts to impose human rights concerns in foreign policy matters. However, individual members of Congress, their staff, the American public, and nongovernmental organizations (NGOs) used their dedication and commitment to human rights to push for the inclusion of human rights in U.S. foreign policy, specifically in foreign aid allocations. Thus, the initial paradox of U.S. human rights policy presented itself in the form of what can be called an "unintended consequence." Indeed, as will be shown below, the formation of the United States' human rights policy at this time was the unintended consequence of the clash between Congress and the executive branch. It can be argued that many in Congress did not embark upon the human rights agenda until they perceived it as a means to restrain Nixon's imperial presidency.

REALPOLITIK

The Nixon foreign policy agenda was based on power and national interests, not on ideological or moral crusades. The Nixon-Kissinger collaboration advanced a foreign policy perspective known as "realpolitik."

Realpolitik is based on practical politics and expediency in addition to the realist sense of power politics devoid of any moral or ideological component. Thus, the Nixon Administration resisted attempts to link U.S. foreign assistance to human rights performance. Realpolitik dictated that human rights were secondary to U.S. national security interests. This viewpoint is clear in the following statement made by President Nixon, as reported in the *New York Times*:

> [T]he "national interest" is the only proper concern of this nation's foreign policy, and the "national interest" should be narrowly constructed to exclude moral commitments or "causes" that do not promise a clear, direct, predictable payoff in increased security or prosperity for the nation. (Nixon 1973)

For Secretary of State Henry Kissinger, the United States' security interests, primarily the containment of the Soviet Union, always had to trump human rights considerations. Foreign policy decisions had to be governed by considerations of national security, not morality. Kissinger's confirmation hearings before the U.S. Senate in 1973 further demonstrated the Nixon Administration's rejection of human rights objectives in U.S. foreign policy:

> I believe it is dangerous for us to make the domestic policy of countries around the world a direct objective of American foreign policy. . . . The protection of basic human rights is a very sensitive aspect of the domestic jurisdiction of . . . governments. . . . If the infringement of human rights is not so offensive that we cannot live with it, we will seek to work out what we can with the country involved in order to increase our influence. If the infringement was so offensive that we cannot live with it, we will avoid dealing with the offending country. (Kissinger 1973, 507)

Nixon's rejection of human rights as part of U.S. foreign policy had important consequences for the politics of foreign aid allocation. In the allocation of foreign aid, the United States under Nixon would be willing to overlook a country's human rights record, in the name of cooperation, security, world peace, and the principle of state sovereignty. Foreign aid was a tool used for geopolitical and strategic purposes—to contain the spread of communism and to keep the power of the Soviet Union in check. Nixon's use of foreign aid was directly related to the containment of communism and the need of furthering his military campaigns. This attitude caused the Senate in 1971 to reject Nixon's foreign aid requests submitted to Congress for approval for fiscal years 1972 and 1973. The congressional decision was a historic event, since it was the first time that Congress refused to fund foreign assistance programs. USAID reports that there were three reasons for the Senate's refusal: "(1) opposition to the Vietnam War, (2) concern that aid was too concerned with short-term military considerations, and (3) concern that aid, particularly development aid, was a giveaway program producing few foreign policy results for the United States" (USAID 2006b). The Executive-Congress conflict over the use of foreign aid can be traced to the Democratic majorities in Congress, who tended to favor foreign aid but also abhorred the human and social costs of the military operations in Indochina and Latin America, which were often secretly supported by U.S. foreign aid. Until Congress legislated human rights provisions into the Foreign Assistance Act (FAA), the president had fairly broad power to use foreign aid monies as he desired.

The Nixon Administration did not remain idle in the face of this congressional rebuttal. The Nixon Administration condemned the idea that the United States should use its vast foreign aid resources to pressure governments to reduce the level of political repression, citing concerns over sovereignty and the illegality of intervention in the domestic affairs of another state. Nixon's realist perspective that human rights were a domestic matter had several negative outcomes for U.S. human rights policy (Cohen 1979). In particular, the United States during this time did not play an active role in the promotion of human rights globally. Although the United States provided strong, passionate leadership in the creation of the Universal Declaration of Human Rights, it failed to ratify the international human rights treaties, the International Covenant on Civil and Political Rights, and the International Covenant on Economic, Social and Cultural Rights. Moreover, the United States rarely condemned human rights violations, either publicly or privately, during this period.

From the perspective of the Nixon Administration, neither U.S. interests nor the cause of human rights would be furthered by public humiliation and damaged relations with aid recipient countries. To deny a state foreign aid due to its human rights abuses would be tantamount to public humiliation. Therefore, human rights violators did not suffer a decrease in the amount of U.S. aid they received.

In the first study of its kind, Lars Schoultz (1981) found that U.S. aid was given disproportionately to those countries that abused the human rights of their citizens.[3] A quantitative study by Stohl, Carleton, and

Johnson (1984) supported Schoultz's findings. Stohl, Carleton, and Johnson determined that during the Nixon and Ford Administrations, there was an unfortunate direct relationship between human rights and foreign aid: more foreign assistance went to recipients with higher levels of human rights abuses. Thus, the Nixon and, later, Ford Administrations flagrantly disregarded congressional intent in the allocation of aid.

CONGRESS AND THE IMPERIAL PRESIDENT

The dissatisfaction of Congress toward the executive branch's blatant disregard for human rights prompted congressional hearings in the Subcommittee on International Organizations (later renamed the Subcommittee on Human Rights and International Organizations; see chapter 4), chaired by Representative Donald Fraser (D-MN), to examine and make recommendations for increasing the priority given to human rights by the United States. In 1973, citing a concern "over the rampant violations of human rights and the need for a more effective response from both the United States and the world community," the U.S. House Foreign Affairs Subcommittee on International Organizations began hearings on the human rights conditions in eighteen countries (U.S. Congress 1973). Fraser's Subcommittee on International Organizations denounced the United States' disregard for human rights for the sake of economic and political interests in relations with foreign governments, notably South Vietnam, Spain, Portugal, the Soviet Union, Brazil, Indonesia, Greece, the Philippines, and Chile. At the conclusion of its hearings, the subcommittee issued a report titled *Human Rights in the World Community: A Call for U.S. Leadership* on March 27, 1974. In this report, the Subcommittee determined that

> human rights factors are not accorded the high priority it deserves in our country's foreign policy. . . . [Human rights] becomes invisible on the vast foreign policy horizon of political, economic and military affairs. . . . Unfortunately, the prevailing attitude has led the United States into embracing governments which practice torture and unabashedly violate almost every human rights guarantee pronounced by the world community. Through foreign aid and occasional intervention—both overt and covert—the United States supports those governments. (United States Congress 1974, 9)

In response to the recommendations issued in the report, the State Department created the Office of Coordinator for Humanitarian Affairs and assigned human rights officers to each of its regional bureaus. The report further "proposed human rights impact statements, forceful private diplomacy, public condemnations, raising of human rights issues at the United Nations and, finally, the suspension of military and economic aid to governments that persistently abused the rights of their citizens" (Cohen 1979, 218–219). The subcommittee had jurisdiction based on Section 116 and Section 502B of the Foreign Assistance Act (to be discussed below). As a result, the subcommittee was to hold hearings on the human rights practices of countries slated to receive economic or military assistance from the United States. As chair of the subcommittee for the 94th Congress, Representative Fraser held a total of forty human rights hearings. The subcommittee's human rights hearings proved to be an important forum for witnessing human rights abuses around the world and in keeping human rights concerns in the forefront of U.S. foreign policy.

Congressional Initiatives

As a result of the civil rights movement and remorse over the Vietnam War, the American public and congressional representatives felt the responsibility to speak out on behalf of international human rights standards. Congress wrote into law formal requirements for the restriction or denial of foreign aid to countries that consistently violated the human rights of their citizens. Thus, U.S. foreign aid would not automatically be given to a country simply because it professed anticommunist sentiments. Congress and the American public believed that U.S. foreign policy should reflect the moral principles of the nation. The intention of Congress was to distance the United States from the morally reprehensible behavior of the governments of foreign aid recipients. The belief was that foreign aid ought to be directed to democratic regimes that respect human rights and fundamental freedoms. But Congress did not greatly decrease foreign aid allocations. Congress sought to exercise greater control over the foreign aid allocations, through the use of such tools as earmarking, legislating conditionality, and requiring informational reports. In this fashion, Congress also reestablished its rightful place as a partner in the making of U.S. foreign policy.

It was during this period that Congress took action to insure that human rights were given priority in decision making on foreign aid issues. Congress enacted legislation linking foreign aid and trade benefits to the status of human rights in foreign countries. By joint action, Congress amended the 1973 Foreign Assistance Act to include Section

32 as a "sense of Congress." The phrase "sense of Congress" refers to Congress' instruction that economic and military aid ought to be denied to governments that imprison or intern their citizens for political reasons. Congress, however, did not make this restriction mandatory. The initiative, introduced by Senator James Abourezk (D-SD), reads as follows:

> It is the sense of Congress that the President should deny economic or military assistance to the government of any foreign country that practices the internment or imprisonment of that country's citizens for political purposes. (Public Law No. 87-195, Section 32)

Although not a binding edict, Section 32 of the Foreign Assistance Act did foreshadow congressional intent in constraining executive license to financially and militarily support governments that violate the human rights of their citizens. Nixon responded to congressional attempts to link U.S. foreign assistance to a government's human rights record by arguing that there was no objective way to distinguish between good and bad countries since human rights abuses were widespread and hidden. In a congressional hearing before the House Foreign Affairs Committee in June 1974, Robert Ingersoll, Assistant Secretary of State for East Asian and Pacific Affairs, testified that the administration had not instituted any measures to satisfy the directives of Section 32 (Ingersoll 1974). Ingersoll explained that the Nixon Administration could not define "political prisoner" and, therefore, could not objectively determine who was or was not a political prisoner. The Nixon Administration simply ignored the wishes of Congress. Stephen Cohen (1982) believes that Congress expanded and amended the human rights legislation as a direct consequence of the executive branch's persistent noncompliance with its wishes.

U.S. Security Assistance

Because the executive branch ignored the mood of Congress, in 1974 Representative Fraser delivered a letter, signed by 105 congressional members, to Kissinger warning that Congress' support for foreign aid would depend on the inclusion of human rights concerns in the president's foreign policy decisions. Nixon and Kissinger ignored the letter. As a result, Section 502B was added to the Foreign Assistance Act, to prohibit security assistance to governments that grossly violate human rights. However, this new section was still presented as a sense of Congress stipulation. 502B(a)(1) of the 1974 Foreign Assistance Act states,

It is the sense of Congress that, except in extraordinary circumstances[,] the President shall substantially reduce or terminate
security assistance to any government which engages in a consistent pattern of gross violations of internationally recognized
human rights, including torture or cruel, inhuman or degrading
treatment or punishment; prolonged detention without charges; or
other flagrant denials of the right to life, liberty, and the security
of the person.

Section 502B was intended to prevent foreign governments from using
U.S. security aid to violate the human rights of their citizens and to distance the United States from repressive regimes. The modification in the
language of the legislation, from military assistance found in Section 32
to security assistance in 502B, reflects Congress' intention to limit not
only military aid but also arms sales and police equipment (S. Cohen
1982). Congress declared that the primary aim of Section 502B was to
promote compliance with internationally recognized human rights.

The use of language directly taken from international documents to
characterize gross human rights violations ("torture or cruel, inhuman
or degrading treatment or punishment; prolonged detention without
charges; or other flagrant denials of the right to life, liberty, and the
security of the person") was a deliberate attempt by congressional members not only to underscore the international character of human rights
against charges of U.S. imperialism, but also to domestically codify
international human rights law (Lawyers Committee for Human Rights
[LCHR] 1989). Thus, it was hoped, the U.S. population would become
acquainted with international standards of human rights by using words
that were very similar to their own domestic civil rights. At the same
time, the United States would be shielded from accusations of applying
its own standards to other cultures.

In order to provide the executive branch sufficient leeway in times of
an emergency that would require exceptional action, Congress wrote Section 502B with some intentional ambiguity and, regrettably, with some
inadvertent weaknesses too. Section 502B suffers from several shortcomings in language. If security assistance was to be granted despite a country's practice of gross violations, the president was required to submit to
Congress a detailed explanation of the "extraordinary circumstances,"
as stipulated in 502B. The inclusion of the phrase "extraordinary circumstances" would allow the president to continue to provide aid to
human rights–violating governments if there were significant reasons
for doing so. Unfortunately, Congress failed to define the meaning of

"extraordinary circumstances" or to place limits on the exclusions. The ambiguity of the wording would open the door for executive abuse. In hindsight, Fraser confesses, "[W]e might as well have opened the barn door and let the horses out right there! The Nixon–Ford Administration walked right through that door" (1979, 179). The LCHR reports that the executive branch broadly interpreted the phrase "extraordinary circumstances" to mean any U.S. national security interest (1989). The United States had (and still has) innumerable security interests throughout the world, be they geographical, ideological, mineral, economic, strategic, or military. Furthermore, this extremely broad interpretation of "extraordinary circumstances" made no distinction between vital or minor national security interests.

A second defect in the wording of Section 502B was the vague guideline of terminating or restricting aid due to a "consistent pattern" of human rights violations. Since there is no universal objective meaning or measure to the imprecise phrase "consistent pattern," the determination of what is or is not a consistent pattern has been unsystematic and politically motivated. The executive branch was able to get around this directive by simply failing to find patterns or by declaring the evident pattern inconsistent.

A third method of avoiding implementation of 502B was the provision that security aid not be given to "any government" that engages in human rights abuses. Terminating aid requires the establishment of a link between the official government and the human rights violations. The LCHR (1989) notes that 502B can be legally ignored if the administration maintains that the civilian government is weak and without effective control over its military force. The civilian government is, therefore, not responsible for the human rights violations committed by the military forces and is thus still eligible for foreign assistance.[4] The LCHR fears that "by providing security assistance under such circumstances, an administration could foster close relations with military institutions in countries with weak civilian governments, thereby bolstering the very elements" that are engaged in human rights abuses (1989, 24). After all, when the United States provides security aid to either a weak or strong government, the actual beneficiary of the military equipment and armaments is the recipient country's military. David Weissbrodt remarks that, at least rhetorically, the State Department and USAID have linked the presence of a consistent pattern of human rights violations to governmental responsibility. USAID writes that "a finding that a consistent pattern exists would tend to refute assertions by the country concerned that violations which occurred were the acts of unauthorized officials and at variances with official policy" (cited in Weissbrodt 1977, 258). Similarly, the State Department understands that, where a consistent pattern occurs, governmental culpability is inferred. Yet, the United States has never denied or restricted aid to any country by officially declaring a violation of Section 502B.

A fourth problem with Section 502B is that the human rights violations must be gross abuses. To be categorized as a gross violation, the human rights abuses not only must be severe but also must affect a fairly large number of people for a long period of time. Prolonged arbitrary imprisonment is a gross violation, but detention without charges for weeks or even months is not considered a gross violation due to its relatively brief period of confinement. Furthermore, isolated violations, even if severe, are not gross in that the numbers of people who suffer are relatively small. Therefore, a small number of incidents of torture and murder by a foreign government would not disqualify it to receive U.S. security assistance. Regrettably, the ambiguity of how many violations it takes to be considered too many allows many human rights–violating states the generosity of U.S. foreign aid programs.

Finally, 502B can also be successfully avoided by redefining what is or is not a military, security, or police article. Electric batons can be cattle prods and military helicopters equipped with machine guns can be classified as postal delivery vehicles, as will be later argued by the Reagan Administration in the 1980s.[5]

Since the 1974 version of 502B was merely an advisory sense of Congress, the Ford Administration was able to legally ignore congressional intent. President Gerald Ford's Secretary of State, Henry Kissinger, as expected, vehemently opposed linking human rights to foreign policy endeavors, and fought against the idea of increasing congressional initiative in the formation of U.S. foreign policy. In a hearing before the House Committee on International Relations, Undersecretary of State for Security Assistance Carlyle Maw testified that no security assistance was denied based on a country's human rights record (1976). In a presidential report submitted to Congress on the steps taken by his administration to comply with Section 502B, Ford used the report to condemn the policy and clearly indicated that he had no intention of denying military aid or arms sales based on human rights violations. Congress' first attempt to make Section 502B obligatory upon the executive branch was vetoed by President Ford. In so doing, the Ford Administration claimed that the implementation of 502B would constrain executive discretion in foreign policy decision making. Congress responded to this veto by legislating a binding provision.

In 1976, the Humphrey-Cranston Amendment aimed at strengthening Section 502B of the Foreign Assistance Act by removing the sense of Congress language in the original section, and replacing it with an explicit mandate for the termination of security aid to gross violators. The Humphrey-Cranston Amendment directed that the president be legally obligated to deny or restrict aid to countries violating human rights, unless extraordinary circumstances could be proven. Congress also reserved unto itself the right to overrule the Executive. Thus, the 1976 amended version of 502B put into place another method of congressional control over security assistance and presidential prerogative. If Congress wished to challenge the president's decision to provide military assistance to a country, it could first request a detailed report from the secretary of state on the human rights situation in the country in question along with a comprehensive explanation for why the Executive claims extraordinary circumstances. If the report was not sent within thirty days, all security aid would be automatically and immediately terminated until the report was filed. Upon review of the report, Congress, by joint resolution, could terminate the security assistance for the country. Despite these cumbersome and time-consuming reports to Congress, the extraordinary circumstances clause was invoked by Ford in 1976 to continue to provide military aid to Argentina, Haiti, Indonesia, Iran, Peru, and the Philippines.

A final congressional initiative during this period that tried to further regulate U.S. human rights in foreign policy was Section 301 of the International Security Assistance and Arms Export Control Act of 1976 (PL 94-329). This act affirmed the promotion of human rights standards as an explicit goal of U.S. foreign policy. The act instructed the president to formulate military assistance programs to promote human rights and to avoid identification with repressive regimes. This legislation reiterated the termination or restriction of security assistance to governments that consistently violate the human rights of their citizens. The act also made it mandatory for the State Department to file complete reports on the human rights situation in every country receiving security assistance.

Congress enjoined the State Department to create an Office of Human Rights and Humanitarian Affairs (HA) to monitor human rights and assemble annual public reports on the human rights conditions in every state that receives U.S. foreign assistance. Later, this mandate was extended to include all countries that are members of the United Nations. In order to ensure executive compliance and promote congressional oversight, Congress directed that the annual reports (referred to as *Country Reports on Human Rights Practices*) that are submitted for economic aid must include the particulars of how the aid will benefit needy people, while military aid reports must establish that the aid is justified by extraordinary circumstances, the national interest of the United States, or both. Congress believed that by forcing the Executive's bureaucracy to prepare and publish the reports, it would prevent the Executive from ignoring the human rights practices in recipient states.

To encourage a proactive human rights policy, these reports must also outline the steps taken by the administration to promote human rights. Moreover, foreign governments would know that the details of their human rights abuses were being collected and that the findings would be made available for worldwide review. The hope was that the foreign government, in order to moderate public criticism, would undertake corrective measures to reduce human rights abuses. Section 301 further made clear that if the reports were not forthcoming, security assistance to violating countries would be terminated.

U.S. Economic Aid

In 1975, the Harkin Amendment (also referred to as Section 116) was added to the International Development and Food Assistance portion of the Foreign Assistance Act. The Harkin Amendment prohibits economic assistance to any country that commits gross human rights violations unless it can be shown that the aid will directly benefit the poor and needy. Section 116 was legislated as a legally binding mandate. Section 116 of the Foreign Assistance Act states,

> No assistance may be provided under this part to the government of any country which engages in [a] consistent pattern of gross violations of internationally recognized human rights, including torture or cruel, inhuman, or degrading treatment or punishment, prolonged detention without charges, or other flagrant denial of the right to life, liberty, and the security of person, unless such assistance will directly benefit the needy people in such country.

Congress legislated Section 116 in reaction to the Nixon and Ford Administrations' use of "economic aid to prolong the staying power of regimes more than to provide help for needy people," particularly the repressive regimes in power in Chile and South Korea (Fraser 1979,

148). Representative Fraser's own report, *Human Rights in the World Community: A Call for U.S. Leadership* (United States Congress 1974), concluded that U.S. economic assistance helped to sustain some of the world's most brutally repressive regimes. An example of the misuse of economic aid to bolster a brutal, authoritarian, yet U.S.-friendly regime was the Food for Peace program (PL 480) providing Chile, post-Allende, with the required cash necessary for Chile to become one of the best customers of U.S. arms manufacturing. Fraser states that "one of the major benefits to Chile of Public Law 480 Title 1 loans is to indirectly assist Chile in purchasing arms from the United States" (as quoted in Schoultz 1981, 186). In the year after Chile's 1973 military coup, which murdered President Salvador Allende Gossens and installed General Augusto Pinochet Ugarte in power, Chile, with only 3 percent of the world's population, was given 48 percent of all the Food for Peace credits.

The wording of Section 116 was forceful in mandating presidential compliance to terminate aid, and thus abandoned the sense of Congress rhetoric found in the initial version of Section 502B. Nevertheless, Section 116 suffers from many of the same defects of language found in 502B of the Foreign Assistance Act. Congress left the vague reference to a "consistent pattern" of human rights violations and the provision that economic aid not be given to "any government" that engages in human rights abuses in the legislation. Section 116 suffers an additional ambiguity, which is referred to as the "needy people clause." Critics refer to this as the "needy people loophole." The clause was included to pacify those in Congress who argued that there were more appropriate methods of promoting human rights than cutting off development aid to the poor. Advocates of foreign aid asked, "Why should the poor be twice penalized . . . once by their government torturing and repressing them, and then by the U.S. by depriving them economic aid?' Nevertheless, it became a loophole because the State Department and USAID, the two bureaucracies charged with the administration and supervision of U.S. bilateral economic aid, would depict virtually all projects to be funded by economic aid in such a way as to appear to directly benefit the poor. Not only did very few projects fail to be funded, but also most were not even scrutinized for their human rights impact. Thus, U.S. economic aid could be used to prolong the staying power of repressive regimes.

Congressional documents specify that the clause "directly benefit the needy people" was "designed to provide safeguards against the possibility that authoritarian governments which deprive their citizens of basic political and human liberties do not divert U.S. assistance from its intended purposes or use such assistance to bolster their repressive regimes" (cited in Weissbrodt 1977, 245). If the Executive Office chooses to exercise the needy people clause, the president must present to Congress a detailed explanation of how the assistance will directly benefit those in need. The Harkin Amendment further legislated that, if Congress was not satisfied with the president's report, either the House or the Senate could, within thirty days, override presidential intent and cut off economic aid. The language of Section 116 made economic aid easier to terminate than military assistance. In addition, Section 116 placed a heavy burden of proof on the president if he wanted to continue economic assistance to human rights–abusing regimes. Section 116 received widespread support in Congress, both by those members of Congress who were genuinely concerned with human rights and by those who wished to see all foreign aid terminated.

However, denials of economic aid were and still are uncommon. This is mainly for two reasons. First, by definition, USAID projects, particularly PL 480 Food for Peace programs, are essentially created to meet the basic human needs of the poor. Therefore, virtually all USAID loans and grants can be given without an assessment of the human rights conditions in the recipient state. Economic aid, by common (but erroneous) definition and assumption, is used to help recipient countries develop and raise the living standard of the poor.[6] Second, and more cynically, economic aid has little to do with altruism. Foreign aid is tied to procurement, denoting that aid recipients must purchase their equipment, arms, materials, supplies, parts, and services or other commodities made in the United States from U.S. corporations. The intent is to increase market opportunities for U.S. business. For example, PL 480, which was originally titled the Surplus Disposal Program, has three goals: to expand U.S. trade, to use the United States' surplus foodstuffs to fight global hunger and to encourage economic growth, and to cultivate new markets for U.S. agricultural commodities. PL 480's primary objective was undoubtedly to eliminate food surpluses from domestic markets. Food surpluses depress market prices for the commodity, consequently reducing the profits to be made by U.S. farmers, retailers, and investors. PL 480 had the added economic benefit of opening new or expanding old markets for U.S. farm products. Food aid was never meant to replace a country's normal commercial food imports.[7] Hoy (1998) concurs with the argument that PL 480 does little to combat world hunger since, historically, over one-third of U.S. food aid goes to countries that have no food shortages.

Another congressional initiative tying human rights to U.S. economic policy is the Jackson-Vanik Amendment to the Trade Reform Act of 1974.[8] The Jackson-Vanik Amendment prohibits the granting of Most Favored Nation (MFN) status and trade credit to nonmarket (communist) countries that deny or restrict the right of their citizens to emigrate. Specifically, the Jackson-Vanik Amendment denies MFN to any communist/socialist country that

1. denies its citizens the right or opportunity to emigrate;
2. imposes more than a nominal tax on emigration or on the visas or other documents required for emigration, for any purpose or causes whatsoever; or
3. imposes more than a nominal tax, levy, fine, fee, or other charge on any citizen as a consequence of the desire of such citizen to emigrate to the country of his choice. (19 U.S.C. 2432, Sec. 402(a))

Country-Specific Legislation

In addition to the general legislation, listed above, linking human rights considerations to U.S. foreign policy initiatives, Congress also held country hearings and enacted country-specific legislations. In 1974, Congress began to pass human rights legislations that applied only to a specific country. Country-specific legislation is used when, in the opinion of David Forsythe, Congress "perceives both a human rights problem and an administration's lack of attention to that problem" (1988, 160). Country-specific legislation is commonly used to deny or reduce security assistance to named countries on human rights grounds. Country hearings are in-depth investigations by the Subcommittee on International Organizations into the human rights issues of a particular foreign aid-receiving country and serve as a determination of the role of the United States in promoting human rights in that country. As chair of the subcommittee for the 94th Congress, Representative Fraser held a total of forty human rights hearings. The Subcommittee on International Organizations has jurisdiction over Section 116 and Section 502B of the Foreign Assistance Act. The subcommittee's human rights hearings proved to be an important forum for witnessing human rights abuses around the world and in keeping human rights concerns in the forefront of U.S. foreign policy.

Country-specific legislation is generally effective for a single year and must be reviewed by Congress annually. Stephen Cohen asserts that although usually applicable only to military aid and of limited duration, the country-specific legislation was also a finding by Congress that the Executive had failed to apply Section 502B to a government engaged in "gross violations" and that "extraordinary circumstances" would not justify past levels of military aid. (1982, 256)

Consequently, country-specific legislation often corrected for presidential impudence in ignoring U.S. law, the manifestation of congressional will. But it also put the president and abusing states on notice that their behavior would not go unnoticed.

It is interesting to note that most congressional initiatives regarding human rights issues were directed at U.S. friends and allies since the United States did not provide economic or military assistance to communist states. Human rights policy with regard to the communist bloc was a different issue altogether. In communist countries, human rights were to be protected and monitored by the Helsinki Accords. The next section examines more closely the procedures and politics associated with these accords.

THE HELSINKI CONFERENCE

In the summer of 1975, the leaders of thirty-five European countries, along with Canada and the United States, met in Helsinki, Finland, for a three-day summit that culminated with the signing of the Final Act of the Conference on Security and Cooperation in Europe (CSCE). The Final Act, also known as the Helsinki Accords, includes the recognition that European states have sovereign and juridical equality and the right to territorial integrity, freedom, and political independence to choose their political, economic, and cultural systems. Furthermore, the thirty-five nations agreed to refrain from direct or indirect intervention in the domestic affairs of other nations. The principle of nonintervention would require states to refrain from using military, political, or economic coercion to impose their interests.

The parties to the Final Act also pledged to "respect human rights and fundamental freedoms including the freedom of thought, conscience, religion or belief, for all without distinction as to race, sex, language or religion" (Basket 1, Principle VII). The state signatories also contracted to undertake programs and policies designed to promote and encourage effective exercise of rights and freedoms, including the right to emigrate. The Final Act was divided into different sections called "Baskets," dealing with different aspects of the agreement. The incorporation of human rights in the Helsinki Accords is found in Basket 1 and Basket

3. Basket 1, Principle VII compels respect for human rights and fundamental freedoms, while Principle VIII recognizes the right to self-determination. Basket 3 explicitly advocates free movement of people, and freedom of ideas and information (through open access to the media).

At the outset, because the Final Act legitimizes the territorial borders of the Soviet sphere of influence, and because the U.S. delegation led by Ford and Kissinger was inattentive to human rights considerations, the United States' response to the Helsinki Accords was halfhearted. Korey (1990) explains that the United States' initial unenthusiastic and indifferent response to the three-year Helsinki discussion was a result of Kissinger's skepticism with the notion of human rights. Kissinger believed that pushing forward the human rights agenda would threaten his détente initiative with the Soviet Union. Meanwhile, the Reagan conservatives believed that the Helsinki Accords sanctioned the Soviet Union's natural sphere of influence in Eastern Europe. Ronald Reagan, at the time a Republican governor from California, denounced the Ford Administration's decision to sign the Helsinki document and criticized this move as a "stamp of approval on Russia's enslavement of the captive nations" (Buncher 1977, 33). Undersecretary of State George Ball referred to Helsinki as a defeat for the West and a betrayal of the people of Eastern Europe. Ford was sharply accused of giving away Eastern Europe. Soviet dissident Andrei Sinyavsky "recalls that he wept bitter tears when he read the text [of the Final Act]" (Korey 1983, 28). Therefore, when Congress proposed the establishment of a committee to monitor compliance with the accords, President Ford vigorously opposed congressional efforts. It was an election year, the issue split the Republican Party, and Ford wanted Helsinki to be forgotten. Ford's retreat from the Helsinki Accords galvanized the Carter campaign.

The Final Act of the Helsinki Accords included a provision for regular, public review of its implementation. The monitoring of the Helsinki Accords scrutinized human rights in Eastern Europe and the Soviet Union. In the United States, reports of the persecution of human rights dissidents and activists disturbed the public and members of Congress. As a result, the U.S. Congress legislated for itself a pivotal role in overseeing the accords. Congress created a joint legislative-executive commission to monitor the implementation of the Final Act, chaired by Congressman Dante Fascell (D-FL). The Helsinki Commission, originally made up of eighteen members of Congress and three members from the executive branch (one each from the Department of State, the Department of Commerce, and the Department of Defense), was charged with monitoring Eastern Europe's compliance with its pledge to ensure the human rights of its citizens and to promote the development of programs to expand East–West economic cooperation. In order to fulfill its monitoring responsibility, Congress mandated that the executive branch provide the Helsinki Commission with a semiannual report surveying European compliance and outlining programs of cooperation. The commission was to report directly to Congress. President Ford, still attempting to distance himself from the Helsinki Accords, signed the legislation creating the Helsinki Commission, but negotiated an observer, not member, status to the executive branch.

Jeffrey Ross (1992) claims that the Helsinki Conference was seen by Leonid Brezhnev, the leader of the Soviet Union, as a means to legitimize the post-World War II division of Europe. In order to expedite Western endorsement, the Soviet Union agreed to the inclusion into the Final Act of what they assumed was an impotent provision: Basket 3. By making minor concessions to Basket 3, the Helsinki Accords facilitated the transfer of technical knowledge, credits, and trade to the Soviet Union. Ross concludes, "Ironically, accords designed to preserve Communist power in Eastern Europe were a major factor in its demise" (1997, 328). The Ford Administration along with the leaders of the Soviet Union were surprised with the strength and influence of the human rights provisions.

As indicated in the previous chapters, the conflict between the president and Congress in the development and implementation of U.S. human rights policy is further complicated by the bureaucratic politics of the large executive branch bureaucracies. The Department of State, under Kissinger, thwarted congressional directives to collect and publish reports on the human rights conditions of foreign client states. The State Department thought that doing so would interfere with the diplomatic purposes of their embassies.

THE EXECUTIVE BRANCH REBUFF

The State Department was often hostile toward congressional initiatives that targeted foreign governments allied to the United States.[9] The State Department traditionally views its primary responsibility to be diplomatic and emissary, building cordial relations with foreign leaders, negotiating agreements, and representing the United States. Reporting on a country's human rights abuses contradicts this noble mission. Accordingly, the collection and publication of critical information on friendly regimes were seen by the State Department as conflicting with its primary duty. Thus, a major barrier to an authentic human rights policy during the Nixon Administration was the disdain for human rights by the head of the State Department, Secretary of State Henry Kissinger. Robert Boettcher (1980) writes that a sense of confrontation and opposition prevailed between the State Department and Fraser's human rights activities at the time Kissinger presided over the bureaucracy.

Congress created a bureaucratic office in the Department of State to monitor and report on the human rights situations in countries receiving U.S. aid.[10] Section 301 of the International Security and Arms Export Control Act legislated the establishment of a Coordinator for Human Rights and Humanitarian Affairs.[11] The Ford Administration largely ignored the Office of Human Rights and Humanitarian Affairs and attempted to subvert its mandate to report on the human rights situations in foreign aid recipient countries. The first Coordinator for HA, James Wilson Jr., "kept a low profile and had relatively little impact on policy" (Maynard 1989, 179). The duties of the newly created bureaucracy were to monitor decisions to provide foreign assistance to gross violators of human rights, formulate U.S. foreign policy toward human rights, and prepare the annual human rights reports.

In 1975, the State Department filed its first report on the human rights situations in countries receiving U.S. assistance. Once published, the *Country Reports* were regarded as generally weak in substance and heavily biased. Weissbrodt (1977) observes that the 1975 *Country Reports* did not allude to a single country as a human rights violator, nor did it record the "objective facts" on verifiable human rights abuses of aid recipient countries. Yet, due to his scorn for the linkage between human rights and foreign policy initiatives, Secretary of State Kissinger attempted to prevent the release of the State Department's *Country Reports* (Cohen 1979, 221) due to their unflattering, but by most accounts understated, portrayals of several U.S. allies. Kissinger believed that a human rights report on countries friendly to the United States would harm the management of U.S. foreign policy. Salzberg and Young report that "during the Nixon and Ford Administrations, the Subcommittee on International Organizations was frequently frustrated in its efforts to obtain frank and complete testimony from the department on human rights violations in particular countries" (1977, 278). Often, when the country in question was a U.S. ally, the process of human rights reporting was stalled or distorted by the regional bureaus and, therefore, the reports and testimonies given to Congress were inaccurate. The State Department was vigorous in its criticism of the human rights situations in communist countries but tended to defend and downplay the human rights violations in pro-American regimes. Congress, by necessity, came to rely on the information provided by human rights nongovernmental organizations.

In response to criticism that the report was fragmentary and rudimentary, Undersecretary of State Carlyle Maw responded that "the Department has 'studied these analyses extensively' and had concluded that, while '(s)ome countries presented more serious evidence of violation than others . . . we have found no adequately objective way to make distinctions of degree between nations'" (Franck and Weisband 1979, 88). According to the State Department, human rights could not be a focus of foreign diplomacy because there was no common definition of what human rights were, although the language of Sections 502B and 116 both clearly inventoried violations of human rights. Nor was there a consensus, claimed the State Department, as to the appropriate standard for human rights achievement. Historians and political researchers, having examined White House records, have concluded that Kissinger believed the reports to be too inflammatory, and directed the State Department to whitewash the human rights conditions in allied repressive states. Kissinger reasoned that "since all but a handful of countries committed human rights violations it served no useful purpose to specify for criticism American allies and friends" (cited in Weissbrodt 1977, 244).

The 1976 *Country Reports* were more candid and detailed, but remained classified by the State Department. The classification of the reports made the reports unavailable to the public. Congressional pressure compelled declassification, making the reports open to the public. Before declassification, the State Department "responded by excising certain material but ultimately acceded to congressional pressure and, in December 1976, the [1976] reports were made public" (Weissbrodt 1977, 265). In keeping with its traditional role as diplomat and envoy, the State Department distanced itself from the derogatory human rights information published in the *Country Reports*. When egregious behavior could not be downplayed or overlooked, the State Department would quote Amnesty International, the International Commission of Jurists, or a country hearing on the violation of human rights standards. This maneuver was used even when the State Department conducted substantial human rights studies and had firsthand information about a specific situation. Furthermore, the early State Department reports neglected to include incidents of country cooperation with international organizations' human rights investigations when the country was not a U.S.

friend or ally. Lastly, the early reports relied heavily on information provided by the foreign government itself.

Realizing that the hostility and indifference to human rights within the State Department were in part due to a lack of bureaucratic careerism—since no agency or career diplomat had a stake in promoting human rights—Congress responded by upgrading the Bureau of Human Rights and Humanitarian Affairs in 1977. The bureau was to be headed by the coordinator for human rights. This promotion in the bureaucratic structure institutionalized human rights issues in the Department of State and foreign policy. But Cohen (1979) identified three stumbling blocks to an effective human rights policy managed by the State Department. First, none of the newly designated human rights officers were of senior grade. Therefore, this corps of human rights officers did not have the authority or influence to integrate human rights concerns in policy planning. In response to this reality, Congress would later upgrade the position of coordinator to that of assistant secretary. The assistant secretary is now responsible for preparing the annual country reports on human rights conditions around the world.

A second problem identified by Cohen (1979) was that many of the human rights officers did not have a commitment to human rights. They were merely Foreign Service officers with an additional title and additional duties. Human rights concerns were secondary to their real responsibility of maintaining amicable relations with foreign governments. Thirdly, due to the lack of support within the State Department, a position in the Bureau of Human Rights and Humanitarian Affairs was seen as a dead-end job. A post in HA was seen as punishment for those who were exiled due to some misdeed or misstep, or it became a place for those simply putting in their time before retirement. Collecting and reporting on human rights violations would not advance a foreign officer's career at the State Department.

THE PUBLIC, NONGOVERNMENTAL ORGANIZATIONS, THE MEDIA, AND THE HUMAN RIGHTS AGENDA

During the Nixon and Ford Administrations, U.S. human rights policy was legislated by Congress, ignored by the executive branch, and hindered by the agency directed to implement the policy (the State Department). Despite this inhospitable environment, nongovernmental organizations (NGOs) and private citizens continued to lobby and promote human rights concerns. Schoultz (1981) explains that, once the Vietnam War ended for the United States, NGOs were able to turn their attention to other violations of human rights committed by foreign governments supported by the United States. These NGOs were supported by an American public that was disturbed by revelations of CIA murder schemes and bloody coups, the use of U.S. economic aid to perpetuate repressive regimes, and the use of taxpayer dollars to purchase tiger cages used to incarcerate Vietnamese peasants suspected of sympathizing with the communists. U.S. citizens wanted their government's foreign policy to reflect a respect for American values, that is, democracy, individual liberty, and human rights.

Since the executive branch was indifferent to or participating in the human rights violations, human rights organizations and activists focused on the U.S. Congress to advocate morality in U.S. foreign policy. "Every piece of human rights legislation that passed the Ninety-fourth and Ninety-fifth Congresses (1975–1978) did so with the active support of human rights interest groups. . . . Most amendments followed the same legislative route from lobbyist's pen to the statute books" (Schoultz 1981, 105–6). Human rights lobbyists would often write up a draft of the legislation that they would like to see become U.S. law, and give it to a sympathetic member of Congress. If the proposed bill appeared to face difficulties with a conservative majority in Congress, a member of Congress with human rights sensibilities or concerned constituencies could simply hold a hearing and invite the national news services. In the post-Vietnam era, this method was often sufficient to get a bill through Congress.

Human rights nongovernmental organizations helped influence the development of U.S. human rights policy in three ways. First, human rights advocates "helped set the stage for the Fraser hearings" (Forsythe 2000, 175). Many activists came to the cause of human rights from the anti-Vietnam war and civil rights movements, repulsed by what they considered to be the immoral foreign policy of the Nixon Administration. Human rights NGOs were able to sustain public interest in and public opinion for an ethically responsible foreign policy. Second, human rights NGOs testified at Fraser's historic hearings, providing a massive quantity of documents and other evidence to corroborate allegations of gross violations of human rights. Schoultz (1981) notes that, during the 1970s, human rights NGOs provided Congress with virtually all of the data on human rights violations in Latin America. Information on the human rights conditions and U.S. involvement in Latin America was often withheld from Congress by the executive branch. Finally, several of Fraser's foreign policy staffers were associated with NGOs too. Most notably, John Salzberg, Fraser's foreign affairs advisor, was a representative of the International Commission of Jurists at the United Nations prior to joining the House Committee on Foreign Affairs staff. Salzberg coauthored the landmark report *Human Rights in the World Community: A Call for U.S. Leadership* (United States Congress 1974) with Fraser. NGOs' major strength lies, in the opinion of Clarke, O'Conner, and Ellis (1997), in their advocacy of human rights and social justice in foreign policy. NGOs run campaigns raising public awareness of their causes, provoking public reaction, and lobbying the government to provide more aid or cut it off to certain countries based on their human rights records.

CONCLUSION

The original paradox in the formation of U.S. human rights policy was a matter of unintended consequences. Although the president and the executive branch fought to eliminate human rights concerns from foreign policy and foreign aid allocation decisions, the idea of human rights and morality as foundations for U.S. foreign policy resonated with or was found particularly useful politically by many members in Congress during this time. U.S. human rights policy was wrought through the constitutional conflict between President Nixon and Congress. Clearly, U.S. human rights policy was not an intentionally planned strategy. It was instead the result of Congress' attempt to rein in an imperial president and modify Nixon's immoral foreign policy behavior.

CHAPTER 3

U.S. Human Rights Policy, the Unintended Victim:
The Carter Administration

After Kissinger and Nixon, Vietnam and Watergate, there has been a yearning for morality in foreign policy so palpable it could be marketed.

Ronald Steel (1977)

One of the most celebrated features of the Carter Administration was its emphasis on human rights. Carter's foreign policy was a definite shift from the realpolitik of the Nixon Administration. President James Earl "Jimmy" Carter was committed to the issue of morality in U.S. foreign affairs. Regrettably, due to the dissension within the White House and in the State Department, the United States' human rights policy during his presidency became the unintended victim of bureaucratic infighting and international power politics. An inconsistent, and often contradictory, human rights policy was the consequence of the opposing ideologies and foreign policy goals of Secretary of State Cyrus Vance and National Security Advisor Zbigniew Brzezinski. Furthermore, a coherent and effective human rights policy was a casualty of the foreign policy bureaucracy backbiting within the Department of State. The State Department bureaucracy is responsible for overseeing human rights legislation. Yet, identifying a foreign government as a human rights abuser is contrary to the State Department's traditional function as diplomat and mediator. Therefore, under Carter, the State Department hampered congressional intent and presidential directives to implement human rights legislation. Additionally, the newly created Bureau of Human Rights and Humanitarian Affairs, headed by a political appointee without foreign policy experience, was seen as an intruder in the established bureaucratic political order. During the Carter Administration, a climate of confrontation prevailed within the State Department, between the regional bureaus and the Bureau of Human Rights and Humanitarian Affairs in particular. And, finally, Carter's ideals fell victim to the reality of power politics and Soviet expansionist behavior. Thus, paradoxically, U.S. human rights policy became victimized at a time when the "human rights president" was sitting in the White House. During the Carter era, U.S. human rights policy became incoherent, inconsistent, and even incongruous at times.

IDEALISM

Jimmy Carter's campaign for the presidency of the United States focused on the need for morality in government and foreign affairs. To an idealist, foreign policy ought to include moral principles because these values reflect the true character of the United States and the American people. The use of foreign aid can be a tool to further these objectives. A moral foreign policy would prevent the United States from becoming associated with or supporting repressive governments that, in the long run, are unstable and dangerous because of their lack of popular support.[1]

In his 1975 book, *Why Not the Best?* Carter expressed his desire to formulate American foreign policy based on morality, ethics, and honesty. Throughout the Democratic presidential primaries, the theme of morality in foreign policy was constant. But, at that point, there was no mention of human rights yet. The spotlight on human rights did not emerge until the preparation of the 1976 Democratic platform. Human rights proved to be a valuable political tool to unite the Democratic Party, both the leaders and the voters. Polls indicated that the American public responded favorably to the issue of human rights. For liberals, the policy promised a crusade against right-wing dictators (especially the military governments of Latin America), and embodied atonement for Vietnam. For conservatives, the policy offered a lever against communism and its abuses—also a way, in National Security Council (NSC) staff member William Odom's words, "to really beat up morally on the Soviets" (Dumbrell 1997, 17). Furthermore, a focus on human rights gave substance to Carter's proposal to restore morality to U.S. foreign policy. Jimmy Carter's appropriation of the human rights momentum moved the protection of human rights from Congress to the White House. Human rights, once little more than a controversy in domestic politics, became the main theme of U.S. foreign policy in all its international and domestic ramifications.

After the Watergate fiasco, the American public sought a leader with strong moral character. They elected Jimmy Carter, a virtuous Christian who taught Sunday school. Americans wanted a return to the virtuous myth of American foreign policy pitting good versus evil, right versus wrong, while, at the same time, avoiding international entanglements. Carter promised to return America to the path of righteousness, vowing never to do anything that would violate his own moral and ethical standards. The moral restoration of America's foreign policy was set in motion on January 20, 1977. In his Inaugural Address, Carter declared the United States' commitment to human rights:

> Because we are free we can never be indifferent to the fate of freedom elsewhere. Our moral sense dictates a clear-cut preference for those societies which share with us an abiding respect for individual human rights. . . . Our commitment to human rights must be absolute. . . . (Carter 1977a)

As an idealist, Jimmy Carter was convinced that human nature is essentially good. In his May 1977 Commencement Address at Notre Dame University, Carter reiterated his commitment to human rights and moral values in foreign policy behavior. Carter lauded the "good sense" of the citizens of the United States and promised to share with them the decision making in foreign policy (Carter 1977b). Meyer reports, "He [Carter] said he wanted to make the U.S. government as good as the American people. He believed that morality had to be the basis of international policy" (1998, 54). Carter believed that the United States' foreign policy should mirror the nation's moral principles. People and governments are capable of mutual aid and collaboration because, fundamentally, they are concerned for each other's welfare. All people and nations hold a common interest (a harmony of interest) in peace. All that needs to be done is to construct the world through international law on the basis of our shared universal values, and to develop international forums to work out our disagreements and provide collective security.

The Carter Administration pledged to implement a foreign policy based on moral considerations. Carter indicated his administration's commitment to human rights by signing, in 1977, the International Covenant on Economic, Social and Cultural Rights and the International Covenant on Civil and Political Rights. Carter argued, in a speech before the United Nations, that the United States has not only a legal right but also a responsibility to speak out against human rights violations wherever and whenever they occur.

Carter backed up these large symbolic gestures with tangible legislation. To emphasize his determination to incorporate morality into the foreign policy process, Carter signed Presidential Directive 13 (PD-13) in May 1977. PD-13 declared that arms transfers were to be exceptional tools of U.S. foreign policy. By presidential dictate, Carter greatly reduced the two largest security assistance programs, Military Assistance Program (MAP) and Foreign Military Sales (FMS), and prohibited the retransfers of U.S. military equipment, with the exception of retransfers to Israel, North Atlantic Treaty Organization (NATO), Japan, Australia, and New Zealand. He also prohibited any commercial arms sales. Furthermore, a proposed recipient's ability to secure U.S. arms would be based on its human rights conditions and the economic impact on the recipient's development. Before arms transfers could be authorized, the Bureau of Human Rights and Humanitarian Affairs would have to determine the human rights consequences of the transfers. Carter affirmed that his administration's absolute commitment to human rights would apply to both pro-U.S. and anti-U.S. regimes.

THE IMPLEMENTATION OF U.S. HUMAN RIGHTS POLICY

The Carter Administration initially stated that there was to be a single standard for U.S. human rights policy, and that this policy would apply to friend and foe alike. In a University of Georgia "Law Day" speech (1977), Cyrus Vance, Carter's secretary of state, defined the administration's understanding of human rights as integrity of the person (the right to be free from governmental torture, nonjudicial execution, and prolonged detention), the right to economic and social goods (the right to food, shelter, and medial care), and civil and political liberties (such as free speech and freedom of religion). Moreover, foreign assistance was to be favorably linked to the human rights performance of the recipient country. The challenge before the Carter Administration was to carry the issue of a single standard of human rights from campaign pledge into foreign policy behavior.

However, a shift from an absolute principle to a case-by-case standard position on human rights took place in just a few short months after Carter's inauguration. Following the Georgia Law Day speech, the rhetoric of a single standard was dropped and quickly replaced by a case-by-case determination of the best way to further human rights in specific countries. The administration realized it would require a certain amount of flexibility in order to further the absolute principle of human rights. Carter, who did believe human rights were absolute, adjusted the ideal to reflect the reality of the international system. U.S. foreign assistance would be considered on a case-by-case basis due to "the limits of our power and of our wisdom . . . [in] a matter for informed and careful judgment" (Vance 1977, 208–209). Defenders of Carter's human rights policy claimed the principle of human rights remained absolute. Only the method of implementation and influence of compliance were determined on a case-by-case manner. The Carter Administration required flexibility to implement a carrot-and-stick approach to human rights policy. Some states responded better to quiet diplomacy, others to public criticism, and yet another set of states responded only to sanctions. Many human rights advocates do agree that human rights strategies should be devised on a country-by-country basis. Roberta Cohen asserts, "Measures effective in one country may prove harmful or ineffective in another" (1982, 230). She uses the example of Chile, where denouncements there resulted in the release of political prisoners, whereas similar denunciations in Uganda led to threats against Americans.

Still, critics believe that the Carter Administration simply created a double standard in the implementation of U.S. human rights policy. The Carter Administration imposed human rights conditions in Latin America while ignoring equally vile human rights practices in countries where the United States maintained strong military, economic, or strategic interests. Among the countries where such interests prevailed were South Korea, Indonesia, and the Soviet Union. The result was that bilateral foreign aid became a means to compel human rights standards in small and weak countries with little strategic importance to the United States. However, countries that were politically and strategically important could violate human rights without the threat of U.S. condemnation or withdrawal of aid.

The Carter Administration's aspiration to an evenhanded, single standard for human rights in the allocation of foreign aid was unrealistic. The United States could only influence, through foreign aid and trade, those countries with which it was on friendly terms. Consequently, foreign aid and trade were focused on right-wing, pro-American regimes. The United States did not provide economic or military aid to its enemies, which during the Cold War were defined as leftist or communist countries. Therefore, foreign aid as leverage for human rights purposes was limited to anticommunist, pro-American governments.

Given this case-by-case approach to human rights and what Joshua Muravchik (1986) believes was a leftist bias among many of Carter's appointees, Carter's human rights policy tended to focus primarily on the abuses in Latin America. Anthony Lake, director of the State Department's Policy Planning Staff, reasoned that the United States had greater influence in Latin America than other regions. Furthermore, there were less intense security and economic interests in the region, and the abuses in Latin America were particularly severe (Kaufman 1998).

Because of the political limitations of foreign aid as a policy tool to further human rights, Carter was criticized from all sides of the political spectrum. Those who believed human rights initiatives did not go far enough or fast enough criticized Carter's policy as mere rhetoric. Conversely, those who believed that human rights were simple-minded, naïve, or even dangerous concerns for U.S. international interests complained that Carter's policy focused on the abuses of friends and allies. Finally, a third group protested that Carter's human rights policy penalized strategically unimportant states while human rights-abusing states viewed as vital to U.S. interests were ignored. For example, the United States temporarily cut aid to Ethiopia, Guatemala, El Salvador, Argentina, and Uruguay while foreign aid actually increased for South Korea, Iran, and the Philippines, states with equally abysmal human rights conditions.

Not surprisingly, then, President Carter's words of goodwill and his desire to implement a moral foreign aid policy proved difficult to implement. In response to the realities of international relations, the Carter Administration's position on human rights was erratic and inconsistent, loudly criticizing human rights abuses at certain times and with certain countries, and falling silent in the face of equally egregious abuses at different times in the case of different countries. Frequently, the inconsistency of censure regarding human rights violations was politically biased and geopolitically driven. In an attempt to renounce Nixon's immoral support of repressive rightist regimes, particularly in Latin America, Carter's human rights policy tended to focus on the abuses of Latin American rightist tyrants and military governments to the virtual exclusion of leftist governments. Zbigniew Brzezinski, Carter's national security advisor, wrote in his memoirs that he was concerned that "our human-rights policy was in danger of becoming one-sidedly anti-rightist" (1983, 128). Arthur Schlesinger believes that political bias had less to do with the inconsistency of human rights denunciation than geopolitical significance. Schlesinger (1979, 515) writes,

Washington was fearless in denouncing human rights abuses in countries like Cambodia, Paraguay and Uganda, where the United States had negligible strategic and economic interests; a good deal less fearless toward South Korea, Saudi Arabia, Yugoslavia and most of black Africa; increasingly circumspect about the Soviet Union; totally silent about China.

Studies have also shown that Carter's good intentions were often undermined by the realities of power politics. Regrettably, in the battle between geopolitical reality and human rights, human rights often lost. The statistical evidence indicates that there was not a significant relationship between human rights performance and U.S. aid during the Carter years. A quantitative study of the Carter Administration's human rights policy performed by Carleton and Stohl concludes,

> [T]here was a great deal of difference between the rhetoric and the reality of the Carter human rights policy as applied to aid distribution. The Carter Administration did not significantly withdraw material support from repressive United States friends. It made ample use of the "extraordinary circumstances" clauses written into human rights legislation. (1985, 216)

In fact, the Carter Administration never formally determined that any country "engaged in a consistent pattern of gross violations of internationally recognized human rights." Although a few countries had their security assistance reduced or denied, they were never formally called gross human rights violators. The request for aid was approved or disapproved with little explanation or clarification.[2] Stephen Cohen (1982) believes that to do so would have restricted the president's desired flexibility. Once a country was named a gross violator, any change in status due to claims of improved human rights conditions would be heavily scrutinized, as would the president's motives for granting security assistance. Consequently, in the provision of security assistance, the Carter Administration divided countries into three categories: the good, the bad, and the ugly. In the first category were governments with decent human rights records. Granting security assistance to these countries was uncontroversial. The second category included countries that, although they had violated human rights, did not exhibit a consistent pattern of gross violations of human rights. These cases presented the administration with little difficulty, and military aid and arms sales could easily be justified. The third group, the ugly, involved countries that routinely murdered and tortured their citizens. So widespread and severe were the violations that these countries would be excluded from any consideration for security assistance due to their engagement in a constant pattern of gross violations of internationally accepted human rights.

Unfortunately, countries with a consistent pattern of gross violations of human rights, such as the Philippines, South Korea, Iran, and Zaire, were found to fit the extraordinary circumstances criteria and consequently did not suffer a reduction of U.S. foreign aid allocations. In a telling example, Vance (1978) reported to the Senate Subcommittee on Foreign Operations Appropriations that, regardless of South Korea's human rights violations, the United States had fundamental security commitments—the deterrence and restraint of North Korea—and that, therefore, it was irresponsible to cut South Korea's foreign aid.

The Carter Administration was able to get around the clause in 502B, which required the denial of aid to countries that display a consistent pattern of gross violations of human rights, by determining that steps, however imperceptible, were taken to curb the violations. Stephen Cohen reports,

> In some instances the Carter Administration adopted a highly strained reading of the statute (502B) which, although not contrary to its literal terms, produced a result contrary to Congressional intent. In other cases the language was simply disregarded, so that decisions violated even the letter of the law. (1982, 264)

Thus, Carter found that in the case of Indonesia, there was not a consistent pattern of human rights violations because there was a plan to someday release the political prisoners. Furthermore, Indonesia fulfilled the extraordinary circumstances clause of Section 502B. Indonesia was a keystone of U.S. foreign policy in Southeast Asia (and a key member of the Association of Southeast Asian Nations, or ASEAN). It was anticommunist, was pro-American, provided a counterbalance to the Soviet and Chinese influence in the region, and had oil reserves.[3] So, in spite of the fact that approximately 100,000 people were murdered and another 30,000 were still incarcerated, Indonesia was not denied U.S. security assistance under Carter. William Burr and Michael Evans (2001) estimate that between 60,000 and 100,000 Timorese were killed during the first year[4] of fighting, and that hundreds of thousands became refugees. Burr and Evans report that "in 1979 the U.S. Agency for International Development estimated that 300,000 East Timorese—nearly half the population—had been uprooted and moved into camps controlled by Indonesian armed forces" (2001, 4).

Secretary Vance admitted that provisions of 502B, linking security assistance to human rights conditions within the recipient country, would be administered on a country-by-country basis as U.S. national security interests dictated (Gwertzam 1977). And this restriction of aid would not impede U.S. commercial interests. Deputy Secretary of State Warren Christopher's testimony to Congress reveals the Carter Administration's acceptance of the realist notion of self-interest in its surprisingly half-hearted application of the congressional requirement for human rights considerations in foreign policy:

> As a general rule, we have sought to implement the human rights policy without interfering with private commercial operations abroad. The primary means for implementing that policy is private diplomacy. Further, we start from a very strong presumption in favor of free trade and against interference. Free and open commercial activities abroad are critical to our economic well-being. (Christopher 1979, 157)

Thus, when U.S. bilateral aid was halted or restricted, private business enterprises and multilateral assistance still continued unabated. The result was that human rights policy was rendered impotent. Lars Schoultz reports that "for every dime halted by the U.S. government, a dollar was sent to repressive governments by U.S. corporations" (1981, 341).

The Carter Administration vowed that foreign assistance would be positively linked to the human rights attainment. Yet, the Carter Administration did not automatically terminate security assistance to gross violators, even if extraordinary circumstances could not be established. In order to maintain flexibility over the use of security assistance, the Carter Administration developed a disingenuous categorization of defense items that was divided into four subcategories:

Category 1: New weapons: tanks, artillery, fighters and bombers, and naval warships;

Category 2: Spare parts for previously acquired weapons;

Category 3: Support equipment: trucks, unarmed aircraft and ships, radios, and radars;

Category 4: Safety-related items: ambulance aircraft and air-sea rescue equipment. (S. Cohen 1982, 274)

The use of the subcategory system allowed security aid to be granted to even the worst human rights-abusing regimes. When the Carter Administration could not politically ignore Section 502B of the Foreign

Assistance Act, due to the severity and consistent pattern of the human rights abuses in the recipient country, the items in Category 1 were generally denied to the abusing government. The denial was an attempt to placate Congress and vocal nongovernmental organizations (NGOs) who demanded that the Executive implement legislative requirements that restrict or deny U.S. aid to human rights-abusing governments. Perhaps more important than the actual weapon, though, are the spare parts and support equipment that keep the military running. Items from Categories 2 and 3, which proved crucial in maintaining a military apparatus, were rarely restricted. Consequently, providing spare parts and support equipment to repressive tyrants "is to continue a significant military supply relationship between the United States and the recipient" (S. Cohen 1982, 274) in violation of 502B of the Foreign Assistance Act (FAA). Category 4 items could easily be justified due to the lifesaving characteristics of the equipment. The result of the Carter category system was that the United States provided military aid to El Salvador, Guatemala, and Argentina, countries that, according to Amnesty International were among the world's worst human rights abusers during this time period (1980).

HUMAN RIGHTS POLICY AS AN UNINTENDED VICTIM
Conflict among Presidential Advisors

Carter's human rights foreign policy was also the unintended victim of the markedly different ideological positions and resultant power struggle of Carter's inner circle. Many scholars believe that the ideological conflict among Carter's advisors weakened his ability to espouse a consistent and effective foreign policy agenda (Rosati 1981). In the early years of the Carter Administration, Secretary of State Cyrus Vance was able to influence many of the essential Carter policies, such as human rights, détente, and arms control. Vance was concerned with human rights, but not to the exclusion of other issues deemed essential to the United States' overall moral foreign policy stance. For example, Vance was the Carter Administration's primary advocate for détente and arms treaties with the Soviet Union. Vance's primary concern was to work with the Soviet leadership to strengthen détente and negotiate a Strategic Arms Limitation Talks (SALT) agreement. Of course, this strategy would require the United States to downplay the brutal human rights conditions in the Soviet Union. On the other hand, Zbigniew Brzezinski, Carter's national security advisor, vocally denounced what he believed to be Vance's excessive willingness to compromise with the Soviets for the sake of arms control. Jerel Rosati reports that Brzezinski's critical standpoint permeated the national security bureaucracy, "resulting in considerable governmental infighting that reached its peak in 1979 [when Vance resigned his post]" (1993b, 471).

However, the implementation of these Vance-influenced policies proved to be disappointing, and the power of Brzezinski increased. Brzezinski did not view human rights as important for U.S. foreign policy. Of course, Brzezinski did see the value of human rights condemnations if those human rights criticisms could be directed toward the Soviet Union. Therefore, Brzezinski recommended that the United States take a firm stance on human rights issues with regard to the Helsinki Commission. Brzezinski was a realist who was not above supporting repressive regimes if this furthered U.S. national interests. As Brzezinski later wrote,

> In the first two years of the Administration, [the issue of human rights] tended to overshadow the pressing requirements of strategic reality. In the last two, we had to make up for lost time, giving a higher priority to more fundamental interests of national security. (1983, 39)

The Carter Administration, under the direction of Brzezinski, "normalized" its relations with China. In a typical realist fashion, Brzezinski convinced Carter to use China as a strategic counterweight to Soviet power. Carter normalized trade relations with China by granting it most favored trading status in 1980. Brzezinski favored building China's military capabilities to balance the military power of the Soviet Union. This course of action would require the United States to ignore the brutal human rights violations in China. Vance opposed using China to counterbalance the Soviet Union since this would antagonize the Soviets. Vance feared that playing the China card was simply Brzezinski's own anti-Soviet politics. Vance's fears proved to be correct, as Alexander Moens reports that Brzezinski "wanted to tie together Sino-American security policy in an overt challenge to the Soviets" (1990, 125).

With every foreign policy crisis, and the resultant move toward a realist response, power shifted away from Vance to Brzezinski. Carter became more dependent on the counsel of Brzezinski. Brzezinski, by far the most hawkish of the president's advisors, orchestrated Carter's tougher stance on the Soviets. Soon after his appointment to national security advisor, Brzezinski pressed for the creation of a military Rapid Deployment Force to defend the United States' vital interests. Due to the administration's devotion to détente, Carter lacked enthusiasm for the proposal (Crabb 1982). However, the Soviet invasion of Afghanistan in 1979 drastically changed Carter's foreign policy. With the Soviet invasion of Afghanistan, Carter sharply increased defense spending and security aid allocations, created the Rapid Deployment Force, and lifted the restrictions placed on Central Intelligence Agency (CIA) covert activities. Carter's doctrine became an openly confrontational declaration toward Soviet expansionism which ended détente immediately and suspended the Soviet-American strategic arms-control agreement (SALT II). The Carter Doctrine was an unmistakably clear warning to the Soviet Union that the United States would protect its interests in the Persian Gulf region:

> Let our position be absolutely clear: An attempt by any outside force to gain control of the Persian Gulf region will be regarded as an assault on the vital interests of the United States of America, and such an assault will be repelled by any means necessary, including military force. (Crabb 1982, 329)

Brzezinski believed that the United States had to counter Soviet adventurism, particularly in the Persian Gulf region. The fact that Carter chose to "draw the line in the sand" in Afghanistan demonstrates that Brzezinski won the battle of the presidential advisors. Afghanistan was for decades prior to the Soviet invasion a client state of the Soviet Union. In 1979, the Soviet Union was simply coordinating a change in Afghan leadership from one communist despot to a more reliable communist hard-liner.

Conflict within the Executive Bureaucracy

Secretary of State Vance did support human rights initiatives. But the State Department's bureaucracy thwarted his attempts at incorporating human rights into diplomacy. Brzezinski wrote that he was "amazed at how skillful the State Department was in delaying the execution of decisions which it had not in the first placed favored" (1983). And what the State Department bureaucracy did not favor was the imposition of human rights concerns in diplomacy. Rosati believes that Carter's human rights initiatives were mainly resisted by the executive bureaucracy because, as the diplomatic corps, the State Department tended to be more pragmatic and more conservative than President Carter, and it attempted to moderate "Carter's more optimistic inclinations" (1993b, 470).

Additionally, the regional bureaus tended to resent the inclusion of human rights in foreign policy, due perhaps to the "client" relationship already discussed in chapter 1. Once again, the Foreign Service officer views his or her job as a matter of promoting and protecting the interests of the client country. Accusations of human rights abuses would undoubtedly offend the client government. Information for the human rights reports, put together by the Bureau of Human Rights and Humanitarian Affairs, is provided by the regional bureaus. Laurie Wiseberg and Harry Scoble admit that

> bureaucracies such as the State Department have tremendous inertia. Careerist officers will change their behavior only when they perceive that the opportunity structure and institutional incentives will in fact reward them for acting in a pro human rights fashion and penalize them for not doing so. (1981, 200)

Early in the Carter Administration, the Executive sought a high-level mechanism to close the needy people loophole in human rights legislation.[5] Thus, in 1977, President Carter created the Inter-Agency Group on Human Rights and Foreign Assistance, commonly referred to as the Christopher Committee or Christopher Group, named after its director, Deputy Secretary of State Warren Christopher. The Christopher Committee was created to examine foreign aid proposals and coordinate the granting of U.S. bilateral foreign aid with a recipient country's human rights practices. The Christopher Committee was made up of representatives of relevant State Department bureaus, the National Security Council, the Export-Import Bank, the Department of the Treasury, the Department of Defense, the Department of Agriculture, the Department of Commerce, United States Agency for International Development (USAID), and the Bureau of Human Rights and Humanitarian Affairs.

The Christopher Committee's mandate was to "examine our bilateral and multilateral foreign assistance decisions as they relate to human rights, to provide guidance regarding specific decisions on bilateral and multilateral assistance, and in general to coordinate the administration's position in this area" (as cited in Franck and Weisband 1979, 93). Aid allocations were approved if the human rights situation in the recipient country was good, if human rights conditions were genuinely improving, or if the project could directly benefit the needy. Franck and Weisband report that the Christopher Group had recommended deferral of several USAID projects and International Monetary Fund (IMF) loans, but the number was "small in comparison to the number . . . recommended for approval" (1979, 90). Nevertheless, on several occasions, countries that were previously advised that their human rights conditions would require a U.S. negative vote voluntarily withdrew their loan applications from IMF consideration.[6]

Even with the Christopher Committee's oversight, the number of denials was small for several reasons. First, by definition, USAID projects, particularly Public Law 480 (PL 480) (the Food for Peace programs), are essentially created to meet the basic human needs of the poor. Therefore, virtually all USAID loans were granted without a comprehensive assessment of the human rights conditions in the recipient state. Second, human rights was just one of the many factors considered in the decision to allocate U.S. foreign assistance. Finally, the major obstacle for the Christopher Committee was that several important aid programs were exempt from the committee's oversight due to intrabureaucratic conflicts.

Among the programs removed over time were military assistance, Economic Support Funds, and the Department of Agriculture's food programs. Undersecretary for Security Assistance Lucy Benson, in a turf struggle with the Bureau of Human Rights, threatened to resign her post if her programs, notably military assistance and Security Supporting Assistance (later, in 1979, it was renamed the Economic Support Funds), were not exempt from review by the Christopher Committee. This did not completely silence the bureaucratic power struggle, however, since the Bureau of Human Rights was represented on the Security Assistance Program Review Working Group and on the Arms Export Control Board. Furthermore, in a classic Warren Christopher compromise formula, the Bureau of Human Rights could appeal the undersecretary's military aid decisions to Deputy Secretary of State Christopher himself. With the removal of several important bilateral foreign assistance programs from the committee's purview because of bureaucratic turf wars, the Christopher Committee was consequently limited to reviewing human rights in relation to development assistance programs and multilateral aid proposals through the international financial institutions, specifically Section 701.

In typical bureaucratic fashion, the bulk of the work of the Christopher Committee was actually performed by the Working Group made up of assistants to the members of the parent body. The majority of cases before the Working Group could easily be decided by consensus and were then simply rubber-stamped by the Christopher Committee. Thus, the Committee only considered those cases that the Working Group could not resolve by consensus. The Christopher Group's Working Group was not immune to interbureau and interagency rivalries:

> Originally seen as a means of arriving at a unified position to take
> to its parent body, the working group proved unable to resolve the
> disagreements among its members . . . . These agencies . . . came to

meetings with only one purpose: to defend, not change, their positions. (Mower 1987, 73–74)

The Christopher Committee and its Working Group used the following criteria for determining Section 701 proposals:

1. The present human rights situation in the recipient country and any positive or negative trends.
2. The political, economic, and cultural background of the country and the level of human rights performance that [could] reasonably be expected of the country in light of that background.
3. The other fundamental U.S. interests with respect to that country; the extent to which a loan [would] directly benefit the needy; and the effectiveness of a decision to defer or oppose a loan in comparison or in combination with other available diplomatic tools for indicating our concern about human rights violations. (As quoted in Maynard 1989, 209)

The Christopher Group's criteria clearly incorporated the "needy people" and "extraordinary circumstances" loopholes written into the human rights legislation, specifically Sections 116 and 502B of the Foreign Assistance Act and Section 701 of the International Financial Institutions Act. The loopholes allow foreign assistance to be granted to gross human rights violators as long as it benefits needy people or if the United States has strategic, economic, or other interests in the recipient country. Criteria Number 2, formulated by the Christopher Committee, is particularly worrisome since it contains the chauvinistic attitude that certain countries, those that are poor or with dissimilar cultural or religious practices, cannot be expected to understand or value human rights.

Additionally, several countries received preferential treatment. Their allocation of aid was not dependent on their human rights conditions (for example, South Korea or Iran). Therefore, aid restrictions were placed only on countries with little strategic or economic importance, primarily in Latin America. In the end, Carter's policy goal of restricting foreign aid to those countries upholding international standards of human rights failed. Clarke, O'Conner, and Ellis conclude that, by the end of his tenure in office, Carter's security assistance policy was simply "what Congress would permit" (1997, 67).

The Arms Export Control Board (AECB), established in 1977, performed a function analogous to that of the Christopher Committee for military and security assistance. The AECB was charged with reviewing

U.S. military aid and human rights. The Bureau of Human Rights sat on the powerful Arms Export Control Board. But, as Lincoln Bloomfield, a National Security Committee staff member, stated, the Bureau of Human Rights' recommendations were generally overruled (Bloomfield 1981). However, as a result of the board's evaluation and report of country performance, military exports did initially drop substantially during Carter's early years compared to previous levels (Heaps 1984). It became more difficult, in the face of human rights legislation and public opinion, to militarily support egregious violators of human rights. However, with the increase in foreign policy crises, Carter's use of military and ESF aid increased.

Conflict within the State Department

Carter's human rights policy was further complicated by the bureaucratic infighting inside the State Department and between the Bureau of Human Rights and other agencies. In 1977, Congress elevated the office of human rights to that of an assistant secretary-level bureau in the State Department. Carter appointed Patricia Derian, a renowned civil rights activist, to the post of human rights coordinator. The post was soon upgraded to the rank of assistant secretary of state for human rights and humanitarian affairs,[7] and Carter increased the staff from the original two to twelve, in 1977. Additionally, a human rights officer was appointed to each regional bureau, and every U.S. embassy was assigned the task of collecting human rights information.

There was little support within the State Department, however, for human rights, for the Bureau of Human Rights, or for Patricia Derian. Maynard (1989) reports that the only reason the other bureaus within the State Department tolerated HA was the belief that HA had direct access to the president. The promotion and increase in staff along with the presidential rhetoric on human rights commitment indicated to bureaucrats that the assistant secretary of state for human rights and humanitarian affairs had the support of and access to the president. Yet, as reported by Hartmann (2001), Derian did not get an appointment to see President Carter until December 6, 1978—almost two years into the Carter presidency.

It should have come as no surprise that the Bureau of Human Rights and Humanitarian Affairs would be enmeshed in bureaucratic conflict. First, the appointment of Patricia Derian as assistant secretary of state for human rights and humanitarian affairs proved controversial in the State Department. Although Assistant Secretary of State Derian was committed to human rights, she was viewed as an outsider with no foreign policy experience. The career officers regarded Derian as an interloper who had not paid her dues. Derian was an outspoken human rights supporter, but, as her critics pointed out, her single-minded devotion to enhancing human rights lacked diplomatic subtlety. Richard Holbrooke was reported as saying that Derian "was myopically fixed on human rights as the only plank in American foreign policy," while the other bureaus in the State Department incorporated economic, security, political, and diplomatic interests (quoted in Kaufman 1998, 54). Rossiter (1984) believes that much of the confrontation between Derian and the regional offices could have been avoided if Carter had appointed a senior Foreign Service officer as the head of HA.

Derian, for her part, was frustrated by the efforts of the State Department to block the inclusion of human rights in foreign policy decision making, by the bureaucratic infighting, with the reduced influence of HA, and by the lack of commitment of the administration with regard to human rights (S. Cohen 1982; Mower 1987; Muravchik 1986). These conditions took their toll on HA, resulting in a number of vacancies within the bureau, including the departure of Senior Deputy Assistant Secretary Mark Schneider. The HA survived the loss of Schneider and later of Derian herself (who fell ill in 1980) due to the recruitment of a respected senior Foreign Service officer, Stephen Palmer. Palmer hesitantly accepted the assignment of acting assistant secretary of HA, but he did not hold the same level of commitment to human rights as Derian (Maynard 1989).

Additionally, the Bureau of Human Rights and Humanitarian Affairs had a specific and limited mandate to formulate human rights policy and to prepare the reports on human rights conditions within countries. Derian was single-minded in her pursuit to promote human rights. In contrast, the State Department had to consider a variety of issues, purposes, and viewpoints in its work. The State Department has the responsibility to develop diplomatic relations with foreign governments, to represent the U.S. government overseas, to provide policy advice to the president, to present the views of foreign governments to the U.S. government, to conduct negotiations, and to analyze and report on events abroad (Clarke 1998, 109). The State Department was rather skeptical and uneasy about the intrusion of human rights into the conventional practice of diplomacy, which it viewed as interfering with its traditional responsibilities.[8]

Human rights were seen as a hindrance to the traditional role of the State Department, which is (once again) to maintain cordial relations with foreign governments. State Department Foreign Service officers traditionally support foreign aid even to repressive governments since "the diplomat without an aid program has to work much harder to advance U.S. objectives" (Zimmerman 1993, 14). Foreign aid is an expedient tool for the diplomat in smoothing the way for mutual cooperation. Under Carter, the career Foreign Service officers found the issue of human rights controversial since it hampered their traditional function of diplomacy and protection of their client states, as seen above. Embassy personnel were reluctant to broach the topic of human rights, fearing that it might disrupt otherwise satisfactory relations. As Rubin has noted, "If relations deteriorate, the honest diplomats will appear to have failed in their mission" (1987, 246). And this would not be a good career move.

The Bureau of Human Rights had to directly counter the Foreign Service officers' tendencies to defend their client countries by understating abuses and overstating positive human rights trends. There are documented cases that, when called to testify to Congress on a country's human rights situation, some Foreign Service officers justified the reported abuses as "merely countering a Communist plot to overthrow the government" (Rubin 1987, 198). Due to the bias in the information received from the embassies, the Bureau of Human Rights often had to rely on reports from human rights organizations like Amnesty International. Human rights NGOs have argued that, in order to please their client state, the State Department's regional bureaus would, on the one hand, minimize human rights violations in the country,[9] and, on the other, exaggerate the progress made by abusing regimes in order to ensure the continued flow of U.S. aid.[10] To facilitate the allocation of foreign aid to human rights-abusing client states, the State Department would make extensive use of the clause "unless such assistance will directly benefit the needy people in such country" found in the human rights legislation. Virtually all aid requests were described by the State Department in a way that would appear to benefit needy people, resulting in very few economic aid requests being denied funding. The State Department also systematically overstated the importance of recipient countries to U.S. national security interests in order to ensure the continuation of military and Economic Support Funding (ESF) aid to human rights-abusing states. Due to the extraordinary circumstances clause in the human rights legislation, any government that is vital to U.S. national security, even a government that engages in a consistent pattern of gross violations of internationally recognized human rights, automatically qualifies for security assistance.

HA would routinely antagonize the regional bureaus by directly challenging their interpretation of the human rights conditions in a potential recipient country. HA developed ties to international and local NGOs and human rights activists, and thereby had access to independent sources of information concerning human rights standards. The Bureau of Human Rights was a counterbalance to the clientism of the regional bureaus because it did not foster a relationship with any foreign government. HA maintained that human rights ought to be a principal determinant in the evaluation of foreign aid allocations. The Bureau of Human Rights was obstinate in its contention that human rights standards had to be met before aid could be granted. When the HA and a regional bureau disagreed on the human rights conditions in a country, a country's strategic importance to the United States, or whether a country ought to be granted security assistance, an Action Memorandum was prepared and sent to the secretary of state for a final decision. The Action Memorandum presented each side's position and reasoning on the issue. More often than not, the secretary of state would side with the regional bureaus.

The State Department was not the only branch of the executive bureaucracy wishing to see the end of the Bureau of Human Rights' mandate. The National Security Council, under Brzezinski, also attempted to conceal human rights violations of friendly but brutal allies. Hartmann reports,

> To avoid the straining of bilateral relations, NSC staff members in late 1978 and early 1979 even proposed unsuccessfully to stop the publication of the increasingly controversial country reports on human rights, and to make these reports available only to selected members and committees of Congress. (2001, 414–415)

This maneuver failed given Carter's and Congress' preferences for a human rights focus in foreign policy. In what can be viewed as a diplomatic blunder, the NSC abandoned the opportunity to press for human rights, or, in realist terms, to publicize the abhorrent human rights conditions in the Soviet Union. With the Helsinki Accords during the Ford Administration, the United States and the Soviet Union had developed the practice of compiling lists of human rights cases for the other side to investigate and correct. The routine began with the U.S. Embassy in Moscow, which would compile the list, send it to the State Department for review, and then give the list to the Soviet ministry (Matlock 2004). Jack Matlock Jr., the deputy chief of the U.S. Embassy in Moscow and later U.S. ambassador to the Soviet Union, reports that this practice did not continue after the inauguration of Carter. Although the U.S. embassy compiled the list and sent it up the bureaucratic chain of command, the NSC never sent it back. Matlock is uncertain whether the blockage of this constructive human rights channel was intentional or simply a matter of negligence, but it is consistent with Brzezinski's intent to cut diplomatic relations with the USSR.

IDEALISM IN A REALIST WORLD

Wood and Peake (1998) reason that presidents use an "economy of attention" when dealing with foreign policy issues. Presidents have an overall agenda that they bring to the office, and will attempt to implement it until other, more pressing foreign policy issues develop. When such issues arise, the attention of the president will shift to the severe problem until it is solved. Furthermore, a president's discretion in setting the foreign policy agenda is often hampered by the problems he inherits from previous administrations. These continuing issues (the Cold War, for instance) must be dealt with despite the president's personal agenda. Carter's preference for his personal agenda, his legacy as the human rights president, stalled when he was confronted with external events that required his immediate and undivided attention. President Carter has been described as a "good-hearted idealist brought up short by the hard realities of the world" (Elving 1996, 110). Carter was faced with a hostage crisis in Iran, a large Soviet military presence in Cuba, the Soviet invasion of Afghanistan, and gas shortages. After the debacles in Iran, Afghanistan, Cuba, and Nicaragua, the Carter Administration's human rights policy was in obvious decline while traditional interests of national security took center stage. These events shifted his human rights agenda toward the traditional realist pursuit of power politics.

With every foreign policy crisis, Carter's political popularity slipped, pushing him, in apparent response to U.S. political polls indicating the preferences of the voting public, to get tougher with the Soviets. "The Administration," according to Hauke Hartmann, "had gravely underestimated the domestic and international problems that resulted from a vocal stand on human rights, and it retreated quickly whenever political costs were to be paid" (2001, 413). The issue of human rights could not sustain continued salience in the face of power politics, and therefore it failed to unify the American public.

This chasm between words and deeds also applied to the American public. The American public, along with its president, would not support human rights when the costs were high. Americans strongly supported the abstract concept of human rights, but they did not favor governmental action. According to Skidmore (1993), a 1978 poll found that 67 percent of Americans and 78 percent of American political leaders believed that the United States ought to pressure foreign governments that systematically violated the human rights of their citizens. But when asked if the government ought to oppose specific countries based on their human rights conditions (for example, the South Africa government with regard to apartheid or the Soviet Union's treatment of its Jewish population), the vast majority of respondents disagreed.

As a result of the Soviet Union's increasingly aggressive international behavior, the Carter Administration's focus on human rights fell under the weight of power politics. In Carter's first two years in office, U.S. bilateral military aid was greatly reduced, compared to the Nixon Administration's levels. But this fact conceals Carter's reliance on ESF. Carter reduced military aid but increased ESF. As has been previously reported in chapter 1, ESF funding, although officially listed as economic aid, is generally recognized as security assistance since it is used to financially support those countries considered politically and strategically important to the United States' security interests. Initially, the Carter Administration sought to increase the development assistance funding and reduce the ESF aspect of U.S. economic aid. But given the realities of the international system, Carter quickly changed his mind soon after the Soviet invasion of Afghanistan.[11] U.S. economic assistance would shift from human rights to security concerns.

Furthermore, with the increase in the Soviet Union's policy of aggression, the much heralded PD-13 was quietly overlooked. Both U.S. military aid and U.S. commercial arms sales increased during the Carter Administration. The link between human rights and military armaments was abandoned for security concerns. Due to the foreign policy failures around the world during the final years of the Carter Administration, the focus was now placed on good relations with Latin America, which meant that attention to Latin America's human rights abuses would also be downplayed or downright ignored. In 1977, the Carter Administration sent $397 million in foreign aid to Latin America. However, by claiming an improvement in human rights, Carter authorized foreign aid transfers in the amount of $519 million to Latin America in 1980. The largest increases went to Nicaragua, El Salvador, and Honduras, countries characterized by continued abuses of internationally accepted human rights. Overall, Carter and Congress held similar views in the provision of aid and the importance of human rights in foreign policy. Ultimately, national security interests trumped human rights.

CONGRESS AS A CONTINUED FORCE FOR HUMAN RIGHTS

Congress, still vexed with past administrations' disregard for human rights considerations, was not convinced with Carter's words of goodwill with regard to human rights. Senator James Abourezk (D-SD) was quoted as saying, "While the President's words sound very beautiful, after the announcements nothing really happens" (quoted in Drew 1977, 59). In any case, Congress was not willing to relinquish its hard-won partnership in the realm of foreign policy. Congress thrust the issue of human rights considerations on a reluctant Executive during the Nixon Administration, and it was not going to abandon its prerogative.

Human rights had become very popular on Capitol Hill. For liberals, human rights provided a moral and ethical component to U.S. foreign policy and became an apologetic mechanism for the Vietnam War and CIA excesses. For conservatives in Congress, human rights were a useful tool for condemning the Soviet Union. In contrast to the Executive's focus on the human rights violations of allied states, congressional human rights rhetoric was unquestionably anti-Soviet. The anti-Soviet focus is apparent by reviewing the Helsinki hearings and the Subcommittee on International Organization hearings. During the Carter Administration (during the 95th and 96th Congresses, 1977–1981), the Helsinki Commission held twenty hearings on the status of the implementation of the Final Act, focusing on the provisions of Basket 3. The majority of the Helsinki hearings concerned violations of human rights in the Soviet Union, but also included inquiries into the human rights conditions in Eastern Europe. Even the Subcommittee on International Organizations, holding hearings on Sections 116 and 502B of the FAA concerning economic and military assistance, reviewed the charges of psychiatric abuse of political prisoners and anti-Semitism and religious persecution in the Soviet Union.

Congressional Initiatives

Congress continued to legislate a series of human rights initiatives during the Carter years. In 1977, as mentioned above, Congress upgraded the post of coordinator for humanitarian affairs to that of assistant secretary of state. The assistant secretary of state for Human Rights and Humanitarian Affairs would be responsible to the secretary of state for matters pertaining to human rights, particularly those matters falling within the scope of Section 502B. Congress felt that issues of human rights were increasingly important in U.S. foreign policy and that the promotion would give added stature and authority to the bureau. Within the State Department bureaucratic structure, HA would have the same rank as the regional bureaus.

In 1978, Congress replaced the old Security Supporting Assistance program with the Economic Support Fund program. The newly renamed program was Congress' attempt at redirecting U.S. foreign aid. ESF funding is prohibited for military or paramilitary programs and should only be used for broad economic development purposes. The U.S. Congress believed that "the name change . . . reflects more accurately the actual use of these funds: to provide budget support and development assistance to countries of political importance to the United States" (1979, 1848). Unfortunately, the State Department has interpreted the restrictions on the use of ESF to mean that politically and strategically important states can use ESF monies to replace their regular budget, which then allows these states to use their own resources to buy U.S. armaments. In this manner, the recipient state can buy both guns and butter. The executive branch favors ESF since, as economic aid, it avoids congressional challenges associated with the granting of military aid to human rights-abusing countries.

In 1979, Congress amended the Foreign Assistance Act by transferring administrative control for most economic aid to the USAID. The intent was to depoliticize the foreign aid decision-making process. USAID's sole raison d'être was economic and humanitarian development free of political or ideological pressure. The State Department still retained control over the Economic Support Funds.

During this time, Congress also legislated that there be an increase in the number of states to be reported on in the State Department's annual *Country Reports on Human Rights Practices*. Originally, only those countries that received U.S. aid were reviewed. But since this only included U.S. friends, not its foes, the reports provided only a partial picture of human rights conditions around the world and one that did not show favorably on U.S. allies. The new reports would now include all United Nations (UN) member states (and later would be expanded again to include all countries). Conservatives in Congress championed the expansion of coverage in the reports. The abuses within communist countries, which were not included in the initial reports, would now be documented. Conservatives believed that "the citizens of the Soviet Union and most other communist countries enjoy far fewer rights than do those of any of the rightist dictatorships of Latin America" (Muravchik 1986, 101), and the State Department's expanded reporting would support their assertions. Conversely, opponents of incorporation of human rights into U.S. foreign affairs hoped that requiring a universal report on human rights would prove so daunting that the matter would simply be dropped. Thus, these detractors hoped, the relevance of human rights in foreign policy allocation would be downgraded.

As the series of legislation acts detailed above indicates, Congress would not be lulled into passivity by Carter's words of goodwill and good intentions. However, the principal congressional directive aimed at implementing U.S. human rights policy during the Carter Administration was the authorization of Section 701 of the International Financial Assistance Act.

The Role of International Financial Institutions

With the issue of human rights abuses mandated in economic and military aid, human rights activists in Congress turned to the question of multilateral aid funneled through international financial institutions, such as the IMF, the World Bank, and the regional banks. Moreover, with the geographical shift in lending from Europe to the developing world, combined with the reduction in U.S. bilateral economic aid, multilateral lending became an important focus of human rights activists. U.S. bilateral foreign aid had been declining in recent years, and multilateral aid was increasing. Nowadays, a large part of U.S. aid dollars are funneled through these institutions, as a form of multinational aid. It was also during this time that Congress became aware of the fact that several countries, notably Pinochet's Chile, were being provided with unusually large World Bank and regional multilateral bank loans to make up for the fact that Congress was restricting U.S. bilateral aid due to human rights concerns.

Because the United States directs a large part of its aid dollars through international financial institutions, Congress sought to utilize U.S. influence in the international financial institutions to secure respect for internationally recognized standards of human rights. Section 701 of the International Financial Assistance Act of 1977 reads as follows:

> The United States Government, in connection with its voice and vote in the [international financial institutions], shall advance the cause of human rights, including by seeking to channel assistance toward countries other than those whose governments engage in—

(1) a consistent pattern of gross violations of internationally recognized human rights, such as torture or cruel, inhumane, or degrading treatment or punishment, prolonged detention without charges, or other flagrant denial to life, liberty, and the security of person; or (2) provide refuge to individuals committing acts of international terrorism by hijacking aircraft.

The U.S. Department of the Treasury administers the United States' multilateral development bank funding and represents the United States on the boards of the international financial institutions. U.S. representatives are instructed to oppose loans, extensions, or technical assistance to any country described in the above provisions, unless the aid is directed to programs that fulfill the basic human needs of the country's citizens. Disregarding Carter's opposition, Congress expanded the requirement that U.S. representatives use their voice and vote to oppose loans to human rights abusers and instead direct loans to those countries that protect the human rights of their citizens. The requirement originally bound U.S. representatives to the Inter-American and African Development Funds, but Congress expanded the requirement to cover the World Bank and the IMF, over the vociferous objections of President Carter.

Multilateral lending institutions use a weighted voting system in determining loans. The countries that provide the greatest contributions get the largest say in where and how the money is distributed. The United States has been the largest contributor to these banks, averaging over 20 percent of the votes, and thus has a substantial, but not overwhelming, influence. The Carter Administration initially attempted to block Section 701, fearing that the restrictions mandated by Section 701 would not only reduce the flexibility the United States needed in negotiating human rights policy, but also politicize the international financial institutions. In the interest of fairness and equality, the charters of the multilateral banks (the World Bank, Inter-American Development Bank, Asian Development Bank, and African Development Bank) require them to restrict funding decisions to economic criteria with no regard to the political characteristics of the recipient state.[12] Opponents of the inclusion of Section 701 in U.S. foreign policy claim that human rights violations are a political matter with no economic ramifications or penalties, and therefore are outside the purview of international financial institutions.

Nevertheless, Section 701 of the International Financial Institutions Act (1977) requires the U.S. representatives to international financial institutions to use their voice and vote to discourage giving loans or grants to gross human rights violators. However, Section 701 has its own loophole. U.S. delegates to international financial institutions were to oppose loans to those countries that violate their citizens' rights,

> except where the President determines that the cause of international human rights is served more effectively by actions other than voting against such assistance or where the assistance is directed to programs that serve the basic needs of the impoverished majority of the country in question.[13]

The Carter Administration believed that the mandate to oppose the loans simply meant that it ought not to vote in the affirmative. Regrettably, when a government that brutally violated the human rights of its citizens (but was an economic or strategic ally of the United States) requested multilateral loans that were not labeled basic human needs loans, the United States adopted a policy of abstaining from the vote in order to avoid its official duty to actively oppose the loan. During the Carter Administration, the United States "opposed" 117 proposed loans by abstaining in 76 votes and voting no in only 41 cases (Mower 1987).[14]

CONCLUSION

Carter was a pioneer president, breaking new ground in the establishment of human rights as a foreign policy issue. He faced many problems, barriers, and resistance in his efforts to formulate a foreign policy based on human rights and morality. Due to the internal strife within the White House and State Department, the United States' human rights policy became the unintended victim of the disunity and power politics of the executive branch. President Carter's failed foreign policy was, in part, an outcome of the divisions and ideological conflicts between the idealism of Cyrus Vance and the realism of Zbigniew Brzezinski, as detailed above. Furthermore, during the Carter Administration, a climate of confrontation prevailed between the State Department and the Bureau of Human Rights and Humanitarian Affairs. The Bureau of Human Rights and Humanitarian Affairs spent so much time battling the other offices in the Department of State that very little was done on the human rights front.

But Carter's efforts in human rights policy, though not always successful, did set precedents that following administrations could not ignore. The goal of Carter's human rights policy was to increase U.S. security in the world by supporting human rights and fundamental freedoms, distancing the United States from abusing regimes, and increasing the number of free and friendly states. Mower believes that Jimmy Carter's leadership role in the promotion of human rights "set the stage for what could well be described as a 'quantum leap forward' in the movement to incorporate this issue into this country's foreign policy" (1987, 3).

Yet, Carter's human rights policy was rarely successful. Critics of Carter's human rights policy are of several ideological persuasions. The first are the liberal members of Congress and the American public who believed that the Carter Administration did not go far enough or do enough to enhance human rights. A second group of critics is made up of those who supported Carter's human rights policy, but condemned the lack of anticommunist application. Carter's human rights policy was a balancing act between defending human rights and pushing through his arms control agenda. Carter could not condemn the Soviet Union's human rights abuses and at the same time improve diplomatic relations with Moscow. Therefore, Carter's human rights policy largely ignored the transgressions within the Soviet Union. Clearly, human rights took a back seat to arms control. Finally, there are those critics who believe that the Carter Administration ignored the reality of power politics and that its human rights policy was both dangerous and simple minded. This group believed that Carter's human rights policy and the perceived weakness of the United States were the cause of the Iranian Revolution, the Sandinista triumph in Nicaragua, the placement of Soviet combat brigades in Cuba, the U.S. hostage crisis, and the Soviet invasion of Afghanistan.[15]

Many believe that Carter's ephemeral commitment to human rights was a matter of political expediency. Although Carter signed the two international conventions on human rights (the International Covenant on Civil and Political Rights and the International Covenant on Economic, Social and Cultural Rights) in 1977, he did not spend his political capital to push the treaties through the ratification process. Critics believe that this is proof of Carter's mere rhetorical commitment to human rights. Hartmann believes that human rights were seen by the Carter Administration as "a low-cost moral infusion, not a hindrance to other important policy goals. Thus, the administration postponed any serious lobbying efforts for the ratification of international human rights treaties" (2001, 414).

When all these considerations are put together, it is obvious that Carter's much touted human rights foreign policy was doomed to fail. U.S. human rights policy was an unintended victim of the bureaucratic and ideological infighting, and, some would say, of the halfhearted application of the Carter Administration. Paradoxically, the human rights president, as Carter was often called, nearly sacrificed human rights to the political realities of power politics. Instead, the success of human rights initiatives during the Carter era was primarily due to congressional effort, the tireless labors of HA, and the support, at least in the abstract, for human rights among the American public. Still, the human rights momentum would continue and become more institutionalized in U.S. foreign policy making, to the chagrin of the Reagan White House.

CHAPTER 4

The Contradictions of U.S. Human Rights Policy: The Reagan Administration

As long as a conservative dictator was not losing his grip on power or was not becoming a household name for evil in the United States, the Reagan Administration was generally happy to be a friend.

Thomas Carothers (1991)

The conflict inherent in the foreign policy process, which during the Nixon Administration was situated between Congress and the Executive, and during the Carter Administration was within the executive branch itself, once again moved to Congress and the Executive during the Reagan Administration. Congress would attempt to maintain its foreign policy gains during the Reagan Administration by using its most powerful tools: holding congressional hearings, placing restrictions on foreign aid allocations, constraining the president's budget priorities, and invoking the War Powers Act. But the Reagan Administration, for the most part, simply ignored Congress' efforts to rein in Reagan's foreign policy adventures. Although Reagan openly ignored congressional will, the tension between Congress and the Executive was less rancorous than it had been under the previous Republican administration. President Reagan was a very popular president among the American public and, therefore, he enjoyed public support for many of his programs. Furthermore, throughout most of his tenure in office, Congress was split. The Republicans controlled the Senate, while the Democrats held the House of Representatives. Finally, while Reagan's rhetoric was resolute, he was often willing to compromise with Congress.

Initially, Congress, even in the face of large deficits and severe recessions, agreed to increase the foreign aid budget as a reaction to the foreign policy setbacks of the Carter Administration. The country as a whole seemed to once again be gripped in an ideological battle against communism, resulting in an increase in military expenditures, security assistance, and arms transfers. In times of perceived external threat, Congress and the American public frequently defer to the president's foreign policy agenda (Lindsay 2003). However, Reagan's foreign policy strategy was often hindered by the human rights legacy he inherited from the previous administration and by continuing congressional initiatives.

The concern for human rights did not come to an end when Carter left office. Upon inauguration, Reagan did endeavor to abandon what he believed was the idealistic, irrelevant, and impractical policy of human rights. But human rights remained a core moral value, which, at least in the abstract, the American public remained highly committed to.[1] Consequently, despite the president's personal agenda, the issue of human rights in foreign policy had to be dealt with by the Reagan Administration. Subsequently, the Reagan Administration strategically planned to usurp the concept of human rights. The Reagan Administration redefined human rights very narrowly to exclusively mean democracy and anticommunism. Furthermore, an ardent anticommunist (Elliot Abrams), not a human rights advocate, was appointed as the chief spokesman for U.S. human rights policy.[2] The Bureau of Human Rights and Humanitarian Affairs was more a propagandist for anticommunism than a promoter of human rights. Under Reagan, human rights were to be put to the service of condemning the Soviet Union. But, contrary to Reagan's attempt to first abandon[3] and then disingenuously redefine human rights, human rights would paradoxically become institutionalized in U.S. foreign policy making under his tenure.

CONSERVATIVE REALISM

Reagan was a man of strongly held, if simplistic, beliefs. The United States, he believed, was engaged in a global crusade of right versus wrong, good versus evil, in its resistance of Soviet communism. Foreign policy, including human rights policy, was formulated to defend the interests of the United States and its allies from the Soviet challenge. For Reagan conservatives, communism was an evil ideology that needed to be eradicated (not simply contained, as Nixon and Kissinger earlier suggested) because it was a vile threat to America's principal moral values of democracy, liberty, and capitalism. Reagan repudiated the Nixon Administration's use of détente as morally bankrupt. Morality and a belief in American exceptionalism were vital components of foreign policy decision making for the Reagan conservatives. Because the Soviet Union was a malevolent threat and the source of all international tribulations, any attempt to cooperate or collaborate with the USSR was a gross miscalculation. Reagan would never collaborate or negotiate with the Soviets since the Soviet Union only understood military might and confrontation.

True to America's crusading heritage, the Reagan Administration viewed the Soviet Union as the evil empire, advancing tyranny and aggression, while the United States sought to free the oppressed, offering democracy and prosperity. Reagan was committed not only to resisting Soviet aggression and expansion, but also to rolling back communism by overthrowing existing communist governments in the Third World. The goal of the Reagan Administration's foreign policy was simply to defeat communism. To this end, Reagan would vastly increase defense spending, raise security assistance to pro-American Third World countries, and initiate several covert operations. Security aid was the first tool in the presidential arsenal. Reagan wanted not only to support states that were threatened by communism, those frontline countries bordering on a communist government, but also to aid freedom fighters, rebels, and insurgents attempting to depose communist regimes. The United States under Reagan would financially support any country that opposed communism, regardless of that country's human rights conditions. U.S. foreign relations with any nation were conditioned by its pro-American anticommunist stance.

Human rights did not disappear during the Reagan Administration, though. Conservative realists of the Reagan variety found human rights rhetoric to be very useful. Human rights proved advantageous in condemning the Soviet Union and remained a valuable mechanism in lambasting the Soviets. Secretary of State Alexander Haig declared that combating terrorism (defined as Soviet-inspired antistate attack) would be the centerpiece of the Reagan human rights policy. Countering terrorism, Haig announced in a January 28, 1981 news conference, would "take the place of human rights in our concern because it [terrorism] is the ultimate abuse of human rights" (As reported by Jacoby 1986). International terrorism was declared the principal threat to human rights. Not surprisingly, the Reagan Administration identified the Soviet Union as the source of international terrorism and, thus, as the provocateur of human rights abuse. Carleton and Stohl conclude,

> By identifying international terrorism as the most significant threat to human rights, and by further identifying the Soviet Union as the chief source of international terrorism, it was possible to bundle

human rights, national security, and international terrorism into a single package that fit neatly (and subtly) into the broader United States fight against global communism. (1985, 208)

Thus, human rights offered a very powerful ideological weapon in the fight against communism.

But Reagan also determined that Congress and the American public would not support a foreign policy based exclusively on fighting communism. Therefore, the administration's policy, particularly in Central America, had to be couched in terms of promoting democracy. A confidential memo to Secretary of State Haig, written by Undersecretary of Management Richard Kennedy, actually advised the administration to reinvigorate the concept of human rights. Kennedy wrote, "Congressional belief that we have no consistent human rights policy threatens to disrupt important foreign policy initiatives." Kennedy suggested that the Reagan Administration should usurp the idea of human rights by redefining the concept. Human rights, for the Reagan Administration, would be defined very narrowly to include only democracy and civil liberties. This strategy would allow the Reagan Administration to use human rights, defined exclusively as democracy and individual freedom, in the ideological struggle against the Soviet Union, while totally excluding economic and social rights,[4] and even the subgroup of human rights that pertains to the physical integrity of the person.[5] Hence, the exploitation of the upstanding reputation and moral appeal of the Bureau of Human Rights and Humanitarian Affairs was the second tool in the presidential arsenal. Elliot Abrams, Reagan's appointee to lead the Human Rights Bureau, was quoted as saying, "You could make the argument that there aren't many countries where there are gross and consistent human rights violations except the communist countries because they have the system itself. It is certainly a plausible way of reading the statute" (as quoted in Maechling 1983, 130). Reagan's human rights policy would be used to counter the USSR and its proxies politically by exposing the Soviet bloc's human rights violations to the world. The Reagan Administration purposely redefined the human rights debate within narrow ideological parameters, downplaying abuses against the physical integrity of the person, and emphasizing one single aspect of political rights, democracy.[6] The 1981 State Department *Country Reports on Human Rights Practices* made clear the administration's intent to use human rights as a weapon against communism.

It is a significant service to the cause of human rights to limit the influence the USSR [together with its clients and proxies] can exert. A consistent and serious policy for human rights in the world must counter the USSR politically and bring Soviet bloc human rights violations to the attention of the world over and over again. (United States, Department of State 1981, 9)

Anticommunism, camouflaged as human rights, led the Reagan Administration to fund and maintain rights-abusing regimes. In order to prevent a fall to communism, human rights violations in a friendly state would often be ignored. The Reagan Administration could overlook human rights abuses in repressive but friendly regimes because it was, in this administration's opinion, a better situation than allowing a greater threat to human rights under communism. Thus, Reagan sacrificed human rights to an ideological crusade against communism.[7] Since communism was synonymous with human rights violations, the most effective human rights policy for Reagan would be to prevent the spread of communism. The Reagan Administration declared, "Our greatest contribution to human rights would be to help prevent a democratic or an authoritarian state from being conquered or subverted by totalitarian forces" (Hartmann 2001, 424).

By dividing oppressive governments into authoritarian or totalitarian categories, the Reagan Administration was able to overlook the outrages committed by human rights violators friendly to the United States. Reagan's U.S. permanent representative to the United Nations, Jeane Kirkpatrick, outlined the administration's understanding of the differences between pro-American military dictatorships and communist totalitarian regimes. In "Dictatorships and Double Standards," Kirkpatrick (1979) argues that not only are authoritarian regimes amicable to the United States, thereby furthering U.S. security interests, but they are also less repressive and more receptive to democratic transformation and liberalization.[8] Authoritarian, unpopular, repressive governments were essentially seen as a transition phase to real democratic governments. Totalitarian regimes (communist governments), on the other hand, were extremely anti-American, and the United States could not hope to influence their behavior. Totalitarian regimes could not evolve into democracies.

Using this twist of logic, the Reagan White House claimed that the United States was actually directly supporting human rights by providing military and economic assistance to friendly, yet repressive, governments. The Reagan team reasoned that a nondemocratic, unpopular, and murderous right-wing government was redeemable, but a nondemocratic, unpopular, and much less repressive left-wing government had to be overthrown. Thus, in order to allegedly further the cause of human rights, the United States emphasized the human rights violations in the Soviet Union and Eastern Europe while largely ignoring equally repressive practices by friendly authoritarian governments.

Reagan's solution to the vile human rights abuses in friendly countries was to use "quiet diplomacy"[9] to encourage political liberties while arming the abusing government with the means to torture. For example, with regard to the murderous regime of Guatemala in 1980, Deputy Assistant Secretary of State for Inter-American Affairs Stephen Bosworth stated, "We are convinced that dialog is the only approach which can be effective in diminishing overreaction by government forces and toleration of illicit rightist activity" (Bosworth 1981, 1333). The fact that right-wing murderous governments were friendly to the United States and antagonistic to the Soviet Union proved their inclination and predilection for democracy and human rights over totalitarianism. Abrams explains, "The United States is at times reluctantly compelled to support regimes which abuse human rights because we think their replacements [leftist regimes] would be much worse for the cause of human rights" (as quoted in Mower 1987, 42).

THE RENEWED COLD WAR WARRIOR

The Reagan White House rhetoric emphasized the return of U.S. strength and prestige. The Reagan foreign policy promised to contain the Soviet Union and reverse its gains in the Third World. Reagan believed that Carter's emphasis on human rights placed U.S. national interest in peril. Instead of supporting—rhetorically, militarily, and financially—anticommunist regimes, Carter's foreign policy had weakened these regimes' hold on domestic power. Thus, Reagan reasoned, pro-American regimes were placed in the unprecedented risk of being overthrown by communist-supported revolutionary factions. In Latin America, all revolutionaries (except anticommunist ones) were by definition terrorists. The Committee of Santa Fe, Reagan's preinaugural policy advisors on Latin America,[10] developed a strategic plan for U.S. foreign policy toward Latin America in a fashion that revived the Monroe Doctrine.[11] The Santa Fe Committee advocated military and economic backing for conservative military regimes in Latin America regardless of their human rights conditions. The Committee recommended total unqualified support for El Salvador's military, and advocated the overthrow of

Nicaragua's leadership. Denouncing the Carter Administration's alleged focus on human rights, the Santa Fe Committee declared that the United States' human rights policy

> must be abandoned and replaced by a noninterventionist policy of political and ethical realism. . . . [Carter's human rights policy] has cost the United States friends and allies and lost us influence . . . [and is therefore] a threat to the security interests of the United States. (Committee of Santa Fe 1980, 2)

Reagan was determined to reverse what he considered to be the Carter Administration's abandonment of Central America and the Caribbean to the Soviets' expanded sphere of influence. Under Reagan, U.S. foreign aid to the region increased dramatically. Since the Monroe Doctrine, the United States viewed Central and South America as its backyard, and the Reagan Administration was resolved to see U.S. hegemony in the region once again reestablished. Therefore, in the opinion of the Reagan team, a judicious U.S. response was intervention—covert or overt—to prevent the loss of Third World nations to the Soviet Union, particularly in Central America. David Cingranelli, in a study of U.S. intervention in Latin America, writes,

> Neither Reagan nor Bush has been particularly concerned about the principle of nonintervention in the conduct of relations with Third World states. Instead . . . both Administrations have made frequent use of overt and covert intervention to achieve U.S. foreign policy objectives. (1993, 206)

A policy of intervention was clearly chosen in the cases of Nicaragua, El Salvador, Grenada, and Panama, to name a few.

Central America was the primary focus of the Reagan Administration's anticommunist crusade. Due to Central America's geographical proximity to the continental United States, if communism was allowed to take hold in Central America, the security of the United States would be imperiled. In a 1983 speech, President Reagan sounded the alarm: "If guerrilla violence succeeds, El Salvador will join Cuba and Nicaragua in spreading fresh violence to Guatemala, Honduras, even Costa Rica. The killing will increase and so will the threat to Panama, the Canal and ultimately Mexico" (Reagan 1983). And after Mexico, the implication was clear. It was imperative, in the judgment of the Reagan Administration, to formulate U.S. human rights objectives with one goal: once again, to resist communism.

The most urgent threat facing the United States was the Soviet objectives in Central America. The key to American security lay in turning back communism in Nicaragua and preventing the Soviet conquest of El Salvador. Reagan feared that Nicaragua would be the nucleus for the destabilization of the rest of Central America.[12] El Salvador would be Reagan's line in the sand. Behind this line, the United States would stand firm to oppose communist expansion.

The Sandinista regime governing Nicaragua, in the view of the Reagan Administration, was a dupe of the Soviet Union. Reagan thought that the Soviet Union would use its advances in Nicaragua to spearhead its expansion into Honduras and El Salvador. The White House charged Nicaragua, as a proxy of Cuba and the Soviet Union, with supplying arms to rebels in El Salvador. As early as his first inauguration into office, Reagan embarked on an ideological war against the Sandinista government by canceling U.S. humanitarian aid,[13] organizing the paramilitary organization known as the Contras, and approving covert CIA activities. The Contras, manned by members of Somoza's National Guard and funded by the CIA, had little support among the Nicaraguan population. The Contras established bases in Honduras and Costa Rica from which they launched raids throughout Nicaragua, often targeting civilians.

In November 1981, Reagan issued National Security Decision Directive 17, which provided funding, recruitment, support, and management of Contra guerrilla forces with $19 million in military aid. The president also authorized covert operations to interdict Cuban arms trafficking to the Nicaraguan government. Soon, Reagan's intent grew from merely intercepting military weapons trafficked by the Sandinista "Marxist guerrillas" to El Salvador, to the overthrow of the Nicaraguan government. In response, Congress passed the first of several Boland Amendments (1982) prohibiting aid to Contra rebels, and ending any U.S. covert operation to aid the overthrow of the Sandinista government. Any U.S. foreign aid directed at the Contras was to be nonlethal humanitarian assistance.

The desire to prevent another communist takeover in the Western Hemisphere, as had happened in Cuba and Nicaragua, motivated Reagan to intervene in El Salvador's brutal civil war. El Salvador was to be the principal battleground in Reagan's war against communist advancement. The Reagan Administration chose to challenge communism's expansion by aiding El Salvador's repressive anticommunist military regime. Reagan substantially increased both military and economic aid, and the number of military advisors, to El Salvador while conducting covert operations in Nicaragua.[14] Human rights violations and whole-sale murders by the military were less vile to the Reagan Administration than the possibility of a communist gain in the region. Hartmann relates an interview with Abrams, who states that "while it was important to us to promote the cause of human rights in Central America it was more important to prevent a communist takeover in El Salvador" (2001, 429). There is evidence that the Reagan Administration knew of and tolerated the notorious "death squads." These death squads were paramilitary organizations made up of off-duty military and police officers associ-ated with the National Republican Alliance (ARENA) political party. In 1983, Vice President George Bush met with the military commanders to explain the difficulties that President Reagan was having in getting Congress to allocate military funding to El Salvador. Bush was reported as stating,

> Providing assistance to you is not a popular cause in the United States. Publicity about death squads, great inequalities of income, the killing of American citizens and military setbacks make it a very unpopular proposition in my country. President Reagan has supported you at considerable political cost, because we know it is the right thing. (Bush 1983)

To quiet the protestations of the American public and of Congress over the death squads, Bush instructed that several military officers con-nected to the death squads be assigned to overseas posts before Congress reconvened. The Reagan Administration knew the leaders of the death squads by name. The reassignment of these notorious military officers greatly reduced the number of death squad victims.

Speciously, Reagan believed that El Salvador deserved U.S. foreign aid. As additional proof that El Salvador's human rights were improv-ing, Reagan claimed that El Salvador was an emerging democracy that had experienced a democratic transformation with the 1984 elections. El Salvador was held up as a democracy "plagued by a Communist insur-gency," even though the military maintained control of the government and killed 70,000 actual or suspected rebels.[15] Democracy was merely a rhetorical device for Reagan to win over Congress and the American public to his foreign policy agenda and to persuade Congress to provide foreign aid. The Reagan Administration very narrowly defined democ-racy as simply the holding of elections, with no understanding that democracy requires the protection of political, civil, and personal integ-rity rights.[16] Eventually, in January 1992, after intense and prolonged negotiations, peace accords would be signed, ending the brutal civil war and placing the military under civilian control.

The Reagan Administration never received the congressional or public support it needed to launch a successful anticommunist campaign in either Nicaragua or El Salvador.[17] During Reagan's first term, Congress was willing to give him the benefit of the doubt and continued substantial economic and military funding to El Salvador and the Contras. Some in Congress agreed with Reagan's get-tough policies, others were thankful something was done to counter Soviet expansion, and yet another group of Congress members simply went with the flow. Reagan won by a large margin and had a well-liked public persona. He was one of the most popular presidents in American history. Although the American public and Congress were troubled by the foreign policy failures of the Carter Administration, which made the United States look weak and the Soviet Union appear to be strong and resolved, they were also uneasy with supporting a country that systematically violated the human rights of its citizens. Moreover, the public and Congress feared a Vietnam-like military mission creep.

U.S. FOREIGN AID

The Reagan Administration understood the power of foreign aid as a foreign policy tool. In Reagan's words, "Security assistance is, quite simply, the most effective instrument we have for helping to shape a more secure international environment. . . . Foreign assistance resources are essential to a successful foreign policy" (Reagan 1985). The first Reagan Administration orchestrated a shift from the use of multilateral programs, which limited the United States' influence in the use and allocation process of aid, to bilateral aid programs, which allowed the United States' economic interests and foreign policy concerns to be the sole determinant of aid allocations. Understanding that the United States could not easily control the allocation of multilateral aid, Reagan cut funding to the multilateral aid institutions. Foreign aid, during the Reagan Administration, was redirected first and foremost toward rolling back communism. Aid would be focused on the regions threatened by a communist takeover or on countries that lay in close proximity to the Soviet periphery. Reagan also used foreign aid to ensure that friendly, pro-American, anticommunist governments stayed in power, no matter what their human rights conditions were. Aid was given to friendly nations fighting to resist leftist insurgents and to relieve social and political unrest emanating from the poor. U.S. foreign aid was used to help allies quash internal security threats even if these threats took the form of democratic, nonviolent protests.

Military rather than economic aid was unquestionably Reagan's preference. Although Reagan was bound by the Camp David Accords that gave priority to Egypt and Israel, Latin America nonetheless received the second largest amount of U.S. military aid. The 1983 National Bipartisan Commission on Central America (known as the Kissinger Commission) determined that poverty, failing economies, and social injustice had made Central America ripe for revolution. Only massive amounts of U.S. military aid and private investment could save the region and allow the regional leaders to plan for its long-term development. Security aid played a large role in Reagan's determination to confront Soviet aggression and topple Central American communist insurgents. To this end, Reagan orchestrated the largest peacetime defense buildup in U.S. history. Providing security aid to anticommunist allies was an indispensable aspect of U.S. defense planning. During Reagan's first term in office, U.S. bilateral military aid jumped from $3.2 billion in 1981 to $5.8 billion in 1985 (with a high of $6.4 billion in 1984). Economic Support Funds (ESFs) rose from $2.2 billion to over $5.2 billion during that same time period (see chapter 1 on foreign aid).

Congress' major role in setting U.S. foreign policy via foreign aid allocations was through amendments and earmarks. Reagan's foreign policy objectives favored U.S. political and strategic interests, and, therefore, his foreign aid requests stressed security assistance to pro-American regimes while downplaying the developmental purposes of foreign assistance. Congress was unsympathetic to Reagan's overreliance on security assistance, and it endeavored to refocus U.S. foreign aid toward development assistance. Even within the category of economic assistance, the Reagan Administration allocated a greater amount of aid under the rubric of ESFs rather than under development assistance. Congress would encumber foreign aid requests with restrictions and earmarks to limit how the aid could be used. However, to circumvent congressional restrictions, Reagan attempted either to reprogram aid (shift aid allocations from one program to his intended program) or to use presidential emergency powers to provide aid to those countries he described as being in dire circumstances. Clarke, O'Conner, and Ellis report that, in addition to the regular foreign aid funding, "the Reagan Administration requested a record number of supplemental appropriations for security assistance" (1997, 75). For example, the Supplemental Appropriations Act (1985) granted additional funds that were "urgently required to our friends. . . . [Aid is] an important element in our overall effort to assist neighboring countries to defend themselves."[18] Congress countered these presidential maneuvers by earmarking entire fund programs and legislating itself veto power for reprogramming arrangements.

Still, the Reagan Administration refused to reduce or eliminate security assistance to repressive, pro-American regimes, thus ignoring both the word and the spirit of U.S. human rights legislation. Within six months of his inauguration, President Reagan rescinded Presidential Directive 13 (PD-13) (Carter's directive to limit the transfer of military arms). No longer would arms sales be an exceptional tool of foreign policy. For the Reagan team, arms sales were an indispensable element of U.S. foreign policy. Arms transfers and military aid were to be greatly expanded to U.S. friends and allies in an effort to regain America's global dominance. Often, to facilitate continued military aid, Reagan resorted to subterfuge in order to avoid implementing Section 502B of the Foreign Assistance Act.[19] The Reagan Administration was thus able to ignore congressional intent through the use of the extraordinary circumstances clause and by interpreting the wording "consistent pattern of gross violations" in such a way that even the worst human rights violators showed some level of improvement.

As was seen above, the ambiguity of the phrase "extraordinary circumstances" does permit the president to continue to provide aid to human rights-violating governments if there are significant reasons for doing so. Reagan interpreted "extraordinary circumstances" to essentially mean any U.S. national security concern. Reagan believed that the United States must confront the aggression and iniquity of the Soviet Union and its proxies. Thus, the United States' national security necessitated the granting of aid and the sheltering of allied governments since ignoring the expansionist behavior of the Soviet Union would jeopardize the security of the United States and its allies. The extraordinary circumstances clause was often invoked to provide aid to rights-abusing Central American regimes.

Reagan's way around the provision that countries be denied security aid if they exhibited a consistent pattern of gross human rights violations was to simply find the pattern not consistent. If a country's record of murder, torture, and detention was slightly less egregious than that of the year before, then the country was, in the opinion of the Reagan Administration, worthy of U.S. security assistance. Forsythe argues that the Reagan Administration would cite

> any statistic or event to show that a pattern of human rights violations was not completely consistent. No matter how poor

the human rights record, there was always the interpretation of improvement. It followed, for the administration, that if anything positive occurred in a right-wing country, Section 502B did not apply. (1988, 55)

When it was believed that congressional objections would be insurmountable, the Reagan Administration simply reclassified the security apparatus. For example, in order to supply military helicopters to the Guatemalan government during the notorious Lucas Garcia regime,[20] the Reagan Administration had the U.S. Department of Commerce classify the helicopters as civilian commodities. As a result, military equipment was sent to a rights-abusing country in blatant violation of United States law.

Although Congress generally went along with the president's requests during his first term in office, by Reagan's second term, lavish foreign aid spending was curtailed because of the enormous federal deficit that had been created during Reagan's first term. The United States' mounting debt and trade deficits required a cut in foreign assistance. Therefore, due to unprecedented federal shortfalls and the general discomfort with an overreliance on military aid to the detriment of development issues, Congress eventually cut Reagan's security assistance funds. The Balanced Budget and Emergency Deficit Control Act (1985), also known as the Gramm-Rudman-Hollings Act, directed the Executive to achieve a balanced budget by 1993. The amendment set a ceiling on the budget deficit. If the Executive exceeded the limit, the amendment authorized automatic reductions in federal spending.[21] Consequently, Reagan became more willing to work with multilateral aid agencies. During the second Reagan Administration, there was a move to cooperate with multilateral foreign aid programs. The use of multilateral agencies allowed the Reagan Administration to cut the total amount of U.S. foreign aid.

Reagan's frustration with Congress cutting his military aid requests (Congress reduced his 1987 foreign aid request by 24 percent) was amplified by Congress' extensive use of earmarks on the proposed security aid funds. To dodge this impediment, Reagan turned to the use of ESF[22] as a complement to and, when subterfuge was required, as a substitute for security aid. Because the ESF allocations, categorized under economic assistance, held fewer congressional restrictions and limitations, the Executive could deploy the aid more easily and with less congressional oversight. Ruttan reports that ESF "programs were relatively free of restrictions (compared to other aid categories), funds could be disbursed very rapidly to countries strapped by the world recession and rising debt crisis, and base-right commitments could be expanded" (1996, 123). ESF resources are often allocated in lieu of military aid in order to avoid a congressional debate on the ethical, moral, or political consequences of providing military aid to certain countries or groups.

The Reagan Administration believed that the best tool for strengthening U.S. security and to stop communist expansion in the Third World was military aid and arms transfers. An unfortunate side effect of pouring millions of dollars' worth of military equipment into nondemocratic countries was the strengthening of the military in the recipient country's political system. El Salvador is once again a prime example. The Reagan Administration supplied the Salvadoran military with billions of dollars in security assistance in its attempt to suppress a left-wing insurgency that threatened the brutal military dictatorship. This influx of security assistance and military training contributed to the 1981 El Mozote massacre, where over 700 peasants in the remote village of El Mozote were killed by the Salvadoran army's elite and U.S.-trained Atlacatl Battalion. In 1981, the State Department issued a white paper stating that the Soviet Union and Cuba planned to provide the Marxist-led guerrillas with weapons to ensure a successful revolution in El Salvador. Secretary of State Haig testified to the House Foreign Affairs Committee that the White House had "overwhelming and unrefutable" (but classified) evidence that the Soviet Union, via Nicaragua, controlled the Salvadoran guerrillas. Congress was not convinced but did compromise with Reagan, providing him with foreign aid for El Salvador, but also requiring him to certify, every six months, that El Salvador was making progress toward improving human rights and political reforms.

By linking aid to a country's pro-American stance and economic policy reforms (privatization), Reagan was able to work with the conservative members of Congress and push through many of his foreign aid requests and programs. The Caribbean Basin Initiative (CBI) proves an illustrative example. Reagan believed that poor countries' primary problem is the bloated public sector, which inhibits the growth and vitality of the private sector in solving social problems. U.S. aid would now be focused on supporting the development of private enterprise. Economic aid would be linked to trade, free-market reforms, and private investment, while simultaneously supporting Reagan's foreign policy agenda of aiding anticommunist governments. The Caribbean Basin Initiative (1982) was a development package of trade concessions, foreign assistance, and investment incentives targeting the Caribbean and Central America (a region of great strategic concern for Reagan). Hastedt believes that the

CBI was not intended to combat the growing poverty and misery of the region, but rather to oppose the "emergence of governments and political conditions hostile to traditional U.S. concerns" (1997, 268). The CBI would provide emergency economic and military assistance, in the form of ESF funds, to those countries in particular need. In other words, the CBI was intended to bypass congressional restrictions and provide El Salvador with additional foreign assistance. The geopolitical intent, and not the humanitarian concern, can be seen by Reagan's intended allocation of the funding. Initially, El Salvador was penciled in to receive 36 percent of the available ESF funding, over $125 million (this amount was severely cut by Congress), while Haiti, a poorer and more populous country, was to be granted only 1.4 percent, or about $5 million, of CBI's funding.

Although U.S. foreign assistance was, for the Reagan Administration, the first tool of foreign policy, it was not the only tool available to the president in his fight against communism. Reagan also manipulated the good offices and integrity of the Human Rights Bureau.

THE BUREAU OF HUMAN RIGHTS AND HUMANITARIAN AFFAIRS

The misuse of the Bureau of Human Rights and Humanitarian Affairs was Reagan's second tool in his struggle against communism. The Reagan Administration attempted to usurp the moral authority and political stature of the Bureau of Human Rights and Humanitarian Affairs by appointing an unwavering anticommunist, not a human rights advocate, as its leader. Having left the office vacant for months, Reagan originally nominated Ernest Lefever to the post of assistant secretary of state for human rights and humanitarian affairs. Lefever, a well-known critic of Carter's human rights policy, advocated the repeal of all U.S. legislation linking human rights with foreign assistance because it interfered with the fight against communism. In 1977, Ernest Lefever wrote,

> The consistent and single-minded invocation of the "human rights standard" in making United States foreign policy decisions serves neither our interests nor the cause of freedom. . . . Making human rights the chief, or even major, foreign policy determinant carries dangers: [It] subordinates, blurs, or distorts all other relevant considerations. . . . We have no moral mandate to remake the world in our own image. (Cited in Heaps 1984, 31–32)

After a loud public outcry, NGOs' (nongovernmental organizations) protests, and congressional denunciations, the Senate Foreign Relations

Committee voted 13 to 4 to reject Lefever's appointment. The rebuff of Lefever demonstrated that the American public and the U.S. Congress still supported the concept of human rights.

Finally, on November 17, 1981, over ten months after Reagan's swearing-in as the 40th president of the United States, Elliot Abrams was unanimously approved as assistant secretary of state for human rights and humanitarian affairs. Abrams, many believe, was simply a more refined version of Lefever (Forsythe 1990). Unfortunately, there is ample evidence that demonstrates that Abrams held similar views as Lefever's regarding the role of human rights in U.S. foreign policy. Abrams, like Lefever, believed that human rights should be subordinated to larger U.S. strategic and geopolitical concerns. Human rights rhetoric was simply propaganda to be used against the Soviet Union. Under Abrams, in the opinion of Caleb Rossiter, the Human Rights Bureau

> was relegated to a low, uncontroversial status. Operating more as a public relations bureau for anti-Communism, the Bureau rarely threatens the interests and domain of the geographic bureaus or the security agencies, and so no longer engenders the conflict it did under Derian. (1984, 22–23)

Forsythe relates an illuminating episode when Abrams testified before a joint hearing of the Subcommittee on Africa of the House Committee on Foreign Affairs and the Subcommittee on International Development Institutions:

> **Chairman Wolpe (D-MI):** Let me ask you this. Do you believe that Angola is, in the language of the statute [Section 701] . . . a gross violator of human rights?
> **Mr. Abrams:** I have never formed an opinion about that.
> **Chairman Wolpe:** More importantly, nor has your own Human Rights Bureau.
> **Mr. Abrams:** We don't actually form opinions about that question because it is not a useful way to spend our time. (Cited in Forsythe 1988, 65)

The assistant secretary of state for human rights and humanitarian affairs, Elliot Abrams, was unable to determine whether Angola[23] was a gross violator of human rights during a time when the Angolan government forcefully relocated civilians into militarized villages; indiscriminately killed, kidnapped, and tortured civilians in rebel-dominated regions; and targeted civilian populations in violation of international law. Furthermore, both the government and opposition rebels (de facto governments in certain regions of Angola) purposely placed land mines in villagers' footpaths and in agricultural fields, while cutting off food supplies to citizens in an attempt to starve each other's supporters (Brennan 1987; United States Congress 1989). Jim Genova (1995) acknowledges that although there is no way to accurately determine how many people were killed in the U.S.-, Cuban-, and Soviet Union-funded Angolan civil war, many analysts nevertheless estimate that at least 750,000 people were slaughtered, hundreds of thousands more were wounded, and perhaps up to a half million were made refugees. Yet, in the midst of the Angolan government's policy of annihilation, Abrams, the chief U.S. human rights envoy, could not form an opinion on whether human rights in Angola were being systematically violated. Rather than form opinions on human rights situations, Cynthia Brown concludes that the Human Rights Bureau, while administered by Abrams, "functioned as a promotional agent and appointments secretary" for anticommunist repressive organizations and regimes (2003).

Abrams's contempt for human rights and his apologist stance for the Reagan Administration's anticommunism crusade conflicted with the duties and responsibilities of his position. Abrams used his official position as chief human rights officer to downplay or simply ignore human rights violations by pro-American governments. Michael Dobbs of the *Washington Post* describes an exchange between Abrams and Aryeh Neier (an internationally recognized expert on human rights, and the founder and former executive director of Human Rights Watch) regarding the El Mozote massacre. Abrams, when confronted with overwhelming evidence of the right-wing death squads' murderous destruction of an entire village, deceitfully alleged that the massacre "never happened." Neier concludes that Abrams was prepared to lie "in order to promote the policy adopted by the administration" (Dobbs 2003, A01). When confronted with criticism from human rights advocates, Abrams's response was shrill and impertinent.[24]

Under Abrams's leadership, many believed that the Bureau of Human Rights and Humanitarian Affairs became an integral tool of Reagan's fight against communism rather than a true advocate of human rights in the United States' foreign policy. When the administration's rhetoric included human rights, it was used as a weapon of political, ideological, and propaganda warfare against the Soviet Union and its client states. Under the direction of the Executive, the State Department redefined the term "human rights." To reiterate, Reagan and his administration collapsed the range of human rights into democracy and anticommunism, refusing to recognize physical integrity rights or economic and social human rights. Heaps reports a confidential interview with a career State Department officer regarding the human rights office:

> [T]he Bureau was weak under Derian, and it is weaker under Abrams. There is inadequate contact with other sectors of the Department, no committee or inter-agency meetings, nor meaningful consultations. There are just memoranda. The idea of human rights is still something of an orphan, adopted periodically when convenient or expedient. (Heaps 1984, 43–44)

Human rights were not given a high priority in the Reagan Administration, with the exception of their ideological use against the Soviet Union. Human rights were vocally supported in the East–West struggle, as they proved to be a good tactical weapon. Abrams, described as a somewhat competent administrator, was clearly not a staunch champion of human rights and was unsuited for the position of chief human rights officer. His primary qualification was his uncompromising anticommunism.

CONGRESS' CONTINUED ROLE

Reagan's Latin American regional security policy, defined as fighting leftist insurgencies, trumped any real human rights concern. Burger-mann (2004) argues that Reagan's adamant ideological stand in Central America was the primary cause of antagonism between the Reagan White House and human rights supporters in Congress and NGOs. During this time, Congress resisted the Executive's use of economic and military aid to support repressive yet U.S.-friendly governments in Central America. But, unfortunately, Congress lacked the political will to exercise its constitutional prerogatives to direct the executive branch's foreign policy initiatives. Many in Congress and among the voting American public felt that the United States had been seriously weakened and humiliated by the Carter Administration's foreign policy debacles. U.S. citizens were held hostage in the Middle East, and the Soviet Union had greatly expanded its military presence in Cuba, Cambodia, Afghanistan, Angola, Mozambique, and, of course, Nicaragua. During Reagan's first term, Congress provided the Executive with large foreign aid allocations and dramatically increased military and intelligence funding as requested by the White House. Amitay Acharya argues that a notable attribute of Reagan's anticommunist campaign

> is the increasing involvement of the [Central Intelligence Agency] CIA and the Special Forces. . . . During the first five years of

William Casey's leadership of the CIA, the intelligence budget has grown faster than the defense budget. . . . The Special Forces are being increasingly used as part of U.S. security aid to its third world clients. (1987, 30)

In an effort to restore U.S. prestige and fend off a perceived Soviet threat, Reagan persuaded Congress to fund every aspect of the U.S. security apparatus.

Every time Reagan faced congressional resistance, he shrewdly took up the rhetoric of human rights and claimed to want to defend them, even if he redefined them very narrowly as electoral democracy. Robert Kagan, deputy for policy in the Bureau for Inter-American Affairs at the State Department, commented that Reagan learned that "support for democracy could overcome congressional resistance" (Kagan 1988, 48). Congress was too easily swayed by the Executive's claims of protecting and promoting democratic governments,[25] improving human rights practices,[26] or granting special exemptions due to U.S. national security concerns. The end result was that Congress provided substantial U.S. funding for military governments or military-controlled governments in Central America. Congress' willingness to defer to presidential fabrication concerning claims of improved human rights conditions is evident in the case of Guatemala. In April 1982, after a military coup installed General Efrian Rios Montt, the Reagan Administration declared a human rights victory in Guatemala. The *New York Times* reports Abrams's contention that

> there seems to be a growing consensus now that Rios Montt really does mean to eliminate political killing and bring the armed forces under control. . . . We want very much to encourage him to continue in that, and one way to do so is to give his government more support. (Kinzer 1983, A3)

From 1982 to 1988, Reagan managed to get Congress to approve $593.3 million in economic aid, nearly half of which ($260.2 million) was in the form of ESF funding. Yet, according to Amnesty International and the State Department's own annual reports on human rights, the killings did not stop. The State Department's career officers collected detailed reports on the human rights situation in Guatemala and documented the fact that Guatemala was among the world's most egregious human rights-abusing countries. While the State Department's estimates of the murders and tortures were lower than those reported by human rights organizations, these estimates were still extremely high. In reality, there would not be any noticeable human rights improvement in Guatemala until 1997.

Despite the apparent naïveté of the U.S. Congress, the U.S. legislature at the time still remained a force to be reckoned with when it came to influencing the human rights policy of the Reagan Administration thanks to the use of congressional hearings. More importantly, during Reagan's tenure in office, Congress passed a series of human rights legislations that, despite Reagan's negative impact on human rights, would nonetheless and rather paradoxically further institutionalize human rights in the U.S. foreign policy making process.

Congressional Hearings

As was seen in previous chapters, Congress regularly uses its power to hold public hearings in order to scrutinize particular issues. It often calls in witnesses to testify in order to determine the accuracy of White House reports. Congressional hearings are powerful tools to publicize incidents, formalize congressional opinion, debate policy options, and shape foreign policy objectives. These congressional hearings always attract much media attention, too. In 1981, the Subcommittee on International Organizations was renamed the Subcommittee on Human Rights and International Organizations. Margaret Galey believes that the name change was intended to "signal to the newly inaugurated Republican Administration that the Subcommittee would give top priority to and serve as a forum for discussing international human rights" (1985, 343). As previously suggested, the holding of hearings was a popular method used to investigate human rights in specific countries, to exert pressure on the administration to make sure it adheres to human rights legislations, and to monitor presidential compliance.

During the 97th Congress (1981–1982), the Subcommittee on Human Rights and International Organizations, under the lead of its chair, Don Bonker (D-WA), held fewer hearings on human rights violations than did the pivotal Fraser Subcommittee during the Nixon Administration. Nevertheless, Bonker continued and even extended the purview of the formal procedures. Bonker's subcommittee heard testimony on twenty-two human rights hearings. Fourteen of these hearings were country specific, and the remainder concerned human rights in bilateral and multilateral forums. But, for the first time, several of these historic hearings focused on the specific types of human rights violations that took place (for example, disappearances and religious intolerance). Congress did not prevent President Reagan from granting foreign assistance to human rights-abusing regimes, as we saw above. But Congress' watch-dog role nonetheless restrained the president's actions. On a few occasions, with regard to Chile in particular and, for a time, for Argentina, El Salvador, and Guatemala too, Congress did make use of its ability to formulate country-specific legislation to limit or bar U.S. military assistance.

At a House of Representatives' Committee on Appropriations Subcommittee on Foreign Operations hearing on foreign aid on February 25, 1981, the deliberations focused on foreign assistance allocations to El Salvador. President Reagan had claimed that the majority of the murders were committed not by the security forces, but by the leftist insurgents. These assertions were publicly and vocally contradicted in the hearing not only by human rights NGOs, including the Catholic Church, but also by members of Congress who had visited El Salvador[27] and even by Salvadoran military officers themselves. Ricardo Alejandro Fiallos, a captain in the Salvadoran military, testified that the death squads were made up of members of the Salvadoran security forces and that the high-ranking members of the military not only knew about the death squads but also actually planned their murderous activities (United States Congress 1981). Because the administration's claims were so insincere, even U.S. Ambassador to El Salvador Robert White testified in front of Congress, "The [government] security forces in El Salvador have been responsible for the deaths of thousands and thousands of young people, and they have executed them on the mere suspicion that they are leftists or sympathize with leftists" (United States Congress 1981, 3; see also White 1981). Testimony in this congressional hearing proved extremely embarrassing to the White House. Nevertheless, Congress was also concerned with preventing the possible victory of a leftist revolution in El Salvador. Thus, Congress did not terminate aid to El Salvador. Congress did not want to be responsible for "losing" El Salvador to communism. Therefore, even in the face of massive murder, torture, and disappearance of political leaders, peasants, nuns, and students, Congress still chose to provide aid. Although Congress may have complained and halfheartedly required certification, it still gave Reagan the money needed to support the brutal military regime in El Salvador. Forsythe (1987) concludes that, overall, Congress had the power, but unfortunately not the will, to terminate or restrict security assistance to anticommunist countries that brutalized and tortured their citizens.

Legislation

As was shown in chapter 1, Congress has the power to legislate the foreign policy behavior of the Executive, to constrain presidential initiatives, and to regulate executive actions. Furthermore, Congress can act through its power of legislation to deny or restrict the use of foreign assistance. Another key method of congressional oversight is the legislation of reporting requirements on the executive branch. Confronted with the atrocities of the Salvadoran military, and yet concerned with losing El Salvador to a communist takeover, Congress compromised by setting conditions for military aid. With the appalling revelations of the mounting death toll in El Salvador due to the paramilitary death squads, Congress passed the International Security and Development Cooperation Act of 1981. Under mandate of Congress, if El Salvador was to receive U.S. assistance, the president had to certify that progress had been made in the human rights conditions in El Salvador. The president would have to certify, in writing to Congress, that the human rights conditions in El Salvador were improving and that the military was making progress in controlling the death squads. The act required the Executive, as a condition of military aid, to certify every 180 days that the Salvadoran government was making "concerted and significant" efforts to improve its human rights conditions, was achieving substantial control over the military, was making progress in its economic and political reforms, and was going to hold elections at an "early date." To certify that a country is eligible for funding, the executive branch must produce a lengthy and detailed report documenting the human rights situation and the improvements or progress made in achieving internationally recognized human rights. The certification process was still another congressional concession since Congress would not cut funding altogether, but instead put the executive branch on notice that it wanted to be kept informed on the human rights situation within El Salvador.

Initially, the Democrat-controlled House of Representatives included a provision granting a veto over the certification if members of Congress found the report deficient or defective. But, in an effort to get the certification procedure through the Republican-held Senate, the veto provision was dropped. Only the president had the power to determine if El Salvador qualified for aid. In January 1983, Reagan submitted a sixty-seven-page document conceding that human rights abuses still continued. However, the report added that the "government of El Salvador has made progress [and displayed] increased consciousness of the importance of more effective action on human rights. . . . The situation is not perfect and progress is not as great as desired, but it is progress nonetheless" (cited in Heaps 1984, 40). Accordingly, in the opinion of the Reagan Administration, El Salvador no longer demonstrated a consistent pattern of human rights abuses, it showed progress toward correcting human rights violations, and therefore it was entitled to U.S. aid. Although El Salvador's progress was "disturbingly slow" and "not as great as desired," it nonetheless met the legal requirements for receiving aid. Thus, when confronted with a blatantly false certification of El Salvador's human rights improvements, Congress was powerless to reject the certification.[28] While the certification process may have eased the conscience of Congress' members, it did relatively little damage to Reagan's counterinsurgency policy.

Congress also passed a series of acts intended to limit U.S. funding of covert operations in Nicaragua. In 1982, Congress would enact the Boland Amendment (named after Edward Boland [D-MA], chair of the House Intelligence Committee), which prohibited the CIA from funding the overthrow of the Nicaraguan government or from provoking conflict between Nicaragua and Honduras. Reagan construed Congress' limitation of humanitarian assistance to include "equipment and supplies necessary for defense against air attack" and "training in radio communications, collection and utilization of intelligence, logistics, and small-unit skills and tactics." Reagan declared that the aid he was sending to the Contras was "material support and guidance to the Nicaraguan resistance groups" necessary to pressure the Sandinista government to discontinue its support of the Salvadoran rebels (Clarke, O'Conner, and Ellis 1997, 107). The aid, Reagan implied, was not funding for the overthrow of the Nicaraguan government but simply the provisions necessary to care for a pro-American organization resisting the legitimacy of the government of Nicaragua.

However, in 1984, Congress and the American public learned of the CIA involvement in the mining of Nicaragua's harbors. Mysteriously, Dutch, Liberian, Japanese, and Soviet ships were damaged as they struck mines when entering ports in Nicaragua in March 1984. As a result of the growing question of exploding boats, the CIA reported that the mines were placed by "unilaterally controlled Latino assets," which later became understood to be a CIA-run operation (Arnson 1989, 156). Congressional anger was ignited by this embarrassing public revelation. Not only was the CIA mining of harbors a violation of international law and U.S. law, but it was also an act of international terrorism meant to destabilize the Nicaraguan government. Furthermore, the Reagan

Administration failed to inform the intelligence oversight committees in Congress of the CIA's covert activities.[29] Congressional intelligence committees, which held the task of overseeing CIA covert activities, were undeniably inadequately briefed, leaving Congress out of the foreign policy-making loop. This situation prompted a conspicuous shift in Congress over Nicaraguan human rights abuses, Reagan's support of the Contras, and CIA tactics. Those congressional members who had previously backed Reagan's Contra policy now decided to join the growing ranks of the Boland Amendment supporters.

The Senate quickly issued a resolution condemning the harbor mining and prohibiting any further CIA activity of this sort. The Boland II Amendment (May 1984) prohibited any lethal aid to the Contras.[30] There would be a total of five Boland Amendments, enacted between December 1982 and December 1985, prohibiting U.S. military or security assistance for the Contra rebels. Now hampered by severe congressional restrictions, the Reagan team would then devise two new schemes in order to continue to support the Contras in violation of the Boland Amendments. The first strategy was for U.S. officials, Lieutenant Colonel Oliver North and Elliot Abrams,[31] to solicit funds from third parties in support of the Contras. North and Abrams solicited money from private individuals and from three foreign governments, Saudi Arabia ($32 million), Brunei ($10 million),[32] and Taiwan ($2 million). A second, perhaps more illegal, and certainly more unethical method was a plan which would later be known as the Iran-Contra Affair.[33] The Boland Amendments undoubtedly succeeded in limiting the Executive. In response, the Reagan Administration desperately attempted to secure outside and illegal funding for the Contras.

Contrary to Carter's position, Reagan also instructed the Treasury Department to vote in favor of repressive right-wing pro-American countries seeking loans from international financial institutions. This was directly in violation of Section 701 of the International Financial Institutions Act.[34] The Reagan Administration simply ignored the provision to vote against loans to countries that practice gross human rights violations contained in this act, unless the provisions could be used against leftist regimes. Again, the Reagan Administration believed that right-wing regimes' human rights violations never formed a consistent pattern. Therefore, the United States could use its voice and vote in the international financial institutions (the World Bank, International Monetary Fund [IMF], and regional banks) to encourage aid to right-wing military regimes. In response to the Reagan Administration's transparent indifference to congressional will, in 1983, Congress decided to drop the word "consistent" from Section 701 in order to eliminate the Executive's manipulation and misinterpretation of the statute. This congressional act was undertaken after Abrams testified to a subcommittee of the House Banking Committee that the State Department did not regard Section 701, a duly legislated law, as compulsory but rather as merely one choice of action. Abrams testified,

> I think 701 does not call for a decision pattern. It calls for us to try to decide among the various means of influencing human rights conditions in a variety of countries. We have to choose when and where to use tools, including these votes. (Abrams 1983)

The Reagan Administration's complete disregard for U.S. law left Congress with no choice but to modify Section 701 by dropping the term "consistent" from the legislation. The Reagan Administration had too often justified supporting loans to right-wing governments allied with the United States by dubiously claiming that these countries showed improvement in their human rights standards. Yet, at the same time, the Reagan White House cited human rights abuses in its opposition to multilateral loans for countries like Angola, Syria, Laos, and Vietnam. However, with the newly amended legislation, the executive branch could no longer point to only intermittent or infinitesimal improvements in the human rights conditions of repressive regimes as a justification for continued assistance.

But perhaps the most successful human rights legislation enacted by Congress during the Reagan era was the Comprehensive Anti-apartheid Act. In 1986, Congress legislated economic sanctions against South Africa, over Reagan's veto.[35] The Comprehensive Anti-Apartheid Act[36] banned direct air flights between the United States and South Africa, further outlawed private U.S. investment and loans to the South African government and white-owned firms, limited imports, and removed tax benefits. The Reagan Administration believed that the Anti-Apartheid Act threatened the billions of dollars owned and invested in South Africa by U.S. corporations. The Anti-Apartheid Act also threatened to weaken a staunch ally in the fight against communism. Congress, aware of the president's political agenda, did not grant executive flexibility normally found in human rights legislation. Congress resolutely refused to include a waiver clause allowing the Executive to set aside the legislation under certain circumstances. In this case, Congress purposefully placed human rights considerations above U.S. economic and strategic interests. Section 501 of the act required that the Executive report on the extent of the progress toward ending the system of apartheid and toward establishing a nonracial democracy in South Africa. Reagan's first report to Congress under Section 501 detailed the lack of progress, but strongly recommended that no additional economic sanctions needed to be applied. Reagan adamantly argued that punitive measures against South Africa were counterproductive and that the economic sanctions in place ought to be repealed. What was needed, in Reagan's opinion, was "active and creative diplomacy" (United States, Department of State 1987). However, Congress stood firm and maintained the economic sanctions.

Congress' imposition of foreign assistance funding restrictions, combined with earmarks, conditions and certification, hearings, and oversight, along with key human rights legislation, all greatly hindered Reagan's ideological campaign and foreign policy adventures. One might wonder what Reagan's offensive foreign policy might have been like if Congress had not preempted several of Reagan's policy designs.

INSTITUTIONALIZING HUMAN RIGHTS

The scorn for and renunciation of human rights during the first Reagan Administration were mitigated somewhat in Reagan's later years as president. In fact, during Reagan's tenure, and as already hinted at above, human rights would, ironically, become more and more institutionalized in U.S. foreign policy (Donnelly 1995). Tamar Jacoby (1986) went as far as to state that the Reagan Administration experienced an about-face in its efforts to nullify human rights concerns from foreign policy decision making. Several reasons have been advanced to explain this phenomenon. Forsythe (1995) credits the shift in Reagan's human rights policy to three factors: new personnel, a modified view of U.S. interests, and a continuing congressional push toward human rights issues. An additional factor, not mentioned by Forsythe, was the professionalization of the bureaucracy. And, finally, human rights legislation existed that had to be fulfilled regardless of the president's agenda.

The most significant factor in tempering human rights rancor was that, particularly during Reagan's transition from his first administration to his second, "a number of ideologues left the Reagan team, to be replaced by more pragmatic persons" (Forsythe 1995, 122). Notably, George Shultz replaced Alexander Haig as secretary of state. Foreign Service officers replaced Jeane Kirkpatrick; and Richard Schifter replaced Elliot Abrams as assistant secretary of state for the Bureau of Human Rights and Humanitarian Affairs. With the retirement of the staunch anticommunist ideologues, the newly installed, more practical and pragmatic personnel concluded that a strict anticommunist policy was contrary to U.S. long-term economic and strategic interests. The president's new team of advisors counseled Reagan to persuade friendly authoritarian leaders to reduce human rights violations and allow limited democratic participation.

Moreover, by the beginning of Reagan's second term in office, the idea of human rights in foreign policy had become a more recognized objective within the State Department. Donnelly and Liang-Fenton write that "the federal bureaucracy is not simply an extension of the president. Policy changes at the top often do not penetrate very quickly, or sometimes even very far, into the foreign policy bureaucracy" (2004, 16). In the case of human rights, the bureaucratic tendency toward policy inertia and entrenchment proved somewhat beneficial. The Bureau of Human Rights and Humanitarian Affairs, created in 1975, slowly became an established fixture in U.S. foreign policy, with its attendant career officers, vested interests, and funding. Moreover, the Human Rights Bureau and embassy bureaucrats became more professional, developing exacting procedures and meticulous routines in the collection of information and data, and reporting on country-specific human rights.

The Reagan Administration's persistent lip service to democracy created expectations as well.[37] Rossiter argues that "the tendency in U.S. foreign policy-making for rhetoric to influence reality" (1984, 244) facilitated the institutionalization of human rights in U.S. foreign policy at that time. Once senior-level policy makers began using the rhetoric of democracy and human rights protection, they often became bound to the concepts. Critics, the media, and the American public in particular wanted to know what the government was doing to achieve these declared goals and how well the process was unfolding. Since the policy was expected to generate results,

> [S]enior officials tend[ed] to respond by telling their subordinates to start doing something in pursuit of the goals, if only to give the impression that they are serious about them. . . . Predictably enough, senior officials began signaling the foreign policy bureaucracy to take up the issue actively. (Rossiter 1984, 244)

Moreover, as Forsythe asserts, "[T]he State Department . . . recognized that if the department does not act on human rights concerns, Congress [would] proceed without it" (1990, 452). The State Department was well aware that if it did not implement human rights legislations, Congress could cut its funding, instigate onerous oversight procedures, and monitor its daily activities.

The congressionally mandated *Country Reports*, initially deficient and biased, became progressively more thorough, comprehensive, and objective during the 1980s. By all accounts, the *Country Reports* vastly improved over time. By Reagan's second term in office, the reports were considered to be accurate and dependable, with a few exceptions. Edwin Maynard (1989) believes that there was still a tendency to underreport human rights abuses in pro-U.S. states and overemphasize communist states' human rights abuses. But, overall, the reports were quite factual. Essentially, the process had become institutionalized. The collecting of human rights data had become a routine part of the normal operating procedure. Ambassador Richard Schifter, the new assistant secretary of state for human rights and humanitarian affairs, notes,

> One of the very important consequences—perhaps unintended—of these legislative provisions (requiring annual human rights reporting by the Department of State) is that they have made human rights concerns an integral part of the State Department's daily reporting and daily decision-making. A human rights officer in an Embassy overseas who wants to write a good annual human rights report on the country in which he or she works must carefully monitor and observe human rights developments throughout the year on a daily basis. (United States, Department of State 1988)

Consequently, the State Department became better at investigating human rights conditions. State Department personnel would no longer rely exclusively on the local government's account of the human rights conditions in their countries. Embassy personnel began talking to more than government officials and would now consult NGOs, human rights activists, and press reports in order to get a more comprehensive picture of the country's situation. Carrying out thorough investigations and writing comprehensive reports made State Department bureaucrats and their bosses look good. Certainly, this helped the Foreign Service officers' careers.

An additional motivation behind the improvement of the *Country Reports* is that the media, human rights organizations, and Congress started to methodically examine the publication. Congress became better at scrutinizing the reports as it had now established its own contacts in the human rights field. Moreover, human rights NGOs would regularly examine and comment on the reports, publicly countering any inaccurate or misleading information. State Department officers were frequently called upon to clarify or justify how the reports were compiled and, often, had to defend their findings and conclusions. Thus, the public scrutiny of the reports encouraged accurate and reliable reporting. Today, the *Country Reports* are one of the most important tools in the analysis of human rights conditions around the world.[38]

The bureaucratic struggle within the State Department was more or less resolved by the time the Reagan Administration took office. Mower (1987) believes that the reduction in bureaucratic antagonism allowed the Bureau of Human Rights to embed human rights within the State Department decision-making processes because it was now accepted as a legitimate component of foreign aid considerations. Mower writes that "the Reagan bureau was reaping the fruits of the intense and often frustrating struggle by its predecessor to win a place of human rights within the bureaucracy" (1987, 78).

The Bureau of Human Rights and Humanitarian Affairs (HA) became more institutionalized too. Previously, HA was routinely excluded from State Department cable traffic. Once the pariah bureau where a transfer meant the end of a career, the Bureau of Human Rights and Humanitarian Affairs now began to attract an elite corps of talented young professionals concerned with human rights and career advancement. When the bureau became established and accepted, it developed typical bureaucratic practices and routines. Like all bureaucracies, HA sought to protect its budget, power, authority, and prestige. The Human Rights Bureau, despite Reagan's foreign policy endeavors (or perhaps because of them), became an established and entrenched bureau with many career Foreign Service officers holding a vested interest in human rights.

However, HA still had to occasionally battle with the regional bureaus of the State Department. Because the Reagan Administration lowered the importance of human rights in diplomatic relations and increased the military assistance budget, many of the traditional career diplomats in the State Department hoped to return to what had been considered their time-honored role of maintaining smooth relations with countries, whether or not these countries had bad human rights conditions. The Bureau of Human Rights still had to counter the Foreign Service officer's tendency to defend his or her client country by understating abuses and overstating positive human rights trends, particularly if foreign aid allocations were at stake. Certainly, the ability to offer foreign aid to the client state made the diplomat's job easier. Thus, any attempt to make large cuts in the military aid programs "elicited massive protests from the foreign policy bureaucracies" (Payaslian 1996, 66). There are documented cases where, when called to testify to Congress on a country's human rights situation, Foreign Service officers during the Reagan years justified egregious human rights abuses as the country's courageous attempt to "counter a Communist plot to overthrow the government" (Rubin 1987, 198). Thus, in an attempt to maintain foreign aid funding levels, some Foreign Service officers would conjure the specter of communist takeovers in order to guarantee U.S. financial support.

Due to the bias in the information received from the embassies, the Bureau of Human Rights systematically relied on reports from human rights organizations like Amnesty International. HA had to sign off on the data collected by the embassy personnel before the *Country Reports* could be published. NGOs' major strength lies in their advocacy of human rights and social justice. At every step in the foreign aid allocation process, the executive branch was countered by the accurate reporting of NGOs and the news media.

In addition, there was a simmering friction between the State Department and the Executive. Reagan exasperated many in the State Department by referring to the bureaucracy as "a hotbed of liberalism" (Rossiter 1984, 204). Many State Department officers thought Reagan was casting doubt on their loyalty. Furthermore, throughout the Reagan Administration, there was a conspicuous increase in "political creep" (the use of political appointees for the plum jobs of assistant secretary and deputy assistant secretary positions). Political creep caused great concern and resentment among the State Department's Foreign Service officers. Promotion opportunities, for the ambitious Foreign Service officers, were lost due to political appointments. During the Reagan Administration, political appointees filled nearly one-half of these coveted positions. Perhaps a trivial incentive for institutionalizing human rights was simply the desire to annoy Reagan and his bellicose staff.

In the words of Daniel Drezner, "[B]y the end of Reagan's second term, human rights were accepted as an important component of the American national interest" (2000, 745), in theory if not in practice. The idea of human rights, once established as part of the bureaucratic standard operating procedure, became an institutionalized feature of U.S. foreign policy.

CONCLUSION

The Reagan Administration's efforts to dismiss human rights as a policy objective were at least partially stymied by Congress, human rights advocacy groups, and public opinion. Mower concludes that "the existence of human rights legislation, the presence in the State Department of a Human Rights Bureau, and other institutional arrangements seemed to ensure the survival of this [human rights] foreign policy element" (1987, 3) with or without the Executive's support. Whereas the State Department was "hampered by the absence of a strong domestic constituency supporting its actions" (Hastedt 1997, 216), the issue of human rights and, therefore, the Bureau of Human Rights and Humanitarian Affairs had strong backing in Congress and within the American public. The Reagan Administration could not eradicate the human rights infrastructure within the State Department that was the result of a congressional mandate. However, Reagan did attempt to coopt the human rights bureaucracy with the failed nomination of Ernest Lefever and later the successful nomination of Elliot Abrams.

But human rights were institutionalized in U.S. foreign policy at a time when the sitting president was vehemently opposed to their inclusion in executive decision making. Even a popular antihuman rights president could not ignore human rights issues in developing his foreign policy strategy. At least in the abstract, the American citizenry supports the idea of human rights and morality in foreign policy. Thus, "the apparent discarding of human rights concerns" by Reagan, Cynthia Arnson believes, "miscalculated the depth of public acceptance of the U.S. role as a moral protector and promoter of human decency" (1989, 53). Despite Reagan's enormous popularity, the American population would not back Reagan's Central American policy because it blatantly lacked a human rights component. The ideological war against communism could not be won with death squads.

The Reagan Administration, wishing to delink the granting of foreign assistance from human rights, claimed that its foreign policy "[was] guided primarily by the criteria of effectiveness, choosing the response that is most likely to improve human rights" (United States, Department of State 1981). Foreign aid was to be given principally for the furtherance of U.S. economic and strategic interests. And it was to be granted only to friends, or to those likely to be bought as friends. The Reagan Administration wanted to legitimize its strategy of creating or maintaining a human rights double standard. With friendly countries that abused the human rights of their citizens, the Reagan strategy was quiet diplomacy and persuasion, while with communist countries it was public denouncements and isolation, if not outright military intervention.

When Reagan could not ignore human rights, he attempted to redefine them as anticommunism. However, by the end of Reagan's eight-year tenure in office, communism was no longer the evil empire it once was said to be. Foreign aid and the continuing military buildup lost their Cold War urgency. Not only was the U.S. economy no longer able to maintain massive defense spending levels, but also relations with the Soviet Union had started to improve by the end of Reagan's presidency. The Soviet Union's military and economic strength had diminished, both in real terms and in comparison to the United States, in large part due to the military buildup of the Reagan era. Mikhail Gorbachev realized that the Soviet Union had to stop antagonizing the United States since his number one priority was to develop the Soviet economy. Gorbachev's objectives could only be accomplished with the cooperation of the United States, and the USSR's relations with the United States under Reagan's second term reflected this new trend.

The Cold War was much less frosty in 1988. The eventual demise of the Soviet Union, and along with it much of the rationale for U.S. foreign aid and military expenditures, would allow U.S. foreign policy to take a "kinder and gentler" turn during the Bush Sr. Administration. However, human rights would still be sacrificed to prudent politics.

CHAPTER 5

Human Rights in the New World Order: The George H. W. Bush Administration

The [Bush Sr.] Administration's policy has been a mix of deluded realpolitik and indifference to human rights.

"What Foreign Policy?" (*The New Republic*, 1991)

George Bush Sr. confronted a dramatically changing world with the passing of the Cold War. The dissolution of the Soviet Union and the collapse of communism initiated important questions concerning the nature and future of the advancement of human rights. During the Cold War's ideological battles, human rights issues were often relegated to a low priority. With the United States' triumph over communism, human rights and democracy seemed assured. Now was the time, many believed, for human rights ideals to be acted upon. Many hoped the United States would now be able to apply a universal standard to human rights and would censure human rights abuses wherever they occurred. However, Bush's tentative, cautious, prudent style tended toward a reactive rather than a proactive response to human rights and international crises.

Undeniably, the demise of the Soviet Union and its proxy governments in Eastern Europe produced serious human rights violations and international crises. Furthermore, Third World countries that were once objects of superpower competition had much of their foreign aid—both economic and military—slashed. With the end of the superpower confrontation, the Third World, heavily armed by the superpowers, experienced the reemergence of ethnic conflicts, civil wars, and genocide. In terms of innocent civilian deaths due to conflict, war, and genocide, the post-Cold War era has been perhaps more lethal than the era of superpower confrontation.

Challenged with the eruption of new human rights crises, George H. W. Bush was neither sympathetic nor antagonistic toward the concept of human rights. Human rights were of little significance in Bush's primary goal of defending the international status quo and maintaining global stability. If the costs of supporting a human rights agenda were small, Bush could be an active proponent. But if there were possible political costs for supporting human rights or if human rights competed with other interests, the Bush Administration would then simply ignore the violations.

Bush's lack of vision and ideological stance, along with his penchant for stability and cautious inaction, greatly reduced the rancor in Washington. Bush's foreign policy strategy included compromise and cooperation with Capitol Hill. The Bush Administration enjoyed a relatively cooperative and conciliatory relationship with Congress, unlike the Nixon or Reagan Administrations. By and large, Bush Sr. knew how important consultation with Congress was if he was to have his way in foreign affairs. Furthermore, there were no debilitating internal struggles within Bush's Administration, as there had been for the Carter Administration for example, since Bush chose advisors who were temperamentally similar to him and ideologically compatible.

Although one of the shortest, the Bush Sr. Administration was, perhaps, the most crucial of all administrations for U.S. human rights policy in the past forty years. The end of the Cold War brought a new promise of peace and prosperity. Expectations once again were high. The United States no longer had a genuine adversary. The world was turning from totalitarianism to democracy—from communism to free-market capitalism. More importantly, Bush enjoyed a friendly relationship with Congress, and technocrats now ruled the White House. The previous two decades of conflict in U.S. foreign policy to try to shape an authentic human rights policy (with the legislating of human rights requirements over the opposition of the Nixon Administration, the failed implementation of a human rights policy during the Carter Administration, and the active usurping of human rights by the Reagan Administration) now placed the policy in a position to yield fruit. Human rights were primed to finally be at the heart of U.S. foreign policy initiatives. The advancements in U.S. human rights policy in the previous administrations, often achieved by default or through defining paradoxes, led human rights activists, scholars, and policy makers in the early 1990s to expect great progress for human rights standards. Yet, despite all this, the Bush Sr. Administration would bring a reversal in the recognition of the importance of human rights in U.S. foreign policy. Bush may have used human rights language, but he actively put the United States on a path toward more human rights violations, an attitude that would continue to dominate U.S. foreign policy throughout the 1990s.

A PRAGMATIC CONSERVATIVE REALIST

Cecil Crabb and Kevin Mulcahy characterize Bush Sr.'s foreign policy as "a distinctive blend of conservative and pragmatic principles" (1995, 256). As a pragmatic conservative, Bush brought to the presidency a group of advisors who shared his convictions and principles of moderation and expediency. Bush's inner circle was ideologically homogeneous in that Bush surrounded himself with cautious, moderate conservatives, thus further ensuring consensus and compromise. James Baker, Bush's secretary of state, testified at his confirmation hearing that he too was indeed a pragmatic conservative:

> Some have described my philosophy as 'pragmatic.' . . I am actually a Texas Republican, all of whom are conservative. I will admit to pragmatism, however, if by that you mean being realistic about the world and appreciating the importance of getting things done. (Baker 1989, 2)

Pragmatism, as a worldview, is characterized by believing in the practical utility of what works. Political pragmatism calls for a straightforward, no-nonsense approach to problem solving that is reactive rather than preemptive. The pragmatist pursues compromise at the expense of the attainment of philosophical or ideological principles. "As a self-described pragmatist," Charles Kegley believes, "Bush succeeded in separating its conduct from the hysterical extremes of Reagan's ideological interpretation of threat" (1989, 720). Prudence, not ideological crusade, was the focus of Bush Sr.'s foreign policy. Bush shunned the divisiveness of ideological politics for consensus building. Bush's rejection of doctrinaire campaigns was largely due to his perception that Reagan's primary foreign policy embarrassments were the result of his excessively ideological approach to politics. Bush intended to formulate a more rational foreign policy, absent the ideological crusade of the Reagan era. Hard-line conservatives bemoaned the pragmatism and moderation of the Bush Administration, believing that it was bringing the Reagan Revolution to an end. Instead, technocrats and bureaucrats were now directing U.S. foreign policy.

As a conservative, Bush was also unsettled by rapid change, preferring instead slow, incremental change in an attempt to maintain the status quo. Bush described his presidency as the "status quo-plus," meaning that he intended to continue the policies of his predecessor with a "kinder, gentler face." President Bush, however, was worried about the speed of change within the Soviet Union, and he was convinced that the best response was slow, cautious policies relying on personal diplomacy. At the same time, some scholars like Kegley believe that Bush, like Reagan before him, was also an enthusiast about interventionist foreign policy, as evidenced by his "extravagant commitment . . . to defense spending in an era of declining resources, staggering deficits and debts, and Soviet retrenchments" (1989, 723). Perhaps this was an effort to prove that the United States was still willing to stand up to challenges to its national interests in an era without a legitimate enemy. Bush thought that it was necessary to maintain a strong commitment to defense spending even though the United States faced huge federal deficits generated by the Reagan Administration. Overall, though, Bush was a moderate realist who believed that the United States ought to utilize its military and economic strength in pursuit of its national interests.

With the end of the Cold War and the dawn of the American unipolar moment, Bush's success in building a true model of collective security, the United States' categorical victory over Iraq in the Gulf War, led many to believe in Bush's declaration of a "new world order." The spread of democracy and capitalism promised to usher in a major transformation in world politics. Bush's new world order drew heavily from the Wilsonian tradition, and the United States' unique military and economic preeminence assured its apparent success. Bush's 1991 State of the Union Address set out his new world order vision, a global order "where diverse nations are drawn together in common cause to achieve the common aspirations of mankind—peace and security, freedom, and the rule of law" (Bush 1991). Again, in a speech before the United Nations, Bush proclaimed the idea of "a new partnership of nations that transcends the Cold War; a partnership based on consultation, cooperation and collective action . . . whose goals are to increase democracy, increase prosperity, increase the peace and reduce arms" (Bush 1990, as quoted in Gardner 1992). However, the anticipation and hope of the new world order were short-lived. A new world order was actually too big a leap for a pragmatic, incremental, and cautious conservative such as George H. W. Bush.

BUSH'S LEADERSHIP STYLE AND RELATIONSHIP WITH CONGRESS

Bush's lack of initiative or innovation assured continuity with the Reagan Administration. Bush's personality prompted him to seek public approval, avoid confrontation, find compromises, take the middle road, and make slow, measured decisions in order to keep all options open (Kegley 1989). This allowed Bush to easily change policy in response to new problems and changing circumstances, as long as these changes involved small, cautious, necessary steps to protect the status quo.[1] Thus, Ryan Barilleaux and Mark Rozell (2004) describe Bush as an "incrementalist" or bureaucratic president, lacking a closely held fundamental ideological doctrine. An incrementalist president first seeks to maintain the institutional status quo and then proceeds with modifications through a piecemeal approach. Modest gains with little or no risk, commitment, or cost were considered a success. Bush clearly adopted this approach. However, when action could not be avoided, Bush would in the end support a more assertive foreign policy (as in Panama, Iraq, and Somalia, for example).

Bush was often criticized for being too cautious and for lacking vision. But even Bush's critics viewed him as professional in foreign policy decision making. Bush was more of a traditional diplomat than a leader. Barilleaux and Rozell (2004) report that Bush identified with the foreign affairs managers and career Foreign Service officers. This identification resulted in the manifestation of values and characteristics associated with the traditional diplomatic corps, that is, the desire for order and stability, a reliance on personal relations, incrementalism, and the need to move prudently. This is often mistaken for inertia. And, unlike Reagan, Bush held the State Department's career officers in high regard, as evidenced by the meetings he held with them within days of his inauguration.

Because Bush knew how important conciliatory relations with Congress were, "President George Bush assembled a professional team to handle liaison operations with Congress" (Fisher 1998, 57). The liaison team included many who had previously served as members of Congress. Additionally, Bush Sr. preferred personal contact with congressional members and often invited groups of congressional members to the White House to discuss policy issues. William Leogrande reports that

> simply by conferring with Congress and treating it like a co-equal branch of government[,] Bush and Baker were quickly able to defuse much of the bitterness left over from the Reagan Administration. Congressional Democrats were so delighted at the contrast

with Reagan's tendency to ignore or berate them they demanded relatively small concessions from Bush as the price for striking bipartisan agreements. (1990, 620)

True to Bush's compromising style, his first action in dealing with the messy situation that Reagan left him with in Central America was to reconcile with Congress. In the spirit of bipartisanship, Bush appointed a Democrat, Bernard Aronson, for assistant secretary of state for inter-American affairs.[2] The newly appointed Aronson, however, had little knowledge or experience in Latin American affairs. On the contrary, Robert Pastor (1991) believes that Bush was more interested in selecting a pragmatic power broker, someone who knew how to get things done, particularly on Capitol Hill, rather than an experienced regional specialist. Aronson's appointment, according to Pastor, was intended to give Bush an ambassador to Capitol Hill.

POLITICAL EXPEDIENCY IN INTERNATIONAL CRISES

The Bush Sr. Administration's human rights policy, in the opinion of Jack Donnelly, "lay somewhere between those of its predecessors" in both word and deed (1993, 116). During the Bush Sr. years, human rights objectives were neither the "heart" of U.S. foreign policy as was said to be the case with the Carter Administration, nor entirely manipulated and usurped as had happened during the Reagan Administration. Bush Sr.'s human rights policy was much less moralistic and more pragmatic, yielding to realism and post-Cold War power politics. In general, the Bush Sr. Administration was inclined to support human rights, but only when the policy was thought to be cost free. Still, this attitude prompted him to frequently ignore human rights. Bush's neglect of human rights can in part be explained by his preference for personal diplomacy. Bush's leadership style rested on the use of personal, or rolodex, diplomacy. As such, the raising of sensitive or embarrassing issues, like human rights conditions, particularly when they are believed not to be imperative to U.S. national interest, was to be avoided. A country may have been vital to the United States, but its human rights conditions were not.

The Gulf War

Bush Sr.'s foreign policy, by and large, incorporated "moral impulses as long as they did not prove inconvenient to expediential concerns" (Forsythe 1995, 126). This administration's preference for political expediency was clearly demonstrated with regard to the Kurdish massacre at Halabja. In March 1988, Saddam Hussein used chemical weapons against Iraqi Kurds, killing over 5,000 civilians and injuring an additional 10,000.[3] During his presidential campaign, Bush Sr. downplayed the incident since, at the time, Iraq was a U.S. ally. It was not until Bush Sr.'s efforts to demonize Hussein in preparation for the first Gulf War that the administration finally condemned Saddam Hussein for using chemical weapons against the Kurds. After the Senate Foreign Relations Committee made public Saddam's policy of genocide toward the Kurds, Senator Claiborne Pell (chairman of the Foreign Relations Committee, D-RI) introduced the Prevention of Genocide Act (September 1988), which would have placed severe economic sanctions on Iraq in order to pressure the Iraqi regime to modify its deadly behavior. Because the embargo would place acute hardships on American business, oil, and agricultural sectors, the Reagan Administration, on behalf of the Bush campaign, managed to have the bill killed (Zunes 2001). At that time, it was far too close to the 1988 elections to risk upsetting farmers, bankers, oil companies, and exporters. Upon entering office, Bush actually doubled U.S. agricultural loans to Iraq ($1 billion in 1989). It is now widely known that Saddam diverted a large part of that money to his military. In order to provide cash to Saddam, in opposition to congressional intent, on January 17, 1990, Bush signed a waiver providing Export-Import Bank loan guarantees ($200 million) to Iraq. Bush's decision was based on his judgment that doing so was in the national interest of the United States. Iraq was a genocidal but effective Middle East ally.

The Gulf War offers an instructive example of the Bush Sr. Administration's inclusion of human rights into foreign policy only to the extent that it proves advantageous. Prior to his invasion of Kuwait, Saddam Hussein was viewed by the Bush Administration as a counterbalance to Iranian power and as a supplier of a vital resource. Thus, the Bush Administration forcefully opposed congressional attempts, in the spring and summer of 1990, to impose trade restrictions on Iraq due to this country's gross human rights violations. In the autumn of 1990, with the invasion of Kuwait, power politics suddenly transformed an American friend and ally, Saddam Hussein, into the personification of evil, a new Hitler. By allying itself with two undemocratic nations, Kuwait and Saudi Arabia, the Bush Administration was nonetheless able to maintain regional security and access to cheap oil. Looking for a rationale for war, one acceptable to the American population, Bush Sr. mixed economic pretenses with claims about the need to protect democracy and human rights. Bush also made vague references to the creation of a new world order. Interestingly, Ross asserts that "popular support increased when the emphasis was mostly on human rights and the need to confront an international evil" (1997, 329). Once the war ended, though, Bush Sr. had to downplay the issues of human rights and democracy since the end of the war did not establish respect for human rights or democracy in either Kuwait or Iraq. Moreover, Bush's Gulf War actually required sacrificing human rights to political expediency in neighboring states in the Middle East. Human Rights Watch maintains that the Bush Administration purposely refused to censure the human rights abuses of Middle Eastern governments that joined the U.S. coalition against Iraq (1992). Two examples will suffice. Rather than question the severe and notorious human rights abuses in Egypt, Bush awarded Egypt's participation in the Gulf War with $7 billion of debt forgiveness. In addition, the United States' coalition partners included Syria, a state that not only was (and still is) recognized as a vicious human rights abuser and a manufacturer of banned chemical weapons, but also was known to support terrorism. The use of American force and the loss of American lives helped to restore the Kuwaiti royal family to power. But this did not serve to advance human rights or democratic reforms in Kuwait.

Furthermore, in the aftermath of the Gulf War, Bush initially deserted the Kurds and the Shi'ites after inciting their uprising and encouraging them to overthrow Saddam. Although the Bush Administration had encouraged the Kurdish uprising in northern Iraq and the Shi'ite uprising in the south, Bush quickly abandoned these insurgents to the postwar vengeance of Saddam Hussein. Bush feared that the Kurdish unrest would spread to Turkey's Kurdish ethnic minority and renew calls for a Kurdish state, thus destabilizing Turkey, a dutiful ally and North Atlantic Treaty Organization (NATO) member. In the south, Bush Sr. feared that a Shi'ite revolt, with Shi'ite direct ties to Iran, could bring about a power shift in Iraq and the Middle East, thus strengthening an enemy of the United States. Therefore, because promoting and protecting human rights proved to be politically inconvenient to Bush's expedient concerns at the time, to paraphrase Forsythe, Hussein's bloody suppression of the U.S.-instigated insurgency was tolerated. When the massacres became public knowledge in the United States, Bush belatedly ordered a no-fly zone in both the north and the south to protect the insurgents from Hussein's murderous wrath.

In the meantime, according to the United Nations Children's Fund's (UNICEF) 1998 publication, the U.S.-imposed economic embargo led to the deaths of approximately 1.2 million persons, including 646,200 Iraqi children. When the human toll of the economic embargo became known, the United Nations authorized an "oil for food program" that permitted Iraq to sell a certain amount of oil on the world market in order to purchase food. However, the oil for food program was too inadequate (and corrupt) to aid the suffering and hungry Iraqi citizens. Human Rights Watch lamented that

since the [Bush] Administration made clear it would not lift the sanctions until Saddam was removed, the Iraqi people remained the innocent victims of a heartless strategy designed to encourage them to rise up out of sheer desperation against a leader who will stop at no atrocity to preserve his hold on power. (1992)

However, encouraging Iraqis to revolt against Hussein had little chance of success given the previous examples of U.S. abandonment of the Kurds and Shi'ites in 1991.

Another illustration of Bush Sr.'s choice to discard human rights for political expediency is the issue of the elimination of journalistic freedoms. It was Bush Sr. who first instituted the policy of press censorship during wartime through the use of press-pool journalists (only chosen journalists were given access to select sites and soldiers) and further established a security review process with all information provided to the press via the military only. This policy helped Bush to sanitize the Gulf War, hiding the deaths of American soldiers and the "collateral damage" of Iraqi civilian deaths. This strategy also allowed the Bush Administration to manipulate continued congressional and public support for the war. Robert Fiske (1991) complains that the United States fought a war for freedom in Kuwait by actually abolishing freedom of the press in the United States.[4]

China's Human Rights Violations

In another part of the world, the case of China is indicative of Bush Sr.'s human rights policy. During the last decades of the Cold War, the United States befriended China in an attempt to block the expansionistic tendencies of the Soviet Union. In the post-Cold War era, the U.S.-China relationship has revolved around trade and investment. Ideology (China is still a communist country) and human rights considerations rarely received official recognition. Thus, the Bush Administration's policy toward China relied on "constructive engagement."

In what many feel was the first clear manifestation of the growing desire for freedom and democracy of the Chinese population, students in China hoped to replace the Communist Party with an elected democratic government. After the death of the reform-minded Communist Party leader Hu Yaobang in April 1989, students took to the streets calling for democratic reforms, respect for human rights, release of political prisoners, and freedom of the speech and of the press. The demonstrations escalated, with as many as 1 million people crowding into Beijing's Tiananmen Square. The Chinese government declared martial law. On June 4, Chinese troops attacked the unarmed and peaceful protesters, using tanks to roll over the demonstrators. The Chinese Red Cross estimated that more than 2,600 demonstrators were killed (as quoted in U.S. House of Representatives Resolution 285, issued on June 5, 1989).

Following the June 1989 Tiananmen Square massacre, President Bush Sr. immediately ceased arms sales to China, suspended all high-level government contacts, and postponed international loans. However, Bush's support for democracy and human rights quickly waned in the face of pragmatic concerns. In a June 5, 1989, speech on the Tiananmen Square massacre, Bush clarified his intent toward China:

> The United States cannot condone the violent attacks and cannot ignore the consequences for our relationship with China. . . . This is not the time for an emotional response, but for a reasoned, careful action that takes into account both our long-term interests and recognition of a complex internal situation in China. (Bush 1989a, 281)

Bush's personal history as ambassador to China and his pragmatic philosophy influenced his handling of the human rights crisis in China and the way the U.S. Congress was to deal with it. Barilleaux and Rozell assume that Bush's pragmatic nature accounts for his lack of action in supporting human rights and democracy in China. These authors conclude, "His [Bush Sr.'s] lack of any strong initiative against Chinese human rights abuses best evidenced Bush's commitment to a cautious leadership approach. . . . Bush did not take harshly punitive actions against the Chinese government" (2004, 27–28). Bush was trying to serve U.S. long-term interests in China by working through quiet, private diplomatic channels, using his personal contacts and acquaintances.

Bush successfully dissuaded Congress from adopting severe economic sanctions against China. Even the claim that the Bush Administration would restrict diplomatic visits in denunciation of China's brutal behavior was only a propaganda device meant to appease the American population and their congressional leadership. In July 1989, a month after the Tiananmen Square massacre, National Security Advisor Brent Scowcroft journeyed to China to reassure Beijing of Bush's continued support

(Dumbrell 1997). Although Congress passed resolutions condemning China's murderous behavior, Bush believed that canceling a few governmental engagements and stalling the sale of technology would suffice. As a result, only military sanctions would be grudgingly enforced, not commercial ones. Consequently, Bush lifted all economic sanctions and then announced the sale of three communication satellites.

At the same time, Bush Sr. opposed the Democrats' efforts to withdraw China's Most Favored Nation (MFN) trading status. Under the Democratic plan, China would have to take action to correct human rights abuses to regain or retain MFN eligibility. Beijing would be required to release its political prisoners, lift the imposition of martial law, account for those missing or arrested at Tiananmen Square, and end the restrictions on the media. But these requirements were strongly and vocally opposed by President Bush, who argued that maintaining trade with China was in fact the best way to encourage democracy and respect for human rights within the Chinese regime. Furthermore, claimed the Bush Administration, it would be American businesses and consumers that would suffer the most if China's MFN status were to be withdrawn. China, as a prospective trading partner, meant large profits to American businesses. China's economy was growing at a rate of approximately 12 percent annually, and its population provided a potential 1 billion additional customers for American products (World Bank 2001). Additionally, the denial of MFN to China meant that the American consumer, in the opinion of the White House, would face sharply higher prices for items traditionally imported from China (toys, apparel, shoes, and so on).

Bush Sr. twice vetoed legislation tying renewal of China's MFN status with the need to improve its human rights practices. Since the United States had important economic and security interests in China, human rights were subordinated to those "larger" concerns. Among these larger concerns was China's support for the U.S. Desert Storm operation.

The suppression of a human rights agenda to preserve good U.S.-China relations was also obvious in the complete disregard for forced labor issues. By 1991, China's use of forced labor to bolster its export profits became public knowledge. Initially, the Bush Administration worked to preempt congressional legislation to end "forced labor" trade with China. Bush Sr. issued a statement claiming that the U.S. Customs Service would diligently bar forced labor commodities from entering the United States. However, the Customs Service did not deny any forced labor product access to U.S. markets until after a CBS *Sixty Minutes* broadcast and some *Newsweek* articles exposed the fact that China's forced labor exports were being shipped to the United States (as reported by Human Rights Watch 1992). Even after the revelation, the Customs Service only restricted those products that had been featured in the media stories. Also, it is important to point out that the term "forced labor" is a misnomer. A more accurate description is "slave labor," since none of the prisoners of the Chinese regime received compensation for their labor and many of the prisoners were held without a judicial hearing or were forced to stay on after their time had been served. Furthermore, many of the prisoners were not criminals, but political dissidents. These political prisoners, often students, were imprisoned only because they supported democracy and freedom in China. China's use of forced labor is in direct violation of the Slavery Convention (1926), to which both China and the United States are signatories.[5]

Somalia and Operation Restore Hope

Although Bush Sr.'s foreign policy leadership style was to simply disregard a crisis until it required a military or diplomatic reaction, the international system in the early 1990s was still highly unstable and repeatedly necessitated international involvement and, often, U.S. involvement, particularly in the context of Bush's proclaimed new world order after the Gulf War. One such area of instability in need of international involvement was Somalia. The Somalia crisis was in no small part due to the decline in superpower rivalry.[6] After the end of the Cold War, a coup overthrew Somalia's leader, General Mohammed Siad Barre, and the country descended into civil chaos. General Barre had maintained a semblance of order by means of brutal force for twenty-one years. However, in January 1991, he was compelled to flee the capital by opposing clans. What followed was civil and political anarchy as various rebel or tribal forces fought for control of the capital, Mogadishu, using sophisticated U.S. and Soviet arms to fight their battles. It is estimated that 25,000 civilians were killed or wounded between October and December 1991 (Hook and Spanier 2002). Over 250,000 people fled the capital to avoid the gang-style, clan-based fighting. The State Department estimated that 20 percent of the population was internally displaced or became refugees (United States, Department of State 1994). The civil war in Somalia degenerated into ruthless warlord gang fights where human rights abuses were widespread. The combination of a severe drought and warfare produced a famine as severe as any in modern times. The many factions were deliberately destroying food crops and killing livestock so their opponents' civilians would suffer widespread famine. It is estimated that 300,000 people died of starvation, with as many as 2 million in immediate danger of death by starvation.

Bush tried to avoid dealing with the civil war, drought, and mass starvation in Somalia. Bush ignored or disregarded reports of a humanitarian emergency and extensive human rights abuses until he was pressured by Congress, human rights nongovernmental organizations (NGOs), media coverage, and the American public to "do something." Almost two years into the humanitarian crisis, in December 1992, the outgoing Bush announced Operation Restore Hope. Operation Restore Hope committed as many as 28,000 U.S. troops to protect and assist UN-led food distribution for the famine-ridden Somalia. The deployment was supported by Congress and President-elect Bill Clinton.

The Balkans

In April 1992, Washington followed the lead of the European Community and recognized the independence of Slovenia, Croatia, and Bosnia. During the Cold War, Yugoslavia held a special place in U.S. foreign policy since Yugoslavia had maintained a level of independence from the Soviet Union. But, with the demise of the Soviet Union, Yugoslavia was now marginalized. In 1989, the Yugoslavian economy fell into shambles, with 40 percent unemployment and an inflation rate of 25,000 percent (Western 2004). This economic crisis was exacerbated by the political problems of rising Serb nationalism and secessionist movements from several republics.

Although the United States quickly recognized the new states created from the breakup of the Yugoslavian Federation, the United States offered no financial or diplomatic assistance. Jon Western reports that "overall the United States pursued a rather passive, minimalist policy [toward Yugoslavia] that was limited almost exclusively to diplomatic démarches and other rhetorical pronouncements" (2004, 221). Although Bush Sr. supported the United Nations (UN) sanctions and embargos that were imposed on the region, condemned the war crimes and ethnic cleansing, and expressed support for UN peacekeeping efforts, he made it clear from the beginning that no U.S. soldier would be sent into this "Vietnam-type" conflict. There would be no "Operation Balkan Storm," even though Serbian aggression inescapably violated Bush's vision of a new world order and international peace and security. Yugoslavia simply was not a foreign policy priority for Bush since its fragmentation did not threaten U.S. vital interests.

Bush ignored the warnings from both the intelligence community and the State Department of the impending human rights and humanitarian nightmare in the region. Western (2004) reports that, although over 200,000 people (mostly civilians) were killed, 2 to 3 million had become refugees, tens of thousands had already been jailed, and thousands of women were raped, these facts did not change Bush's attitude. Bush did, however, extend the UN arms embargo against Yugoslavia to include the Bosnian Serbs and Muslims, a situation that later would prove even more deadly for the Bosnian Muslims.

Western (2004) also maintains that the Bush Administration used secrecy and deception vis-à-vis the American public and their political representatives with regard to the Balkan crisis. The Bush Sr. Administration did not simply ignore the evidence of human rights abuses resulting from the fragmentation of Yugoslavia. President Bush anxiously attempted to hide from the American public evidence that the Serbs were developing and maintaining concentration and rape camps. Warren Zimmerman (the U.S. ambassador to the Conference on Security and Cooperation in Europe and Bush's appointee as ambassador to Yugoslavia in 1989) reported in an interview with Western that the president had actual knowledge of the concentration and rape camps six weeks before the information was finally leaked to the public. But with the election so close, Bush Sr. simply wanted to avoid having to send U.S. troops into Bosnia in response to another public outrage. Bush chose to privilege his political fortunes (unsuccessfully) over the lives of thousands of innocent men, women, and children.

THE WAR ON DRUGS AND HUMAN RIGHTS ABUSES

Bush's initial presidential campaign platform was based on the eradication of drugs. Polls indicated that drugs and drug crimes were at the top of the list of the American population's domestic concerns. One of the most important aspects of Bush's security policy was to reduce the flow of drugs coming into the United States, even if this meant supplying weapons to military units known to be human rights violators. With regard to Andean countries, drug trafficking was considered the principal threat to the United States' vital interests. Fearing that the aid would be used for unauthorized or illicit purposes, Congress restricted the use of U.S. military and law enforcement aid when it enacted the International Narcotics Control Act (1989). Congress took an unusual precaution by placing the human rights provision into the act twice. First, Congress authorized aid only to countries that were governed by democratic regimes and whose military and law enforcement agencies did not engage in a consistent pattern of gross human rights violation. A subsequent clause required the president to submit a determination to Congress that the armed forces and law enforcement agencies of the recipient country were "not engaged in a consistent pattern of gross human rights violations and [that] the government of such country has made significant progress in protecting such rights" (House Resolution [HR] 5567). Furthermore, it required that the government had actual control over the military and police operations. Bush, when signing the legislation into law, complained about the "unreasonable" restrictions and "cumbersome" reporting requirements (Bush 1990, 1). However, these burdensome requirements were necessary and important because, in the opinion of the U.S. General Accounting Office, the United States did not "have sufficient oversight to provide assurances that aid is being used as intended for counternarcotics purposes and is not being used primarily against insurgents or being used to abuse human rights" (as reported by Human Rights Watch 1993, 133).

U.S. policy with Colombia was, and still is, substantially shaped by counternarcotics priorities. During the Bush Administration, the war on drugs became the sole element of U.S.-Colombian relations. Unfortunately, the problem of drugs has dominated U.S.-Colombian relations to the detriment of human rights issues. Colombia's human rights tragedy has been primarily the result of the internal conflict between the state and several insurgency groups, the Revolutionary Armed Forces of Colombia (FARC), the National Liberation Army (ELN), and the United Self-Defense Forces of Colombia (AUC). The AUC is a collective term for the many paramilitary groups or militias with ties to the Colombian military. The AUC and the military have been responsible for the majority of the political killings and disappearances (Shifter and Stillerman 2004). Insurgency groups are known to have allied with the drug cartels in order to finance their struggle against government forces.

In 1989, Bush kicked off the Andean Initiative, a five-year, $2.2 billion strategy designed to eliminate drugs. The Andean Initiative was meant to attack drugs at their source by eradicating coca production, eliminating labs, and preventing transportation into the United States. The Andean Initiative aid package provided military equipment for the army and police, and thus, indirectly, the AUC. Both the Bush Administration and the U.S. Congress sought to militarize the war on drugs within Colombia by assigning the U.S. Department of Defense as the lead agency in counternarcotics operations. Human rights NGOs feared that strengthening the military and the police would further damage democracy and human rights in the beleaguered country (Sweeny 1999). Andrew Borowiec, executive director of Amnesty International, believes that because the United States provided training and equipment to military groups associated with human rights abuses, the United States was morally culpable for the killings in Colombia. Borowiec asserted, "There is now good reason to believe that the United States has been a collaborator in the charade, that much of the U.S. aid intended for counter-narcotics operations has in fact been diverted to the killing fields" (1994, A1) with the knowledge, if not consent, of the Bush Administration.

The Colombian government even told the United States that it intended to launch "Operation Tri-color 90" against the guerrilla insurgents using U.S. counternarcotics funding, in clear violation of U.S. law. With the president's dubious determination (a report to Congress certifying that Colombia met foreign assistance conditions), the United States provided the Colombian security forces over a half billion dollars' worth of military equipment from 1990 to 1992. The U.S. government knew that the money was going to military units acknowledged as participating in human rights abuses. Thomas McNamara, U.S. ambassador to Colombia, erroneously responded to criticisms, "I don't see the utilization of the arms against the guerrillas as a deviation. The arms are given to the government in order that they may use them in the anti-narcotics struggle . . . but this is not a requirement of the United States" (1991). But the International Narcotics Control Act (1992) clearly restricted the use of counternarcotics funds from being used against insurgent activity. Again, in 1993, the General Accounting Office (GAO) warned that the executive branch had not yet established any monitoring procedures to prevent U.S. aid from being used by Colombian military units to violate human rights. In fact, the GAO found "two instances where personnel who had allegedly committed human rights abuses came from units that received U.S. aid" (United States General Accounting Office 1993).

Yet, the Bush Administration submitted to Congress a determination claiming that Colombia was meeting the human rights requirements set out in the International Narcotics Control Act. Bush alleged that not only were the Colombian military and law enforcement forces not engaged in a consistent pattern of gross violations but, moreover, the Colombian government was actively and earnestly protecting internationally recognized human rights. However, the institutionalization of human rights issues in foreign policy compelled the State Department to provide a candid and accurate depiction of the human rights condition in Colombia.

In clear contradiction of President Bush's claims, the State Department's *Country Reports on Human Rights Practices, 1990* maintains,

> Members and units of the army and the police participated in a disturbing number of human rights violations including extrajudicial executions, torture, and massacres. . . . Official human rights abuses contravene government policy, but so far efforts by security forces to end such abuses have been inadequate.

In other words, the State Department established that, contrary to what the White House certified, ongoing abuses defied official governmental rhetorical policy, and the Colombian government's meager efforts to control its military and other security forces were insufficient and ineffective. Nevertheless, Congress still provided Colombia with over $27 million in military aid, $20 million in policy assistance, and an additional $50 million in Economic Support Funds (ESFs). For the White House and Congress, the United States' drug problem was of greater concern than protecting human rights.

Similarly, U.S.-Peruvian relations at that time revolved principally around the eradication of drugs to the neglect of development issues or human rights concerns. Without question, during the Bush Administration, Peru was one of the most politically besieged countries in the Western Hemisphere. Peru suffered massive human rights abuses from both the military and the insurgent group, the Shining Path. In 1991, President Bush penciled in Peru to receive $95 million for antinarcotics operations. Bush presented a determination to Congress stating that Peru met the human rights requirements of the International Narcotics Control Act. However, the human rights abuses in Peru were so egregious and flagrant that Congress had to suspend the funding. Ten senators, including the ultraconservative Jesse Helms (R-NC), wrote a letter to the executive branch requesting that the obviously falsified determination be withdrawn. In congressional hearings, the executive branch justified funding to the vicious Peruvian military and police by ludicrously declaring that Peru's human rights abuses, although substantial and brutal, were fewer than the abuses committed in El Salvador during the 1980s (where over 70,000 Salvadorans were known to have been murdered by the military). Human rights organizations credit Congress' resolve for beginning Peru's long, slow progress toward democracy and human rights improvements.

A KINDER, GENTLER CENTRAL AMERICA POLICY

Bush, unlike his predecessor, held no strong feelings regarding Central America. Therefore, his foreign policy toward the region was more modest. The low priority Bush assigned to the region can be seen by the lack of urgency in filling positions associated with Latin America. Leogrande maintains,

> Mid-level posts in the national security bureaucracy that dealt specifically with Latin America were among the last to be filled. . . . No assistant secretary of state for Inter-American affairs was appointed until May [1998,] and the senior Latin American specialist on the National Security Council (NSC) was hired even later. (Leogrande 1990, 597)

Bush still opposed the elimination of military aid to El Salvador despite that government's continued human rights abuses. In fact, Bush Sr. vowed to continue Reagan's policy in El Salvador and requested Congress to continue providing large sums of foreign aid to the newly elected Cristiani government (led by Alfredo Cristiani of the extremist National Republican Alliance [ARENA] Party). Nevertheless, the government's human rights violations were still an ongoing problem, even though there were significantly fewer murders, disappearances, and incidents of torture than during Reagan's first term. Congressional members were in a quandary: "Congress, as before, was caught between a reluctance to give military aid to a government connected to heinous political crimes and an unwillingness to cut off aid and risk a leftist takeover" (Carothers 1991, 38). When the ARENA Party (associated with the notorious death squads) won the 1988 elections in El Salvador, the number of politically motivated murders abruptly increased. Although the killings connected with the death squads continued throughout the civil war, the numbers of those murdered were not at the levels associated with the early 1980s. The brutal bloodbath drastically diminished after then Vice President Bush traveled to San Salvador in 1983 to warn the military regime that Congress would restrict or halt U.S. funding if the murders did not stop. In March 1989, Bush sent Vice President Dan Quayle to renew the warning to the Salvadoran government and military that security aid depended on improved human rights conditions. Bush persuaded Congress to provide funding without placing human rights conditions on the aid.

However, in November 1989, the opposition (Farabundo Marti para la Liberacion Nacional, or FMLN) launched an urban offensive against the Salvadoran government. The FMLN set up strongholds in the poor, densely populated urban sectors of the country. When the military could not eradicate the opposition by ground assault, it resorted to air strikes against its own people. The result was the destruction of whole neighborhoods, deaths of thousands of civilians, and extensive homelessness of El Salvador's already poor and disadvantaged. The government raided churches, claiming that they provided sanctuary to the guerrillas. With this mind-set, government security forces murdered six Jesuit priests, their housekeeper, and her teenage daughter. Leogrande writes,

> The military's brutal disregard for civilian casualties and its tolerance of death-squad killings demonstrated that not much had really changed since the dirty war in the early 1980s. . . . [The] military [has] no regard for the rule of law and is unable to distinguish between dissent and insurrection. (1990, 610–611)

The Bush Administration blamed the rebels for forcing the government to kill innocent civilians and claimed that the murder of the priests was committed by the opposition. Bush not only refused to consider restricting military aid to El Salvador, but he also further pledged to expedite pipelined[7] weapons deliveries. Congress demanded a full investigation but was unwilling to restrict aid.

In Nicaragua, Bush, in an effort to end the bitter dispute over U.S. policy in Central America, did not request large sums of foreign aid for the Nicaraguan Contras. Bush's pragmatic inclinations can once again be seen in the funding compromise of the Contras. Realizing that Congress was wary of continued funding for the Contras, Bush wrought the "Bipartisan Accord," where he pledged to fully support the Arias Peace Plan through diplomatic negotiation and economic pressure in an effort to encourage democracy in Nicaragua. In typical fashion, "Bush said he would neither support nor abandon the Contras—a scintillating, pragmatic compromise, a splitting of the difference, a recognition that both sides had half of a point" (Pastor 1991, 9). Bush promised to not seek military aid for the Contras, and the Contras were in fact banned from conducting military operations in the months prior to the 1990 Nicaraguan elections. The bipartisan agreement provided for a veto by any of the four congressional committees (the Senate Foreign Affairs and Appropriations Committees, and the House of Representatives Foreign Affairs and Appropriations Committees) if the president or the Contras violated the terms of the agreement. Under these circumstances, Congress relented and agreed to provide the Contras with $4.5 million in monthly humanitarian aid until the end of February 1990 (approximately $50 million).

FOREIGN AID

Bush Sr.'s foreign policy approach did not include the active promotion of human rights. Bush's tendency toward caution resulted in military aid allocations that remained somewhat constant, reflecting the last years of the Reagan Administration, even in the face of the dissolution of the fifty-year justification for foreign aid—the containment of communism in the form of the Soviet Union. Yet, with the demise of the Soviet Union and, subsequently, of foreign aid's primary rationale, Congress and the American public sought to reduce the amount of military aid.

With the end of the Cold War, Congress and the American public did not see the necessity of squandering large amounts of tax dollars on what many believed was simply a form of international welfare giveaway when there was no longer a supreme enemy. As a result, Congress passed the Budget Enforcement Act of 1990 (PL 101-508), which greatly reduced security assistance so that, by 1992, the majority of small recipients of U.S. bilateral security aid no longer received any money. The Budget Enforcement Act of 1990 set strict limits on budgetary outlays and restrictions on authority for the international affairs function of the federal budget. This meant that additional funding for military aid would be taken from other international affairs accounts or from supplemental appropriations directly from Congress. The Camp David Accords participants, Israel and Egypt, would be protected from the post-Cold War reduction in foreign aid and the redirection of aid toward the transition countries. Therefore, Israel and Egypt would still remain the beneficiaries of the lion's share of U.S. foreign assistance. But this also implied substantial cuts in funding levels for everyone else.

As a bureaucratic president, Bush Sr. understood that indeed "the diplomat without an aid program has to work much harder to advance U.S. objectives" (Zimmerman 1993, 14). Congressional restrictions and reductions in foreign aid could jeopardize the United States' ability to influence other countries' behaviors and further U.S. interests. Economic and military assistance are convenient practical tools for maintaining U.S. hegemonic leadership. Therefore, in 1991, the Bush Administration attempted to reform the onerous statutory requirements of the Foreign Assistance Act (FAA). Bush Sr.'s rewritten version of the FAA endowed the executive branch with extensive power in the allocation and distribution of U.S. foreign aid, leading to a corresponding reduction in the authority of Congress' power of the purse. The proposed legislation would also be less encumbered by human rights considerations or the need for certifications. Congress, however, defeated the legislation.

It was hoped that U.S. economic aid would then be directed toward tackling regional instabilities, fostering development, and promoting democracy. With the end of the Cold War, Congress wanted to focus U.S. economic aid more toward development than ESF. Lee Hamilton (D-IN) and Benjamin Gilman (R-NY) formed the Hamilton Task Force (House Foreign Affairs Committee) to investigate the possibility of redirecting aid. The Hamilton Task Force found that

> changes in the international environment . . . domestic budgetary pressures . . . and the loss of public and Congressional support for the aid program all demand major changes in foreign aid legislation. U.S. foreign assistance needs a new premise, a new framework, and a new purpose to meet the challenges of today. (House Foreign Affairs Committee 1989, 29)

During this time, Congress also sought to regionally redirect U.S. foreign aid to help support the transition of the Eastern European countries now free from Soviet domination. Congress championed the transition to capitalism and democracy by passing the East European Democracy Act (SEED; PL 101-513) and the Freedom Support Act (PL 102-511). Due to the United States' federal deficits, however, this new foreign aid program required a reduction in foreign assistance to Latin America, Asia, and Africa.

CONCLUSION

George Bush Sr. was clearly a pragmatist who had served as director of the CIA, had been U.S. ambassador to China, and had served as the United States' representative at the United Nations. Bush Sr.'s presidency coincided with an era of immense changes in world politics with the passing of the Cold War. His foreign policy style was based on management and administration, that is, careful planning, avoiding new commitments, and personal diplomacy. President Bush Sr. was not necessarily critical of human rights as long as they did not prove awkward or inconvenient. Despite this mixed record on human rights, the Bush Sr. Administration did support the Senate's 1992 ratification of the United Nations International Covenant on Civil and Political Rights. Bush also signed the Torture Victim Protection Act of 1991 (PL 102-256), which allows victims of human rights abuses to use U.S. civil courts to seek remedy against their abusers. However, on signing the act, Bush also expressed fears that U.S. courts "would become embroiled in difficult and sensitive disputes in other countries and possibly ill-founded or politically motivated suits . . . and would also be a waste of our own limited and already overburdened judicial resources" (Bush 1992).

Unfortunately, Bush Sr., like Reagan before him, defined human rights as political and civil rights, and thus declared that the rights contained in the International Covenant on Economic, Social and Cultural Rights were goals, not rights. Thus, he resisted attempts to have this second covenant ratified. The policy instituted by the Reagan Administration to exclude economic rights from the State Department's *Country Reports* continued through the Bush years.

With the end of the Cold War and the United States' victory over the Soviet Union, conditions were finally in place for the implementation of a consistent and coherent U.S. human rights policy. Perhaps now was the time for the application of American ideals of democracy and human rights, so long delayed due to the need to contain communism and Soviet aggression. Indeed, Bush Sr. had the opportunity and the goodwill of Congress to redefine U.S. foreign policy.

Yet, Bush would soon drop the concept or vision of the new world order, and, more importantly, his actions would belie hopes of a moral foreign policy that could further human rights. Instead of creating a new world order, as his rhetoric implied, Bush stubbornly reverted to his pragmatic conservatism. Believing that, with the passing of the Reagan Administration, the worst was over, human rights activists, scholars, and sympathizers were caught off guard. Retrospectively, it was perhaps too much to expect of Bush to actively change American foreign policy when his own personality and management style were hell-bent on maintaining the status quo at all costs. Thus, Bush mismanaged the opportunity to redirect America's foreign policy toward human rights concerns due to his renowned lack of vision and his desire to remain convivial with foreign nations regardless of their human rights record. Consequently, Bush befriended China despite its human rights violations, abandoned the Kurds and the Shi'ites to Saddam's retribution, ignored the plight of the Bosnian Muslims, and discounted the humanitarian crisis in Somalia until it was too large to ignore. Bush did not just squander an opportunity to support human rights. More crucially, he actively reversed human rights guarantees by, among other actions, restricting freedom of the press in the United States and sacrificing human rights situations abroad to a "war on drugs" crusade. For the Bush Administration, without a moral commitment to human rights, human rights became just another policy choice, which could easily be bargained away when it proved politically expedient or convenient to do so.

CHAPTER 6

Selling Off Human Rights:
The Clinton Administration

American satellite makers, aircraft builders, cell-phone manufacturers, computer makers—not to mention insurance and financial
services providers—wanted in on the rich Chinese market. The
Clinton machine wanted huge amounts of cash for its campaign
war chest. Let's make a deal!

Robert Kagan (2001)

Clinton's foreign policy rhetoric was reminiscent of Carter's idealism.
In language true to Carter's optimism, Clinton announced that "U.S.
foreign policy cannot be divorced from the moral principles most Americans share. We cannot disregard how other governments treat their
own people" (Clinton 1991). Clinton believed that democratic enlargement,[1] market economies, and international cooperation would inaugu-
rate global peace and prosperity, thus producing international security.
Clinton backed up his rhetoric by appointing human rights advocates
to positions of power in his administration. For example, Clinton chose
Warren Christopher, who chaired the Inter-Agency Group on Human
Rights and Foreign assistance under Carter, as his secretary of state.[2]
John Shattuck, who served as director of the American Civil Liberties
Union and was vice chair and board member of Amnesty International,
became head of the newly renamed Bureau of Democracy, Human
Rights, and Labor (DRL).[3] Equally important, as Julie Mertus (2004)
reports, is the fact that the Clinton Administration also filled midlevel
positions with people knowledgeable about and sympathetic to human
rights.[4] To the surprise of human rights nongovernmental organizations (NGOs), the State Department actually wanted NGOs' advice and

participation. Aryeh Neier, the founder and former executive director of Human Rights Watch, expresses the euphoria felt among human rights groups at that time:

> The advent of the Clinton Administration aroused great hopes among proponents of human rights. It was not only his campaign statement; it was also appointments of such reliable human rights advocates as John Shattuck, now Assistant Secretary of State for Human Rights and Humanitarian Affairs. This seemed a sign that a concern with rights would weigh heavily in the Administration's foreign policy. (Neier 1994, 79)

The expectations of the human rights community were quite high, higher than during the Carter Administration even, not only because the Clinton Administration sought their counsel but also because of the institutionalization of human rights in foreign policy that had taken place during the Reagan Administration. However, the crushing of these expectations would be all the more painful for human rights advocates, as Clinton clearly would follow, in foreign policy practice if not in rhetoric, Bush Sr.'s unsatisfactory policies for human rights.

Although Clinton was elected with a mandate to fix America's domestic economic troubles, foreign issues, often involving massive human rights violations and humanitarian crises, could not be ignored. The Clinton Administration's general belief was that political freedom would be best guaranteed by economic liberalization, which in turn would ensure global stability. The key, then, for Clinton was to enlarge the number of market democracies. Clinton's concept of "democratic enlargement," designed to cheaply—with little or no political, military, or economic cost—encourage states to become democratic, proved to be the source of the United States' reluctant involvement in civil wars and complex emergencies in the 1990s. Democratic enlargement would require U.S. participation in humanitarian interventions in civil conflicts in countries where the United States did not hold vital interests. However, like Carter before him, Clinton's rhetoric of idealism would soon face the harsh realist reality of power politics, economic interests, intractable conflicts, and massive human rights violations. Clinton's idealism would shift to a more realist position with each new foreign policy crisis during his tenure. As a result, William Hyland believes that "the conversion from idealism to trial and error became the story of [Clinton's] foreign policy" (1999, 197). In their investigation of Clinton's policy beliefs, Aubrey Jewett and Marc Turetzky found that, although the economy held priority, "Clinton took the issue of human rights seriously and considered democracy to be at the core of basic human rights. . . . Clinton saw human rights as intertwined with expanding markets and resolving various ethnic and political conflicts" (Jewett and Turetzky 1998, 652). This was the case when Clinton took office. However, two trends would emerge as Clinton's years in office advanced. First, Clinton's concern for human rights would fall off. Second, by 1996, security and defense issues would become the number one issue for the Clinton Administration, surpassing even the economy. The economy would remain a very important issue for Clinton. But global crises now forced the president to focus on traditional security and defense matters. The movement from an idealist promotion of human rights to a realist approach focusing on security and defense ominously recalls the ideological shift of the Carter Administration.

In a way that may remind us of Carter's own paradox, the paradox of the Clinton Administration centers on the fact that his use of an idealist rhetoric and his focus on domestic issues would soon be sacrificed on behalf of his repeated use of realist power politics in the international realm. Clinton's early foreign policy actions and rhetoric raised expectations that human rights would have a central place in the new administration's guiding principles. However, his later foreign policy decisions and his narrow focus on the economy, often to the detriment of human rights, quickly crushed the rising expectations of the human rights community. The Clinton Administration traded human rights protections to further the United States' economic prosperity and to boost the profit margins of American big business. Furthermore, Congress, the source of support and often the sole advocate for human rights, would now prove to be a serious constraint on the full implementation of U.S. human rights policy, something that had not happened in previous administrations. The Republican majority of the 104th Congress had a mandate to reduce government spending on foreign affairs—including foreign aid.

LIBERAL INTERNATIONALISM

Liberal internationalism, or what Walter Mead (2002) refers to as "Wilsonian internationalism," is a worldview based on idealistic assumptions about the goodness of the rule of law, human rights, democracy, multilateral cooperation, and open trade. Furthermore, liberal democratic states founded on human rights, particularly individual liberties, are seen as essentially peaceful. This is because government leaders must respond to their citizens' wishes if they want to remain in power. The justification for conflict must be imperative if citizens are expected to bear the burden of war in both blood and money. The key for world peace is thus democratic enlargement. The Clinton Administration followed this Wilsonian belief. Clinton thought that "building on the old Wilsonian gospel . . . was that such an [democratic] expansion would encourage an upward cycle of global peace and prosperity, serving American interests and allowing the United States to de-emphasize its own military strength" (Dueck 2003–2004, 6).

Moreover, from a more liberal economic perspective, international conflict is also found to be bad for trade and employment. Citizens enjoy the benefits of free and open trade and thus understand that war and conflict restrict their access to foreign commodities. Additionally, many jobs are tied to the production of merchandise intended for export. In the late twentieth century, the Clinton Administration held that U.S. economic prosperity depended upon lucrative export markets and hospitable trade relations with foreign countries. To ensure that economic issues received priority in foreign policy decision making, Clinton established the National Economic Council (NEC), a parallel structure to the National Security Council (NSC). Further demonstrating his desire to incorporate economic policy considerations into every foreign policy action, Clinton expanded the NSC membership to include the secretary of the treasury.

Additionally, to more closely link democracy, trade, and human rights, the Clinton Administration also restructured the Bureau of Human Rights and Humanitarian Affairs and turned it into the DRL. Headed by John Shattuck, as mentioned above, the DRL was charged with developing new strategies linking the building and preserving of democratic structures with the protection of human rights. Shattuck, in testimony before the House Subcommittee on Foreign Operations, stated that "the promotion of human rights and democracy is one of the fundamental goals of our foreign policy, a goal that reinforces the objectives of preserving America's security and fostering our prosperity" (1998). What makes the United States safe and strong was seen as benefiting the entire world.

For the Clinton team, U.S. foreign policy was thus the servant of domestic economic needs, something that was not illogical from a liberal economic perspective, but was harder to sustain from a more Wilsonian internationalist one. In order for foreign policy to serve America's economy, the world had to be incorporated into a global marketplace. Hence, the United States needed to export democracy and free market reforms. In this fashion, Clinton was able to apparently reconcile the economic argument with the Wilsonian liberal internationalist imperative because promoting global democratic reforms was still crucial. As McDougall declared, "[T]he disappearance of geopolitical threats persuaded the Clinton Administration, staffed as it was with Carter veterans such as National Security Adviser Anthony Lake and Secretary of State Warren Christopher, that Meliorism's moment had arrived" (McDougall 1997, 142).

Convinced of the benefits of free and open trade, and claiming that these objectives were in line with Wilsonian ideals, Clinton chose to champion economic globalization despite the misgivings of many of his supporters, particularly those in the human rights community, the labor unions, and even his own political party. In fact, Clinton often had to rely on the Republicans in Congress to pass his trade initiatives, specifically the terms of General Agreement on Tariffs and Trade (GATT), the new World Trade Organization (WTO), and the North American Free Trade Agreement (NAFTA). The Republican Congress keenly supported global free, fair, and open trade.

Despite his Wilsonian rhetoric (democratic enlargement, assertive multilateralism, and so on), Clinton's foreign policy would stress trade expansionism and the opening of foreign markets at the expense of human rights. Clinton's primary foreign policy strategy was to expand U.S. business abroad. Clinton, who was elected with a mandate to fix America's domestic troubles, often seemed "to view foreign policy as a distraction" (Oliver 2004, 53).[5] Clinton's secretaries of state and national security advisors understood that their primary responsibility was to keep foreign policy issues noncontentious and undemanding so that Clinton could concentrate on domestic policy (Drew 1994). Thus, under this plan, unless and until a humanitarian crisis emerged that captured the media and public awareness, Clinton would simply ignore it.

Like the Carter Administration in the late 1970s, the Clinton Administration also experienced an internal split over the inherent conflict between the interests of commerce and human rights concerns. The economic agencies, the Department of Commerce, the Department of the Treasury, and the National Economic Council, supported the primacy of economic enlargement. But the State Department administrators (notably Christopher and Shattuck) and the U.S. representative to the United Nations (Madeleine Albright) argued for a strong human rights agenda. In fact, Christopher was not an enthusiast of enlargement at all. Christopher considered enlargement to be trade policy camouflaged as foreign policy. Consequently, "Christopher just refused to use the 'E' word" (Richard Holbrooke, as quoted in Brinkley 1997, 121). However, unlike in the Carter Administration, the conflict between all the foreign policy makers under Clinton did not paralyze foreign policy decision making. Instead, Clinton would privilege the supporters of global economic enlargement over the human rights advocates.

President Clinton believed in the virtues of multilateralism. He came to office calling for strengthening the United Nations and regional security groups. And, initially, he claimed that he would be willing to subordinate U.S. decision making to multinational organizations. Yet, Clinton failed to act during the Rwandan genocide and the ethnic cleansing in Bosnia. The Clinton Administration, fearing another failed African peacekeeping operation after the debacle in Somalia, avoided undertaking military or humanitarian action to prevent the Rwandan genocide, which killed up to 1 million people. In Bosnia, it took three years of political pressure from nongovernmental human rights organizations and the international community before Clinton finally determined that Bosnia endangered U.S. vital interests by undermining North Atlantic Treaty Organization (NATO) and the United Nations (UN) peacekeeping. Once the link to U.S. national interest had finally been made, Clinton instituted a massive air campaign targeting Serb posts throughout Bosnia, and he used extensive diplomatic and military control that finally resulted in the Dayton Peace Accords.

REPUDIATED IDEALISM: THE SELLING OFF OF HUMAN RIGHTS

The Clinton Administration was free of the national security constraints of the Cold War. It did not need to contain communism, maintain a large defense, or preserve an iron grip over U.S. strategic allies. Thus, as many have noted, the post-Cold War era presented an unprecedented opportunity for the development of a universal acceptance of human rights. Human rights and development aid in the 1990s could have been the beneficiaries of the much touted peace dividends. However, human rights advocates soon found themselves pitted against economic and business interests for control of U.S. foreign policy.

While campaigning for president in 1992, Bill Clinton reproached George Bush for his indifference to democracy and human rights in foreign policy considerations. In particular, Clinton criticized Bush for his policy of returning Haitians fleeing the repressive military regime following the 1991 coup d'état that ousted democratically elected Jean-Bertrand Aristide. Clinton also reproached Bush for failing to take decisive action in Bosnia and for renewing China's Most Favored Nation (MFN) status following the Tiananmen Square massacre. In a speech before students at

Waseda University in Japan, Clinton declared, "The movement toward democracy is the best guarantor of human rights" (Clinton 1993). Clinton later announced, "Mine will be a foreign policy of engagement, one that strengthens democracy, promotes economic reform, opens markets and stands up to aggression and intolerance" (Clinton 1994). Clinton's rhetoric also included the 1993 warning to China that human rights was the cornerstone of his foreign policy. However, Clinton would continue to expand on a number of George Bush's policies. Clinton would even develop affable relationships with the dictators that he disparaged Bush for coddling. Clinton's policy toward China reflects his preference for U.S. commercial and economic strategic interests to the detriment of human rights. China engaged (and still does engage) in extensive and systematic human rights abuses. Yet, in 1994, trade privileges to China were renewed despite the lack of any human rights improvements. In fact, Robert Kagan states that the "China policy was taken away from the State Department and the Pentagon and given to the money boys at Commerce, at Treasury, at the U.S. Trade Representative's office" (2001, 26). Thus, in the case of China, Clinton's enthusiasm for the priority of human rights was quickly renounced in the name of trade profits.

The trend toward prioritizing economic considerations in foreign policy became a matter of official policy strategy. Commerce Secretary Ron Brown promoted "commercial diplomacy," a modern version of dollar diplomacy,[6] which meant, in Brown's words, "simply the merging of this nation's political and economic interests" (as quoted in Wickham 2000). However, this equating of corporate interests with U.S. national interests frequently meant suppressing human rights, women's rights, labor rights, and children's rights. To foster economic globalization, a developing country will frequently suppress wages to encourage foreign investment and corporate profit. Furthermore, the restriction of rights "frees government bureaucracies to implement the economic austerity measures and wrenching structural adjustments" required by the World Bank and International Monetary Fund (IMF) (Ballinger 1998). Jeff Ballinger, director of Press for Change, an NGO created for the protection of workers' rights, testified before the Bureau of International Labor Affairs that

> despite the Clinton campaign's criticism of the Bush Administration for disregarding human rights as it promoted U.S. business interests, commercial diplomacy quickly became paramount in Clinton foreign policy, particularly in its approach to the developing world. . . . Commercial diplomacy now dominates U.S. foreign

policy, to ensure that U.S. business maximizes opportunities for profit provided by the new global model. (1998)

China is an example of Clinton's decision to prioritize commercial interests over human rights considerations. In 1994, Clinton supported China's MFN trading status with no apparent concern for China's human rights record. Clinton, like Bush Sr. before him, argued that the best way to promote human rights in China was to "engage" Beijing, that is to say, to bring China into the family of rights-guaranteeing states through trade and diplomatic contacts.

Many in the human rights community believe that Clinton squandered the United States' most effective tool to encourage human rights in China. After all, in the 1990s, the United States purchased one-third of all Chinese exports (BBC 1998). The United States could have forced a link between economic progress and political freedom—no Chinese exports until basic human rights are protected. But, by extending the MFN status, the United States was left with little political or economic influence to ensure protection of human rights standards in China. In fact, the delinking of human rights and MFN status can be traced to the concerted lobbying efforts of business groups and multinational corporations who viewed China's cheap labor and potential consumer markets as vital to their own economic interests. Not to extend MFN status to China would have cost U.S. business interests numerous export opportunities. Corporate interests obviously benefit from American involvement with China. Although the economic engagement of China may have proven beneficial to government leaders and the business elite, for the average worker, either American or Chinese, the use of cheap labor to produce cheap commodities that would flood markets, further reducing wages, was not a welcome engagement. Clinton's critics attribute his about-face on the issue of human rights in China to the fact that, by conservative estimates, the United States would have lost about $10 billion if it had withdrawn China's MFN status (Dumbrell 1997). Donald Schaefer reports that, prior to Clinton's determination to delink human rights and MFN status,

China bought $800 million in aircraft from Boeing, $160 million of cars from the Big Three, $200 million in oil exploration equipments; signed a $750 million agreement with Hughes Space Communication; and signed an agreement with AT&T that could be worth billions. (1998, 412)

Shoring up U.S. economic interests by maintaining and expanding overseas markets clearly trumped human rights concerns. It was, after all, using Clinton's catchphrase, "the economy, stupid."[7]

A foreign policy that stressed trade expansion and the opening of foreign markets at the expense of human rights can also be seen in the creation of business lobbies. Under Clinton, business interests and some nongovernmental groups were extremely efficient at persuading the White House to promote their demands. And these groups demanded economic opportunities free of moral considerations. Regrettably, these demands, which Clinton was eager to satisfy, often held foreign policy hostage to the wishes of a few vocal, well-organized, and affluent business groups. Jacob Heilbrunn (1998) implies that the president actively supported the creation of a business lobby, USA*Engage, to further his calls for economic engagement.[8] Among USA*Engage's membership was Unocal, a U.S. multinational corporation accused of using forced and slave labor in Burma and doing business with the Taliban to build a natural gas pipeline through Afghanistan.[9] Heilbrunn quotes a former congressional trade staffer who described USA*Engage as a bunch of "oil barons who want to operate without regard to human rights or labor practices" (1998, 23). U.S. legislation forbidding the operation of U.S. businesses in human rights-abusing countries where slave labor was commonplace was simply ignored because abiding by such a law would lower the profit margins of corporations like Unocal. The White House believed that "corporate interests are the national interest," even at the expense of foreign citizens (Heilbrunn 1998, 26). Without a doubt, big business, business lobbies, and business-promoting NGOs played a significant role in the Clinton White House's foreign policy decision making.

Another example of Clinton's lack of concern for human rights in promoting trade can be seen in the domain of the international sale and exportation of weapons. On February 17, 1995, the Clinton Administration announced its Presidential Decision Directive 34 (PDD-34) on Conventional Arms Transfers. In this document, Clinton recognized that arms transfers were a useful tool and would be used profusely to secure the United States' national interest and to strengthen U.S. friends and allies. Eric Newsom, principal deputy assistant secretary of state in the Bureau of Political-Military Affairs, issued a press briefing outlining the White House policy for arms transfers (1995). The Clinton Administration had determined that sales of conventional weapons were a legitimate tool of U.S. foreign policy since they allowed friends and allies to defend themselves. Equally important for the Clinton Administration was the fact that arms sales would boost America's defense industrial base. The reductions in defense spending in the post-Cold War era amplified the importance of finding new export markets for U.S. arms manufacturers. The export of U.S. arms was vital in balancing the U.S. trade deficit, while also providing high-paying jobs for American workers. However, Newsom claimed, decisions to transfer arms would not be determined solely by commercial considerations.[10] John Dumbrell (1997) notes that, although the Clinton Administration professed that arms sales would be contingent upon adherence to human rights standards, the U.S. share of world arms sales rose from 42 to 70 percent from 1990 to 1993. Ignoring human rights, U.S. arms transfers were based primarily on safeguarding America's competitive and technological advantage in arms production and gaining a larger global market share. The sale or grant of U.S. weapons programs was driven by the lobbying efforts of the private defense manufacturers, who were receiving increasingly favorable treatment in and unprecedented access to the American defense and economic decision-making process.

In order to get around congressional mandates restricting the amount of foreign aid given to human rights-abusing states, Clinton copiously issued waivers to avoid sanctions. For example, although the Clinton Administration had agreed to the provisions of the Helms-Burton and the Iran-Libya Sanctions Acts,[11] it was quick to utilize waivers to dismiss the requirements specified in these legislations (Eizenstat 1998). According to the Clinton Administration, not applying sanctions proved to be the best way of helping U.S. allies against enemies on human rights issues. Once again, the Clinton Administration's position was that economic engagement was the best method to encourage repressive regimes to modify their human rights abuses. Congressionally imposed coercive enforcement mechanisms, such as sanctions, linkages, or conditionalities, in the opinion of the Clinton Administration, were of dubious value in the pursuit of the White House's foreign policy goals of democratic enlargement (Shattuck 1999). Sanctions could restrict the Clinton Administration's ability to economically engage brutal regimes. Furthermore, third party sanctions, like the Helms-Burton Law, greatly reduced U.S. corporations' ability to conduct trade. USA*Engage calculated that, because of sanctions, the United States' economy lost approximately $19 billion every year in exports and 200,000 high-wage jobs (Wright 2001, A1). Hence, economic issues again dominated foreign policy behavior.

Nevertheless, human rights advocates like Kenneth Roth of Human Rights Watch believed that the threat of sanctions in U.S. foreign aid legislation (Sections 116, 502B, and 701) was a necessary tool of U.S. human rights policy. In testimony before the U.S. Senate Task Force on Economic Sanctions, Roth stated,

> When diplomatic pressure fails to curb egregious abuses, however, the U.S. and other nations claiming to uphold human rights must retain the ability to employ limited and targeted sanctions to express their condemnation of violations, press for a change in abusive government policies, and avoid complicity in abuses. (1998)

Of course, Roth acknowledged the need to narrowly target sanctions. That is, sanctions ought to target the leadership in the intended country, and not the people. Nor should the sanctions ever involve restrictions on food, medicine, or other necessities for life.

Still, in order to further its preferred foreign policy strategy, "the Clinton Administration . . . fought sanctions in Congress, and it . . . fudged when the time came to enforce them" (Heilbrunn 1998, 22). In a 1998 *New York Times* article, Clinton was quoted as saying that legislative mandates to restrict aid to countries whose behavior is unacceptable to America "[put] enormous pressure on whoever is in the executive branch to fudge an evaluation of the facts of what is going on" (Sciolino 1998, A1). In so many words, Clinton admitted that it would be tempting for the Executive to falsify or misrepresent the levels of abuse, no matter how much this would violate U.S. law, in order to provide aid to economically or strategically important governments that torture, kill, or falsely imprison their citizens. This, Clinton believed, was necessary to facilitate presidential flexibility in foreign policy issues.

Consequently, human rights scholars charge the Clinton Administration with enacting a new double standard. Aryeh Neier argues that the Clinton Administration willingly denounced human rights violations in "pariah states or the governments of countries that are not considered politically or economically important," but refused to condemn repressive governments deemed to be economically important for U.S. interests (1996–1997, 96). As a result of Clinton's new double standard, the White House failed to resolutely condemn Russia's oppression in Chechnya,[12] it remained silent to China's subjugation of Tibet, and it ignored Turkey's repression of the Kurds.

What is more, even the human rights causes adopted and championed by the Clinton White House were often forfeited for economic, political, or strategic gain. Under the Clinton Administration, the United States increased attention to promoting and mainstreaming women's human rights. Nevertheless, Human Rights Watch noted that the issue of women's human rights suffered from Clinton's new double standard in human rights condemnation. Clinton's commitment to women's human rights was jeopardized, according to Human Rights Watch, by the president's intent to promote advantageous economic and strategic relations with other governments regardless of women's human rights considerations. The Human Rights Watch *World Report 2000* stated that

> the Clinton Administration was a steadfast critic of women's rights violations in areas where the sheer scale and severity of the physical violence could not be ignored. However, the U.S. government was much less critical about blatant sex discrimination practiced in places like Mexico, its second largest trading partner. (Human Rights Watch 2000)

By contrast, where condemnation of the abuse of women's rights, such as the discrimination against women in Afghanistan by the Taliban, helped to bolster U.S. foreign policy objectives and was widely voiced by the international community, Clinton did not hesitate to be a vocal critic. The Human Rights Watch report continued by noting that

> rather than making women's human rights 'mainstream,' as promised by President Clinton and Secretary of State Albright, the U.S. instead allowed women's rights to become the bargaining chip whenever other interests—from trade and investment to national security—came to bear. (Human Rights Watch 2000)

Economic and political concerns would once again trump issues of human rights crucial to women. Regan Ralph challenged the Clinton Administration to put its pronouncements about women's rights into action:

> The Department of State and the Clinton Administration have made some very strong and important pronouncements. What you don't see is what it means in practice. How publicly is this raised with some of the worst offenders? What we have seen is that other issues trump women's human rights. If the administration wants to maintain that it is promoting women's rights, it can't continue to do that. Let's see something beyond the words. (Regan Ralph, as quoted in Lippman 1997, A01)

ASSERTIVE MULTILATERALISM

Clinton's tenure in office coincided with an era when the United States' traditional enemy vanished along with conventional threats to U.S. national security. However, U.S. military operations increased dramatically during the 1990s. As the sole remaining superpower, the global policeman, the United States was called on to send troops around the world to protect civilians, restore order, and foster the reemergence the United Nations. The Clinton Administration appeared to favor multilateralism and the use of the United Nations in confronting the growing array of human rights problems. Yet, global multilateral enforcement of human rights on the part of the Clinton Administration was often a matter of rhetoric and very little more.

An illustration of this rhetorical semblance of global democratic enforcement on the part of the United States under Clinton was the famous Clinton Doctrine. Unlike previous presidential doctrines, the Clinton Doctrine was not a clear, single statement of policy. The Clinton Doctrine was instead an amalgamation of words, statements, speeches, and actions meant to signal Clinton's foreign policy intent. The Clinton Doctrine was supposed to be the humanitarian and human rights justifications for U.S. military intervention in foreign countries. Clinton helped clarify his policy in a speech to U.S. troops in Macedonia:

> We can say to the people of the world, whether you live in Africa, or Central Europe, or any other place, if somebody comes after innocent civilians and tries to kill them en masse because of their race, their ethnic background or their religion, and it's within our power to stop it, we will stop it. (Clinton 1999)

Yet, in a manner reminiscent of Secretary of State Cyrus Vance's clarification of Carter's change of policy from an absolute principle of human rights to a policy based on a case-by-case assessment of human rights, Clinton's second secretary of state, Madeleine Albright, quickly modified the Clinton Doctrine from one confirming a global commitment to one that maintained a case-by-case determination for U.S. involvement as U.S. national security dictated. In a speech before the Council on Foreign Relations just days after Clinton's declaration to protect human rights anywhere around the globe, Albright assured listeners that "every circumstance is unique. Decisions on the use of force will be made by any president on a case-by-case basis after weighing a host of factors" (Albright 1999). Later, the Clinton Administration attempted to backtrack altogether from the concept of humanitarian intervention developed in the Clinton Doctrine. In a White House press briefing, Sandy Berger, Clinton's national security advisor, stated, "I don't think anybody ever articulated a doctrine which said that we ought to intervene wherever there is a humanitarian problem. That's not a doctrine, that's just the kind of prescription for America to be all over the world and ineffective" (Berger 1999).

As a result of Clinton's semblance of assertive multilateralism, or what William Thornton (2000) described as "militant idealism," the U.S. military became nonetheless involved in humanitarian activities around the globe. But, Clinton would find it difficult to mobilize and maintain domestic support for his humanitarian interventions since these adventures rarely involved vital U.S. national interests. Neoconservative critics referred to the Clinton Doctrine of assertive multilateralism as "Gunpoint Democracy," claiming that it would amount to using the United States' military power to forcefully create democracy in regions without a historical or cultural understanding of democracy (Hutchison 1999). More realist detractors of a policy of aggressive multilateralism were concerned that such a policy would drag the United States into open-ended international commitments, risking American lives, resources, and interests. Despite conservatives' and realists' worries about Clinton's new doctrine, there was probably not too much to cause such concerns in practice. Indeed, after a failed multilateral incursion in Somalia, Clinton soon became mindful of the political risks involved as a result of the use of assertive multilateralism. And, once again, he started to turn assertive multilateralism more into a rhetorical strategy than a forcefully sustained path of action.

Clinton chose to deploy an often rhetorical, rather than actual, assertive multilateralism for many reasons. First, there might have been some sincere liberal humanitarian motivations, rather than a purely geopolitical impetus, in his desire to end ethnic conflicts that disrupt food production and distribution, target civilian populations, exacerbate human rights abuses, and destroy weak states' already vulnerable infrastructures. Second, and more importantly, the multilateralism doctrine was Clinton's attempt to appear to "do something" when foreign crises demanded foreign policy decision making. Yet, this multilateralism would never sidetrack his domestic agenda. Third, the use of multilateral operations was believed to be cheaper for the United States since Europe and Japan would pay part of the international security costs. However, the assumption that multilateral peacekeeping operations would save the United States money was soon proven false. Contrary to what Clinton hoped, peacekeeping became an enormous drain on the U.S. economy. The U.S. share of peacekeeping assessments increased tenfold from 1991 to 1995 because the number of peacekeeping operations greatly increased (Rosner 1995). These UN peacekeeping missions, meant to be the practical implementation of the Clinton Doctrine, sometimes involved the United States in tricky situations in foreign lands where immediate U.S. interests were not apparent.

The first, and perhaps only, purely humanitarian intervention (and actual usage of assertive multilateralism) was Somalia. The acting chairman of the Joint Chiefs of Staff, Admiral David G. Jeremiah, stated that there was "nothing of geopolitical value in Somalia that should engage U.S. interest . . . the intervention had only one motivation—humanitarianism" (as quoted in Natsios 1997, 78). Operation Restore Hope seemed to be driven in large part by a humanitarian and human rights objective: to save millions of starving Somalis. The Bush Sr. Administration, which initiated the operation, assumed that Somalia would be a quick and easy operation that would create a "secure environment" for food distribution. Bush Sr. sent in 28,000 American troops to protect food delivery. Congress, the American public, and President-elect Clinton also approved of the mission. However, Clinton was soon convinced that the mission's goals needed to be modified to include capturing Mohammed Farah Aideed (the dominant rebel clan leader), disarming the fighting clans, and rebuilding Somalia "as a proud, functioning and viable member of the community of nations" (Madeleine Albright, as quoted in Bolton 1994, 62).

Clinton's initial liberal agenda of democratic enlargement prompted him to exceed the strictly humanitarian agenda of the initial Bush policy over Somalia. Consequently, the U.S. mission in support of the UN peacekeeping and humanitarian operation became a military combat operation. Following the June 1993 ambush and murder of twenty-four Pakistani UN peacekeepers as they were inspecting a weapons storage site, the American public began questioning the rationale for U.S. involvement in Somalia. The expansion of the mission, along with an increase in Western casualties, soon created a backlash, and the American public and congressional members began calling for the removal of U.S. troops from Somalia. The subsequent death of four U.S. soldiers in August 1994 when their vehicle was destroyed by a remotely detonated mine led both houses of the U.S. Congress to pass nonbinding resolutions demanding the end of any U.S. military involvement in Somalia. During the hunt for Aideed, in what is known as the Battle of the Black

Sea or, more commonly, the Battle of Mogadishu (October 3, 1993), two U.S. helicopters were shot down. The battle to rescue the crews resulted in the death of eighteen American soldiers, and another seventy-nine were injured. As a consequence of the international news reports showing the bodies of the dead soldiers dragged through the streets of Mogadishu, the U.S. public demanded the immediate removal of U.S. troops. Congress voted to cut off funds for the Somali operation. In the face of continuing and vehement opposition to the Somali operation in Congress, Clinton announced the removal of all U.S. troops from Somalia. Clinton finally withdrew the troops by March 31, 1994.

The result of Clinton's initial involvement in UN peacekeeping operations was an aversion to any foreign policy action that may have negative political repercussions. On September 27, 1993, just days after the deaths of the Rangers in Mogadishu, Clinton stated, in a speech to the UN General Assembly, that "the United Nations simply cannot become involved in every one of the world's conflicts. If the American people are to say yes to UN peacekeeping, the United Nations must know how to say no." This was a major change to his previously seemingly prointerventionist rhetoric. As a consequence of the political costs suffered by Clinton following the deaths of eighteen U.S. Army Rangers, the White House announced a rigid set of criteria for determining whether to involve U.S. military in future multilateral peacekeeping operations. On May 3, 1994, Clinton issued PDD-25 that outlined U.S. policy regarding multinational peacekeeping operations.[13] Clinton would maintain the assertive multilateralist rhetoric, but he would no longer become involved until vital U.S. political or economic interests were involved. The United States' subsequent inaction during the Rwandan genocide can be traced directly to the political penalty Clinton suffered as a result of the assertive multilateralist Somalia calamity.

During the Cold War, Rwanda occupied a small but valuable place in the United States' fight against communism and, therefore, received modest amounts of U.S. foreign aid. The Rwandan genocide began when a plane carrying President Juvénal Habyarimana of Rwanda, a moderate Hutu, was shot down in April 1994. The ensuing violence left upward of 1 million Tutsis and moderate Hutus dead. Roughly 2 million people were made refugees, and another million became internally displaced. The killing officially came to an end on July 16, 1994. Once the situation was no longer dangerous, the United Nations, in cooperation with the United States, established Operation Support Hope.

Even in the face of UN, Central Intelligence Agency (CIA), and NGO reports about the growing violence and unprecedented slaughter of Tutsi civilians, and despite the relentless insistence of human rights organizations, the Clinton Administration, fearing another disastrous African peacekeeping operation (like Somalia), failed to act. The Clinton Administration downplayed the humanitarian crisis in Rwanda and actively impeded international actions to stop the genocide. In fact, Alison Des Forges reports that the United States, in April 1994, "opposed strengthening the [UN peacekeeping] mandate, and several days later they advocated withdrawing most of the peacekeepers, a position that became complete withdrawal" (2004, 35). This action sealed the fate of the over 1 million victims of the genocide. The Somali debacle created an unwillingness among the president's staff, some members of Congress, and Pentagon officers to once again become involved in an African peacekeeping operation. Rwanda certainly did not conform to the requirements set out by the newly rendered PDD-25. Having been stung by a failed peacekeeping mission in Somalia, Clinton and "the United States did not favour either direct or United Nations military intervention to stop the killings, as it maintained that the process of peacemaking had become dangerously overutilized, and that Rwanda was of marginal strategic importance" (Klinghoffer 1998, 91). Holly Burkhalter supports this conclusion and asserts that the Clinton Administration responded to the Rwandan genocide "not as a human rights disaster requiring urgent response, but as a peacekeeping headache to be avoided" (1994–1995, 53). Moreover, there was little domestic pressure for U.S. involvement in Rwanda.

In Rwanda, the Clinton Administration viewed its job as being a neutral peace broker, and, as an impartial agent, it refrained from condemning Rwanda's Hutu government's genocidal behavior. The United States refused to acknowledge for many months that the massive killings were ethnic genocide because using this terminology would have required some type of U.S. intervention, particularly in the context of the Clinton Doctrine. In order to avoid having the American public realize that something needed to be done and then demand action, the Clinton Administration rejected outright the use of the term "genocide." It was not until mid-June, when a few vocal members of Congress and the press persistently pleaded for action, that Secretary of State Warren Christopher finally used the term "genocide" in describing the situation. U.S. involvement in the humanitarian crisis in Rwanda would finally occur, but after the genocide, when a massive refugee flight of Hutus escaping reprisals by Tutsis escaped to Eastern Zaire.

To meet the humanitarian requirements of the refugee crisis, the United States organized and implemented Operation Support Hope. Only because the crisis intensified and the number of dead mounted, which heightened international and domestic concern, was the Clinton Administration finally compelled to act. In July, Clinton closed the Rwandan embassy in Washington and froze Rwandan assets in the United States. Later, after the Tutsis had taken control of the Rwandan government, they too engaged in mass slaughter and committed crimes against humanity in acts of revenge against the remaining Hutu population. The Clinton Administration, supporting the new government, tolerated the slaughter of innocent civilians and too easily accepted the excuse that the Rwandan military was unable to "distinguish civilians from insurgents" (Des Forges 2004, 42). Clinton also readily accepted the government's denials of involvement in the retaliations.[14]

Another in a series of Clinton's purported assertive humanitarian operations was the United States' belated involvement in Bosnia. Bosnia was one of the five republics of Yugoslavia until the latter's disintegration. In 1991, Slovenia and Croatia declared their independence and were immediately recognized as sovereign nations. Bosnia-Herzegovina, a region populated by Serbs, Croats, and Muslims, followed suit via a referendum for independence from Yugoslavia in February 1992. The referendum was boycotted by the Bosnian Serbs, who hoped to unite Bosnia with the Serb majority in Yugoslavia for a "Greater Serbia." Slobodan Milosevic, leader of Yugoslavia, provided the Bosnian Serbs with men and arms. The Bosnian Serbs attempted to force out the Muslim population in what is now known as "ethnic cleansing." The ethnic cleansing was performed in a number of ways, either by killing the Muslims or by forcing them to flee the region. The systematic use of murder, torture, and rape resulted in the deaths of more than 200,000 people and forced more than 2 million people out of their homes.

During the 1992 election campaign, Clinton had criticized the Bush Administration for "turning its back on violations of basic human rights" in Bosnia (Zimmerman 1999, 221). However, after the difficulties Clinton experienced in Somalia, the Clinton White House promptly declared that Bosnia was not a vital U.S. interest, and, therefore, it did not conform to the requirements of PDD-25. The Clinton Administration quickly backed away from calling the Bosnian crisis a genocide and downgraded it to a "human tragedy."

After three years of the United States ignoring the human rights abuses in Bosnia, Clinton finally decided to provide extensive diplomatic and military control that would eventually result in the Dayton Peace Accords. In what might appear to be a counterintuitive move, the U.S. Congress lifted the arms embargo on Bosnia and authorized immediate military assistance to the Bosnian Muslims. With pressure coming from the U.S. Congress, the American public, and the international community, Clinton finally determined that Bosnia jeopardized U.S. vital interests by undermining NATO and UN peacekeeping in general. On a nationally televised news program, *Peter Jennings Reporting*, Clinton stated that he supported the lifting of the arms embargo against the Bosnian Muslims and the commencement of U.S.-led NATO air strikes. Clinton declared that the United States, with the backing of the United Nations, ought to do "whatever it takes to stop the slaughter of civilians and we may have to use military force. I would begin with air power against the Serbs" (Clinton 1994). The result was a massive air campaign targeting Serb posts throughout Bosnia and, finally, a long-awaited cease-fire. The U.S.-supported and NATO-performed peacekeeping operation, Operation Joint Endeavor, began with the signing of the Dayton Peace Accords (December 1995). Sixty thousand NATO troops were deployed as part of Operation Joint Endeavor into Bosnia. This force separated the fighting factions, protected civilians, and delivered humanitarian aid. But, once again, it took many deaths, untold rapes, other severe human rights abuses, and public outrage before Clinton would be goaded into action.

FOREIGN AID

Clinton's initial faith in liberal internationalism was demonstrated in his foreign aid agenda. In a statement before the Senate Foreign Relations Committee justifying Clinton's foreign aid budget, Warren Christopher stated,

> Supporting the developing world's efforts to promote economic growth and alleviate chronic conditions of poverty serves America's interests. Nearly $1.4 billion of this budget will fund through USAID and multilateral programs activities that will, among other things, promote economic growth and free-market economies. . . . By helping nations to emerge from poverty, we can help them become stable pillars of regions at peace, and closer partners of ours in diplomacy and trade. (1995)

After the Cold War, the traditional justifications for aid (the national security issues of fighting communism and supporting allies) were no longer valid. Absent these traditional national security reasons for foreign aid, the United States Agency for International Development (USAID) emphasized aid's benefit to U.S. business interests. Robert Fleck and Christopher Kilby report that, under Clinton, aid agencies had to "increasingly focus on domestic commercial benefits when presenting their case to lawmakers" rather than highlight the standard humanitarian or strategic reasons (2001, 598). USAID emphasized the direct economic benefits to the United States when pushing for foreign aid allocations from Congress. As explained in chapter 1, U.S. bilateral aid is tied to the procurement of U.S. goods and services. This means that the majority of U.S. foreign aid has to be spent in the United States by purchasing equipment, commodities, and services made, produced, or provided in the United States. Thus, foreign aid actually helps to open foreign markets for U.S. products. The purpose of foreign aid is to subsidize domestic business, open foreign markets, and provide employment for domestic workers. Furthering U.S. commercial objectives was the primary foreign policy goal of the Clinton Administration.

With the Republicans gaining control of both houses of Congress after the 1994 elections, there was significantly more support for defense spending and less for economic aid, unless that aid was directed toward U.S. national security issues. As part of its agenda of fiscal management, Congress saw fit to cut foreign aid budgets. Republicans in Congress wanted to concentrate on domestic issues and reduce the size and expenditures of the international affairs budget. Consequently, Congress withdrew funds for Clinton's humanitarian actions in Somalia and put up roadblocks when Clinton sought to secure funds for Rwanda, Bosnia, and later Kosovo. Taking to heart Clinton's assertive multilateralist rhetoric, the Republican agenda would require the United States to reduce the number and duration of Clinton's international entanglements. They were concerned that Clinton's liberal internationalism would increase U.S. expenditures abroad. In an effort to drastically reduce foreign aid allocations and downgrade the authority of USAID, the Republican freshmen cut assistance to Turkey, citing its deplorable human rights record (Greenberger 1995, 162). But Congress did not confront Turkey on its continuing human rights problems, choosing instead to maintain its tradition of ignoring Turkey's violations. The reduction in foreign aid, particularly military aid, had more to do with Congress' goal of cutting the foreign aid budget than promoting human rights and fundamental freedoms. The Clinton Administration believed that cuts in foreign aid programs would be a mistake. Not only was foreign aid good for the domestic economy, Clinton argued, but it would also increase U.S. influence in countries dependent on U.S. economic or military aid. Aid was, for Clinton, a good way to win friends and gain influence internationally.

During the Clinton Administration, the former Soviet Republics and Eastern Europe received increasing amounts of U.S. military aid. In addition, Congress created and funded foreign aid programs to assist Russia's denuclearization, continued to heavily fund the modernization of Turkey's military, and financed Colombia's counternarcotics campaign. In Latin America, much of the aid was directed toward antidrug activities and political stabilization. The majority of the aid was given to the military and the police forces, the primary perpetrators of human rights abuses. Michael Klare (2001) reports that, among the reasons for providing Colombia with foreign aid, such as to subdue armed rebels and disrupt drug trafficking, was another covert reason for providing guns and money to Colombia. Colombia had oil. Certainly, Colombia does not have the plentiful oil fields that are located in the Persian Gulf region of the Middle East. But, with America's insatiable appetite for oil, every barrel counts. Furthermore, the U.S. government had (and still has) an economic and strategic interest in reducing U.S. dependence on Middle Eastern oil. Klare writes that "beginning in 1993, the Clinton Administration made the diversification of U.S. oil supplies a major strategic objective" (2001, 20). Consequently, and in line with Clinton's desire to further U.S. economic interests, the United States had to protect the oil industry from the militant attacks of rebels looking to undermine the Colombian economy and further discredit the Colombian government. In 2000, Colombia was the number one recipient of U.S. economic aid (receiving even more aid than either Israel or Egypt that year). Although Colombia was ineligible for U.S. aid under the Leahy Amendment (see below), Clinton waived the provision, citing national security.

In 1994, President Clinton also attempted to reform the convoluted and onerous Foreign Assistance Act. The real motivation in Clinton's attempt to reform the massive, often ineffectual foreign aid bureaucracy was to eliminate Congress' control over a valuable tool in foreign policy, and specifically foreign aid. The Peace, Prosperity, and Democracy Act (PPDA)[15] would have repealed the Foreign Assistance Act and replaced it with a new account structure for foreign assistance. In the opinion of the Executive, the Peace, Prosperity, and Democracy Act of 1994 would have legislated an active role for the United States in promoting democracy, and acknowledged the development of democratic institutions as a means of achieving worldwide respect for human rights. Brian Atwood, former director of the National Democratic Institute for International Affairs (NDI) and Clinton's director of USAID, integrated democracy into USAID's overall mission. Under Atwood's leadership, USAID attached a high priority to strengthening democratic institutions and popular participation in decision making (USAID 1994).

The Peace, Prosperity, and Democracy Act was to fund the many international development programs from a single account. Consequently, the Clinton Administration hoped, the coordination and accountability for U.S. bilateral foreign assistance would be improved. But this reorganization of the aid bureaucracy did not please the Republicans, who concluded that "for all of its rhetoric about change, the Administration [was] not talking about serious reform. The highly touted principles [were], in fact, merely restatements of the status quo" (Bandow 1996, 17). Indeed, the executive branch included significant allowances and exceptions to permit the administration to fund whomever or whatever it wished without any congressional oversight. Congress refused to consider this bill since it did not reduce foreign aid functions but merely renamed them. Moreover, the Peace, Prosperity, and Democracy Act granted the president broad authority to grant aid, thus assuming Congress' power of the purse. Furthermore, the PPDA would have ended Congress' authority to earmark foreign aid funds. Thus, the bill never made it out of committee in the House of Representatives. In 1995, Jesse Helms (R-NC) sought to eliminate the foreign aid bureaucracy altogether. Helms's viewpoint on foreign aid was clearly evidenced in a 1994 *Washington Post* article, where he stated that

> the so-called foreign aid program . . . has spent an estimated $2 trillion of the American taxpayers' money, much of it going down foreign rat holes, to countries that constantly oppose us in the United Nations, and many of which reject concepts of freedom. (Goshko and Williams 1994, A1)

Clinton's animosity with Congress extended beyond the issue of foreign aid budgets, as will be seen in the next section.

CONGRESSIONAL HUMAN RIGHTS INITIATIVES

John Dietrich (1999) reports that the hundreds of newly formed interest groups that were created in the 1990s, along with the more established business lobbies, human rights nongovernmental organizations, and religious groups, framed the foreign policy debates of the executive branch under Clinton, assisted Congress with foreign policy oversight, and acted as a valuable source of congressional information and analysis. "When groups discover what they perceive as problems," Dietrich argues, "they bring their concerns to the attention of Congress for redress in hearings, new legislation, or other action" (1999, 283). The expanded power of these interest groups under Clinton could be seen in the case of the granting of MFN status to China once again (a foreign policy option backed by the Clinton Administration) and with the enactment of several important pieces of human rights legislation (that were passed by Congress despite Clinton's reservations and objections). When national security is not threatened, congressional members become more willing to push legislation favored by their constituents and by interest groups in order to win reelection. The end of the Cold War and the need to contain communism not only brought "soft" foreign policy issues (non-security-related concerns) to new prominence, but also opened a larger political space for interest groups to lobby for their own particular concerns. When Congress is less deferential to the Executive's foreign policy prerogatives, interest groups, NGOs, and lobbyists have a much greater influence in the foreign policy process.

Allen Hertzke and Daniel Philpott credit the creation of the 1998 International Religious Freedom Act (IRFA) to "the emergence of a formidable network of determined activists who document persecution and press for vigorous U.S. action" (2000, 75). The IRFA makes the protection of religious freedom a primary goal of American foreign policy. The act established an Office on International Religious Freedom, headed by an ambassador at large, within the State Department. The IRFA also created a bipartisan Commission on International Religious Freedom. The commission was charged with monitoring religious persecution and recommended policies to promote religious freedom. The act also required the Executive to restrict or deny U.S. foreign assistance to any country that violates the religious freedom of its citizens, similar to Sections 701 of the International Financial Institutions Act and Sections 116 and 502B of the Foreign Assistance Act. Specifically, the International Religious Freedom Act states,

> Section 2B(2) To seek to channel United States security and development assistance to governments other than those found to be engaged in gross violations of the right to freedom of religion, as set forth in the Foreign Assistance Act of 1961, in the International Financial Institutions Act of 1977, and in other formulations of United States human rights policy.

The IRFA also required the State Department to issue an annual report on religious persecution. The Office on International Religious Freedom was charged with the responsibility to compile reports in concert with the human rights reports on religious freedoms around the world. This report parallels the State Department's *Country Reports on Human Rights*, detailing the level of religious protection or persecution in foreign countries. The State Department, then, has to identify countries "of particular concern." The act specifies a list of punitive actions the president must choose from, unless he opts to issue a waiver for countries vital to the U.S. national interest. Although Clinton had considerable reservations concerning the requirements for punitive action listed in Section 405 (a) of the IRFA, which he felt constrained his policy options, he nonetheless signed the IRFA because of the IRFA's overwhelming support in both houses of Congress.

In October 2000, the Trafficking Victims Protection Act (TVPA) was also signed into law despite concerns by the Clinton Administration. The TVPA was designed to combat trafficking in human beings, required effective punishment for traffickers, and aimed to protect victims. Although the bill corresponded to the Clinton Administration's efforts to protect victims and prosecute offenders, the provisions calling for punitive action against governments that were incorporated into the legislation by Congress went well beyond the initial proposals outlined by the president. The Trafficking Victims Protection Act[16] prohibits nonhumanitarian U.S. assistance to foreign governments that tolerate or condone severe forms of trafficking, unless the prohibition is waived by the president. Additionally, the Trafficking Act requires annual reports on trafficking as part of the State Department's *Country Reports on Human Rights*. The TVPA sets up a three-tiered measure of governmental compliance: governments that fully comply, governments that do not yet fully comply but are making significant efforts, and governments that do not fully comply and are not making significant efforts. The Clinton White House strongly opposed the bill's mandatory sanctions and imposition of nonhumanitarian aid restrictions on countries that failed to prosecute the most severe forms of trafficking. Clinton argued that these requirements limited the president's flexibility to work with countries to improve their efforts to thwart human trafficking. However, the TVPA received unprecedented support in Congress and was fervently backed by both the religious right and feminist organizations. Attached as a rider to the TVPA, the Violence against Women Act (to combat domestic violence, stalking, and sexual assault) was also passed.

Congress also passed, again over Clinton's objections, one of the most potentially important human rights edicts, the Leahy Amendment. The Leahy Amendment to the 1997 Foreign Operations Appropriations Act (PL 104-208), named for Senator Patrick Leahy (D-VT), sought to ban security aid and training to military or police forces if these security forces were involved in gross violations of human rights, unless effective measures had been taken to bring the offenders to justice. Candidates for training would have to be screened to determine if they were involved in any human rights abuses or criminal acts prior to attending or participating in any U.S.-sponsored training exercises that were funded through U.S. foreign assistance. The Leahy Amendment was expanded in 1998 to include all security assistance programs funded through the Foreign Operations Appropriations Act.[17] Thus, the Leahy Amendment became one of the most important tools for the promotion and respect of human rights in U.S. security assistance programs. The Leahy Amendment of the Foreign Operations Appropriations Act states,

> None of the funds made available by this Act may be provided to any unit of the security forces of a foreign country if the Secretary of State has credible evidence that such unit has committed gross violations of human rights, unless the Secretary determines and reports to the Committees on Appropriations that the government of such country is taking effective measures to bring the responsible members of the security forces unit to justice. (PL 104-208)

Interestingly, the Clinton Administration claimed the amendment was unnecessary since the U.S. government supposedly already withheld military aid to human rights-abusing military forces. However, human rights groups provided evidence that the U.S. government continued to provide security assistance to military units implicated in gross human rights violations.

The introduction of the Leahy Amendment would restrict the Clinton Administration's ability to provide Turkey with security aid. The Leahy Amendment substantially slowed the sales of U.S. military equipment, specifically armored personnel vehicles, to Turkey in 1999. Turkey was and still is unique among U.S. military aid recipients. Turkey is a long-time ally, a NATO member, but also an egregious human rights abuser. But the introduction of human rights and democracy were never strongly encouraged by U.S. foreign policy since these matters were thought to potentially destabilize a strategically located ally. The protection of Turkey's secular government and of its territorial integrity was in the United

States' vital national interest. Therefore, criticisms of Turkey's human rights violations had to be muted. In an effort to continue directing security aid to Turkey, Clinton simply worked out a disingenuous deal to continue sending military aid, despite the Leahy Amendment, by stating that the armored vehicles would not be sent to Turkish provinces that were associated with human rights violations directed against the Kurdish population (Barkey 2004). However, once the vehicles were delivered, the United States could no longer be responsible if Turkey chose to later drive these vehicles into restricted, human rights-violating regions. The provision of sophisticated U.S. weapons and other military equipment to Turkey, notorious for its oppression of the ethnic Kurds, is additional evidence of Clinton's selling off of human rights for strategic purposes.

CONCLUSION

Clinton came to office with the promise that human rights would finally be a cornerstone of U.S. foreign policy. With human rights now institutionalized in foreign policy, it was no longer a question among State Department officers of whether to include human rights, but rather of how to include human rights in their official duties. And with a new president declaring his support for human rights, human rights advocates, in Clinton's early years in office, were optimistic that internationally recognized human rights norms would be realized and respected in U.S. foreign policy. Although several of Clinton's appointees were associated with the promotion of human rights and, more importantly, despite the fact that his rhetoric declared that human rights and democracy were going to be primary pillars of U.S. foreign policy, in practice Clinton never really gave human rights any priority in his foreign policy decision making. Paradoxically, Clinton, liberal internationalist sweet talk notwithstanding, clearly attempted to circumvent human rights legislation by fudging reports on human rights, by excessively using waivers, and, more crucially, by frequently reducing human rights considerations to economic interests. In retrospect, the Clinton Administration only supported human rights when they were compatible with other, mostly economic, foreign policy preferences. Human rights considerations were quickly abandoned when they conflicted with more pressing economically or politically important issues.

Clinton sacrificed human rights to U.S. economic interests. For Clinton, liberal internationalism became economic liberalism. Humanitarian interventions were undertaken with the aim of encouraging the growth of new, stable economic markets and trading partners. Regrettably, trading with nondemocratic and often repressive regimes, for instance China, required abandoning U.S. human rights policy that linked trade and foreign aid benefits with human rights standards. Clinton's Administration caved in to the desires of big business and important trading partners and forced the United States to ignore human rights. Jeffrey Garten, undersecretary of commerce for international trade, finally admitted,

> We [the Clinton Administration] mounted massive trade missions to help U.S. companies win big contracts in emerging markets. Strengthening economic globalization became the organizing principle for most of our foreign policy. And American corporations were de facto partners all along the way. I'll admit that the Clinton Administration probably went too far in conducting a foreign policy so oriented to commercial and economic interests. (2002, 3 of 5)

The overall result of Clinton's general neglect (in deeds if not in words) of human rights was the growing misery and poverty of many vulnerable groups throughout the world forced to integrate even further into the globalizing economic order. Clinton's selling off of human rights expanded misgiving among many people in the world that the United States' "lip service" paid to human rights was nothing more than a way of fostering U.S. economic interests. Clinton squandered opportunities for reassessing and redirecting international efforts toward establishing and protecting human rights. Clinton's deliberate failure to advance human rights in U.S. foreign policy is perhaps the most discouraging paradox of all. Clinton's legacy would be left for his successor, George W. Bush, to deal with. U.S. human rights policy would further suffer under the direction of America's 43rd president, who would not hesitate to aggressively implement U.S. hegemonic desires.

CHAPTER 7

U.S. Human Rights Policy, the Calculated Victim: The George W. Bush Administration

The roots of the Abu Ghraib prison scandal lie not in the criminal inclinations of a few Army reservists but in a decision, approved last year by Secretary of Defense Donald Rumsfeld, to expand a highly secret operation, which had been focused on the hunt for Al Qaeda, to the interrogation of prisoners in Iraq.

Seymour Hersh (2004)

George W. Bush began his presidency under the shadow of illegitimacy (Kane 2003). In a highly contested and bitter election process, Bush won the unenviable distinction of being, some would claim, the second president in U.S. history not to have been elected by the American constituency.[1] Possibly due to his dubious election victory, George W. Bush did not benefit from the traditional honeymoon period enjoyed by every newly elected president. Prior to September 11, Bush's approval rating was the lowest of any president.[2] David Frum, a Bush speechwriter, believed that "on September 10, 2001, George Bush was not on his way to a very successful presidency" (2003, 272). The economy was suffering, Americans were losing jobs, American corporations were caught in felonious business ventures, and the United States' unilateralist arrogance infuriated most of America's allies. Although Bush had little experience in, or indeed knowledge of, international issues, the terrorist attack of September 11 became for George W. Bush the vehicle for the development of his foreign policy interests. Bush's secretary of defense, Donald Rumsfeld, declared that the events of September 11 proved an "opportunity to refashion the world" (2001).

With the September 11 terrorist attacks, the United States once again had an enemy. Unlike the enemy of the Cold War, the Soviet Union, or communism, the post-September 11 enemy was a more ambiguous entity. The United States' new enemy was evil itself. Evil would be personified at various times and in various fashions, as terrorists and their organizations (such as al Qaeda, the Taliban, and Osama bin Laden), as tyrannical leaders like Saddam Hussein, or as rogue regimes now referred to as the "axis of evil" composed of Iraq, Iran, and North Korea.[3] Fighting terrorism—the crusade of good over evil—was the primary and often sole focus of George W. Bush's foreign policy. The fight to defeat terrorism and to eradicate evil required U.S. foreign policy to be at once global and exclusionary. Bush's rhetoric assumed a simplistic yet antagonistic dichotomy: you are either with us, or you are against us. Addressing a joint session of Congress, Bush declared, "Every nation, in every region, now has a decision to make. Either you are with us, or you are with the terrorists" (2001a). This polarizing sentiment was repeated on numerous occasions, reiterating the new ideological division. Bush repeated, "Nations are either with us or against us in the war on terror" (2002d). And again, on October 3, 2002, Bush (2002e) maintained that "[the] doctrine that says, either you're with us or with the enemy, still holds. It's as important today as it was thirteen months ago." Thus it was now America's duty, its mission, and its primary objective to destroy evil and eradicate the evil ones.

With the acquiescence of Congress, President Bush issued a series of executive orders, introduced several pieces of legislation, and issued exemptions that, in effect, victimized human rights guarantees, both domestically and internationally. Congress consented to the USA Patriot Act, a war in Iraq, military tribunals, a historically high federal deficit, and a Department of Homeland Security with virtually limitless powers. The Bush Administration balanced the legitimate concern for security and a commitment to human rights by concluding that America's traditional values of civil liberties and the protection of human rights must yield to the dangerous realities wrought by the evildoers.

Regrettably, the George W. Bush Administration is not the first U.S. presidency to engage in objectionable foreign policy behaviors that restrict or deny human rights standards. However, this Bush presidency is the first to have the opportunity to do so without the restraint and arbitration of Congress, the American public, or the media. The paradoxes formerly shaping previous administrations' human rights policies were completely and purposefully eradicated by Bush's war on terror. As a result, during Bush's terms in office, the paradoxes of U.S. human rights policy were violently and forcefully resolved. U.S. human rights policy was now the calculated victim of George W. Bush's war on terrorism.

NEOCONSERVATIVISM

George W. Bush's campaign rhetoric tended toward classical realist power politics. Bush proudly declared that "a president must be a clear-eyed realist" (1999). Kaplan and Wildman also characterized Bush's foreign policy advisors, specifically National Security Advisor Condoleeza Rice, Secretary of State Colin Powell, and Vice President Dick Cheney, as "devotees of realpolitik who view the United States as a country with no special mission other than to safeguard its material interests" (2000, 25). The United States had to rely on its own resources and power to promote and protect its national interests after the Cold War. The U.S. hegemonic power was to be used to protect its material interests in a dog-eat-dog competitive world. Power was of primary importance in international politics in the twenty-first century; such were the beliefs of realist foreign policy makers at the time Bush came into office. Bush promised a foreign policy based on strength and humility. Under Bush, the United States would not be involved in foreign military interventions for humanitarian concerns or democracy building. U.S. foreign policy was to further U.S. economic and strategic interests, and would not advance or promote universal moral principles. Bush, directly criticizing the Clinton Administration, promised to be more cautious when sending U.S. soldiers into conflicts overseas. U.S. involvements would only be considered if the conflict threatened U.S vital national interests or if it was likely to disrupt or unbalance existing power structures. John Kane, in a biting commentary on Bush's humble foreign policy rhetoric, states that

> strength appeared to translate simply into a dogged intention to use the freedom of action afforded by superpower status to American interests (as interpreted by conservative Republicans) . . . humility translated into a rejection of well-meaning Clintonesque 'meddling' in other nations' business. (Kane 2003, 793)

At the same time that Bush seemed to display a mostly realist rhetoric back in 2000, several of his foreign policy advisors were drawn from a prominent group of neoconservatives associated with the New American Century. The neoconservatives in Bush's entourage, which included Deputy Secretary of Defense Paul Wolfowitz, Undersecretary of State John Bolton, Undersecretary of Defense Douglas Feith, and the Director of the Defense Policy Board Richard Perle, believed that U.S. security lay not in the balancing of power, but rather in the forceful extension of America's power abroad by making the world a reflection of the United States. Thus, Richard Haass aptly summarized what would soon become Bush's main foreign policy objectives: "the principle aim of American foreign policy is to integrate other countries and organizations into arrangements that will sustain a world consistent with U.S. interests and values, and thereby promote peace, prosperity, and justice as widely as possible" (2002). International peace and prosperity could only be assured if America maintained its hegemonic position and military predominance.

Wolfowitz wrote that "the core of American foreign policy is in some sense the universalization of American principles" (2000, 335). American values were seen as universal by the neoconservatives. They ascribed to the dogma of chauvinistic morality in foreign policy and argued that the United States is the measure of righteousness and virtue in the world. Therefore, for the neoconservatives, the United States had a moral responsibility to spread its values and power globally. The United States had to move unilaterally to transform the world into democratic capitalist states reflective of America's virtues. The purity of American motives remained unquestionable. William Bennett explains that, because America's motives were thought to be pure, its decision to preemptively attack Iraq in 2003 would be laudable too. Bennett claims that "because the political values that are at the core of the U.S.' existence are honorable and estimable, the judgment of history is likely to be positive" (2003, 95).

September 11 unmistakably changed Bush's initially realist rhetoric and made the neoconservatives' influence increasingly dominant.[4] Post September 11, the United States' foreign policy would quickly turn into an ideological crusade to protect and extend American values and influence overseas. The global crusade of right versus wrong, good versus evil, in its resistance to terrorism fit well into Bush's religious dogma. Islamic fundamentalism became an evil ideology that needed to be eradicated because it was a vile threat to America's principal moral values of democracy, liberty, and capitalism. In this religious and moral crusade, championed by the neoconservatives and endorsed by Bush, there could be no compromise or concession.

Neoconservative defense strategy, as explained by Wolfowitz (2000), required that the United States prevent a hostile power from gaining regional hegemony and control of any vital resources. This strategy also was aimed at obstructing any hostile state from acquiring weapons of mass destruction (WMD) since these could threaten the United States' exclusive global power. Iraq, in the view of the neoconservatives, was a hostile power seeking regional domination and was also actively developing weapons of mass destruction. Hence, the need to eradicate the regime of Saddam Hussein became imperative. Alex Callinicos adds a more rationally integrated and economically imperialistic argument to the neoconservative rhetoric by stating that

> an American client regime in Iraq not only eases concerns about America's long-term access to oil; it also increases Washington's leverage over allies and rivals such as Germany and Japan that are even more dependent than the US on imported oil . . . [and] enhances Washington's ability if necessary to choke off oil and gas supplies to China . . . [the] grand strategy of American imperialism. (2003, 98)

Bush's neoconservative advisors promptly became proponents of the doctrine of preemptive intervention, a doctrine that is now known as the Bush Doctrine. The intention of this doctrine is to use military force whenever there may be a "potentially materializing danger," that is to say, speculative allegations that some country may develop programs that are not in the best interests of the United States. Bush explained his doctrine of preemptive intervention by claiming that

> if we wait for threats to fully materialize, we will have waited too long. . . the war on terror will not be won on the defensive. We must take the battle to the enemy, disrupt his plans, and confront the worst threats before they emerge. (2002b)

A defining characteristic of the conservative movement (both traditional and neo) is the enmity shown toward multilateral institutions and international law. The liberal acceptance and reliance on such institutions, according to conservatives, results in costly and nonproductive foreign entanglements. A rejection of mulitlateralism in favor of unilateral action preserves the United States' freedom of action in international interventions designed to maintain the United States' hegemony and reform the international system. At the same time, because the United States is the uncontested hegemonic power, realism is not useful because it tends to restrain American military adventures (in realist thought, the hegemon uses its power position to maintain the status quo). Conversely, as indicated above, the neoconservative position requires the use of military action to spread the values, principles, and doctrine of America.

THE NEW IMPERIAL PRESIDENCY: BUSH'S GRAB FOR POWER

Bush's grab for the unilateral authority to wage war, precluding any judicial review of executive action, made a mockery of the separation of powers and the structure of checks and balances that undergird the framework of the American political system. The September 11 terrorist attacks provided the Bush Administration with the opportunity to greatly expand the power of the Executive at the expense of the courts, the legislative branch, and the Constitution. Bush's claimed status as a war president supplied him with the pretext needed to assume those expanded powers. The Bush White House contended that, during wartime, an increase in presidential power is a rational and appropriate course of action that keeps the homeland safe. Furthermore, a fearful public, a surrendering Congress, and a hesitant judiciary allowed and often encouraged Bush to grab ever more power. After 9/11, Congress willingly allowed the president to concentrate foreign policy power into the hands of the Executive by enthusiastically surrendering foreign policy prerogatives to the White House. The American population and the U.S. Congress unreservedly accepted the argument that, in times of crisis, national security requires strength, speed, and often secrecy on the part of the president.

The defiant and rebellious Congress of the Clinton Administration quickly transformed into a group of deferent, retiring followers of President George W. Bush in the aftermath of 9/11. During times of crisis, Congress and the American public typically believe that the country needs a strong president unhampered by congressional meddling. Lindsay (2003) argues that congressional resistance to the Executive during times of trouble is seen as obstructive and unpatriotic. Lindsay describes the sentiment in Congress after 9/11 by suggesting that "members of Congress who previously took pride in standing up to the White House suddenly saw the better part of good policy and good politics lying in a willingness to rally around the president" (2003, 530). No one wanted their patriotism questioned or to run the risk of being depicted as a terrorist sympathizer. Hence, post–September 11, Congress eagerly abdicated its responsibility to check the unbridled power of the Executive. The global crusade of good versus evil also justified all U.S. actions undertaken to exterminate terrorists and their sympathizers, even if this meant dispensing with the Constitution and sacrificing human rights.

The president also quickly moved to seize power from the other branches of government through a strategy that relied on the use of executive orders, through fast-tracking legislation, by intimidating the judiciary, and by claiming executive privilege to create an unaccountable bureaucracy. Each strategy will be examined in turn.

Use of Executive Orders

The Bush Administration's overutilization of executive orders was a direct reflection of the neoconservatives' attempt to run the government by fiat. From 2001 to mid-2005, President Bush issued 178 executive orders, far more than any other president in U.S. history. By doing so, Bush clearly indicated his desire to appropriate legislative powers. These executive orders ranged from the routine dictates relating to issues like seasonal (nonpandemic) influenza to classified terrorism-related commands.[5]

Bush's justification was, once again, that the war on terror required swift, surprise, and perhaps covert operations that would be impossible to undertake if the White House had to get advance approval from Congress. Bush warned congressional members, "[I]t is not possible to know at this time either the duration of combat operations or the scope and duration of the deployment of U.S. Armed Forces necessary to counter the terrorist threat to the United States" (Bush 2003b). Therefore, Bush simply assumed sole authority to launch any policy, operation, or other action allegedly designed to secure U.S. interests. The following briefly reviews the major executive mandates that confiscated congressional prerogatives.

In the Military Order of November 13, 2001, without the advice or consent of Congress, Bush declared war and the right to detain suspected enemies incognito and without representation, in violation of both domestic and international human rights standards. Bush stated that the terrorist attacks "created a state of armed conflict that requires the use of the United States Armed Forces" (2001b). Citing the exceptional and new nature of the war on terrorism, Bush determined that enemies had neither nationality nor citizenship and that, consequently, the conflict also had no territory or geographical boundaries. Therefore, the Geneva Conventions no longer pertained.[6] This presidential decree did not have a provision allowing detainees to challenge their detention. It allowed foreign citizens suspected to be involved with terrorism to be tried before military tribunals. And it removed the principles of law and rules of evidence respected in U.S. civilian courts. Simply put, the Bush Administration assumed the sole authority to determine the detentions.

In a highly unusual move, Bush issued Executive Order #13233, also entitled Further Implementation of the Presidential Records Act (November 1, 2001), which allowed a sitting president to block the release of previous presidential records, thus overturning a law that Congress had passed stating that the U.S. government, not an individual president, owned presidential records. In the name of executive privilege, the Bush Administration now refused to release to Congress or to the American public past presidential papers. Jonathan Turley commented that this executive order rewrote the Presidential Records Act [44 USC 2201–2207], converting it from a statute guaranteeing public access of presidential papers to one that effectively blocks it perpetually (2003). It is generally believed that the records Bush was attempting to shield from public scrutiny pertained to the Iran-Contra scandal, which may prove embarrassing to the many Reagan and Bush Sr. members of George W. Bush's own administration. Additionally, this executive order would also forever keep the documents related to the war on terrorism, the Abu Ghraib torture scandal, and the treatment of prisoners at Guantánamo Bay, Cuba, from public scrutiny.

Legislation

As previously indicated, Congress and the American public, shocked and traumatized by the terrorist attacks, rallied around the flag and supported without any question the policies of George W. Bush. Congress passed several pieces of legislation relating to terrorism and counterterrorism, the most prominent being the USA Patriot Act. Congress also consented to military tribunals, accepted a historically high federal deficit, and allowed a Department of Homeland Security with virtually limitless powers. Under the authority of homeland security, the Federal Bureau of Investigation (FBI) was given the unfettered ability to scrutinize and surveil the lives of average Americans. Using "National Security Letters," the FBI was allowed to investigate anyone who had come into contact, however innocent, with a suspected terrorist. Barton Gellman of the *Washington Post* writes,

> The FBI now issues more than 30,000 national security letters a year . . . [which] do not need the imprimatur of a prosecutor, grand jury or judge. . . . The bureau needs only to certify that the records are "sought for" or "relevant to" an investigation "to protect against international terrorism or clandestine intelligence activities" (2005, A1)

Furthermore, in 2003, Attorney General John Ashcroft rescinded the practice of destroying citizen information that was not relevant or no longer important to the investigation. Now the FBI could retain and disseminate the information, even of blameless, harmless citizens, to other federal agencies. A majority of Americans approved of the series of legislations that would greatly reduce their civil liberties and would allow greater governmental intrusion into their private lives, mostly because they wanted to feel safe.

The USA Patriot Act, formally known as the Uniting and Strengthening America by Providing Appropriate Tools Required to Intercept and Obstruct Terrorism Act (HR3162), enabled the curtailment of individual rights and privacy, the expansion of federal powers, unfettered governmental access to personal information, unrestricted surveillance, and limitless intelligence activities. According to the USA Patriot Act, sneak-and-peak searches, and searches of a person's home, office, or vehicle without the person's knowledge, would not be limited to suspected terrorists, but would be expanded to any and all criminal investigations, thereby greatly reducing the protections afforded by the Fourth Amendment. However, for the Bush Administration, the ends justified the means. In order to facilitate an "ordered liberty,"[7] civil rights and protections had to be terminated. After 9/11, the Bush Administration had declared the United States to be at war. This declaration of war once again justified the emergency measures that would limit not only the rights and liberties of enemies and foreigners, but also those of American citizens.

The Courts

Bush's efforts to restrict judicial review of cases of human rights abuses against corporations, foreign officials, or even U.S. government officials greatly contributed to the expansion of executive power too. Beth Stephens has warned that

> the Bush Administration's aggressive opposition to human rights litigation threatens to undermine the global campaign to punish and deter human rights violations. Combined with the broad assault on judicial review [this will] undermine the assigned role of the judicial branch. An abdication of judicial oversight would endanger the constitutionally mandated balance of powers, leading to the unchecked executive branch power. (2004, 171)

Bush would grant to the Executive the authority to decide whether a case had standing or merit. The use of out-of-country detention centers in Guantánamo Bay, Cuba, was an obvious attempt by the Bush Administration to circumvent judicial review. The Bush Administration claimed that U.S. courts did not have jurisdiction in Cuba since the United States does not have sovereign control of Guantánamo. Furthermore, foreign nationals did not have the right to sue in U.S. courts. To support this claim, the Bush Administration actively sought to discredit the Alien Tort Claims Act (ATCA; 1789).

The ATCA allows foreign victims of internationally protected human rights abuses to seek damages in U.S. federal courts through civil lawsuits under specific conditions. The Bush Administration believed that the use of judicial review under the Alien Tort Claims Act would seriously hinder the war on terror. The Bush Administration claimed, "The potential impact of [the use of the ATCA] on the actions of the Executive abroad is great and further heightened by the Nation's ongoing war against terrorism" (Stephens 2004). Bush also attempted to quash claims of torture and human rights violations filed on behalf of prisoners held in Guantánamo suspected of being al Qaeda or Taliban members. As of 2005, the courts have dismissed Guantánamo claims because they have no jurisdiction over aliens outside the United States (one of the ATCA's provisions is the physical presence of both the victim and the defendant inside the United States).

To further avoid judicial review in Bush's war on terrorism, the administration also developed a new classification of detainees as enemy combatants, enemy aliens, or unlawful combatants. This new categorization of prisoners was created so that both the Geneva Conventions and American law would be rendered inapplicable. As Stephens reports, "[T]he Administration claims that combatants captured while fighting with groups that do not abide by the laws of war are entitled neither to prisoner of war status nor to any military or civilian legal process" (Stephens 2004). Enemy combatants were thus placed in a judicial netherworld whereby they were neither civilians with political or civil rights, nor prisoners of war covered by the Geneva Conventions.

DEMOCRACY AT THE POINT OF A GUN

As a presidential candidate and later as the newly installed president, George W. Bush criticized Clinton (and the Clinton Doctrine) for his global peacekeeping operations and his attempts at nation building. Bush clearly expressed his disdain for peacekeeping operations to protect foreign citizens and rebuild failed states in an interview given to the ABC News Network. Bush stated, "We should not send our troops to stop ethnic cleansing in nations outside our strategic interest" (Garfinkle 2001, 503). As a presidential candidate, Bush promised that there would be no nation-building campaigns in his foreign policy if he were elected. Neoconservatives, such as Kay Bailey Hutchison writing for the Heritage Foundation, also disparaged Clinton's assertive multilateralism and referred to it as "Gunpoint Democracy" (Hutchison 1999). Neoconservatives believed, at least while they were critiquing the Clinton Administration, that it was impossible to create democracy and implement the rule of law by using the United States' military power. Thus, they argued, nation building was bound to fail.

However, the Bush Administration would soon use Clinton's apparent precedent for humanitarian operations as a historical justification for its own nation-building operations. Secretary of Defense Donald Rumsfeld clarified, "The United States has organized armed coalitions on several occasions since the Cold War for the purpose of denying hostile regimes the opportunity to oppress their own people and other people. In Kuwait, in Northern Iraq, in Somalia, Bosnia, and Kosovo" (as quoted in Mertus 2004, 121). Yet, Julie Mertus (2004) maintains that the Bush version of nation building was far more invasive than Clinton's. The post–September 11 nation-building campaign would become programs to entirely rebuild countries after America's image, once the United States was done preemptively bombing and later invading them. Using the nation-building models of post-World War II, the rebuilding of the unconditionally defeated, conquered, and occupied nations of Japan and Germany, Bush believed the United States could remake Afghanistan and Iraq into fully functioning democratic and capitalistic nation-states. Bush believed that creating democracy in Iraq, even at the point of a gun, would act as a trigger for more democratic changes throughout the Middle East. Still, as of the writing of this book, only two of the nineteen countries in the Middle East and North Africa are democracies (USAID 2002).

In the case of Afghanistan, the immediate target of U.S. antiterrorism efforts following September 11, there was a direct link between the Taliban, al Qaeda, and the terrorist attacks. The U.S. invasion of Afghanistan, with the United Nations' subsequent approval, quickly deposed the brutally repressive Taliban and appeared to have significantly damaged al Qaeda's organization and training camps. Unfortunately, many of al Qaeda's leaders, including Osama bin Laden, managed to escape. After the collapse of the Taliban, the Bush Administration was considerably less intent on rebuilding Afghanistan than on hunting down bin Laden. To facilitate the capture of Taliban and al Qaeda leaders, the Bush Administration negotiated with Afghan warlords and restricted UN peacekeepers from setting up operations in areas thought to house bin Laden supporters. This move assured U.S. military control of the countryside to search for the terrorists. With Bush's attention diverted to Iraq, NATO became the lead agency to provide security to the Afghan people.

Although the war on terrorism began as a response to the events of 9/11, it soon became a global and permanent condition. Even though it was not connected to al Qaeda, the Taliban, or Osama bin Laden, Iraq was the second target of the war on terrorism. The Iraq invasion was, for the Bush Administration, a war for democracy, a war of liberation, and a war to remake the Middle East. The Bush Administration wanted to transform the Middle East and make it more in line with U.S. interests and values. The strategy chosen to do so was nation building through military force. Iraq was the true test case for this nation-building effort. Bush convinced a majority of the American public to support the war by confusing the source of the terrorist attacks on the United States. In his January 2002 State of the Union Address (Bush 2002a), Bush acknowledged that the war on terror had only begun. U.S. policy was to first strike the terrorists directly, as in the war in Afghanistan, and then "our second goal is to prevent regimes that sponsor terror from threatening America or our friends and allies with weapons of mass destruction." Iraq was seen by neoconservative foreign policy makers as a legitimate target of U.S. military action. The door was still left open, though, for the other members of the axis of evil, Iran and North Korea.

The Bush Administration predicted a democracy domino effect. As Bush explained to listeners from the American Enterprise Institute, "[A] new regime in Iraq would serve as a dramatic and inspiring example of freedom for other nations in the region. . . . Success in Iraq could also begin a new stage for Middle Eastern peace, and set in motion progress toward a truly democratic Palestinian state" (Bush 2003a). The Bush Administration maintained that the presence of American soldiers and the example of a successful Iraqi democracy would rouse the popular masses in neighboring Iran to demand liberalization, modernization, and democracy, thus toppling the mullahs. Syria's autocratic regime was also expected to fall under the demand for democracy. To date, this has proven to be a false prediction. But Bush's desire to spread democracy worldwide did not make room for democracies that would not support American values and interests. When confronted with the possibility of a democratic election of a Shi'ite-controlled theocracy in Iraq, Rumsfeld responded, "A regime like that in Iran is not compatible with our vision of Iraq" (as reported by Bozorgmehr and Dinmore 2003, A1). Clearly, it was not democracy that the United States wished to impose on Iraq, but rather an American version of democracy, one that could support American interests and was tied to a free market economy. The result of Bush's democracy at gunpoint in Iraq was the demise of 2,471 U.S. soldiers with an additional 17,648 wounded (as of May 31, 2006), the death and injury of thousands of Iraqi citizens, the detention and violation of uncounted numbers of secret prisoners, and the creation of covert interrogation camps run by Central Intelligence Agency (CIA) agents.

Critics believe that Bush's claims of the moral obligation to extend the virtues of American democracy to the uninitiated Iraqi people and to eliminate weapons of mass destruction were not the exclusive motivations for the Iraq war. If the idea was to protect the United States and the world from crazed human rights-abusing and WMD-wielding madmen and to bring democracy and freedom to the oppressed, then it should not even have been a toss-up as to who should have been targeted, Saddam Hussein in Iraq or Kim Jong Il in North Korea. In fact, there was no credible evidence that Iraq supported terrorism or had weapons of mass destruction. On the other hand, there was (and still is) convincing intelligence that North Korea was in possession of viable nuclear warheads. In fact, North Korea publicly announced its possession of nuclear weapons. Therefore, critics were led to ask, could the reason to go to Iraq be oil? Iraq had the second largest oil reserves at the time of the U.S. invasion. The May 2001 National Energy Plan, written under the direction of Vice President Cheney, underscored the economic and political security issues associated with the United States' dependency on foreign oil. The United States' increasing reliance on foreign oil created "a condition of increased dependency on foreign powers that do not always have America's interests at heart" (White House 2001). Furthermore, controlling Iraq's oil would not only protect U.S. access to oil but, as Callinicos reports, would also provide the United States with greater authority over the distribution of oil to its friends and allies (2003). In truth, the Bush Doctrine of preemptive intervention was used against a country that posed no serious threat to the United States, or at least no larger threat than it had for the previous twelve years.

When presidents experience foreign policy disappointments, Congress and other foreign policy elites are more likely to question the motives, methods, and objectives of the foreign policy activity. While Bush experienced little congressional opposition to his Iraqi policy initially, the unrelenting resistance encountered in the guerrilla war in Iraq,[8] the continuing loss of American lives (that the Bush Administration attempted to conceal from the American public), the revelation of egregious human rights violations committed by American soldiers, the administration's admission that the occupation of Iraq would be measured in generations, the absence of WMDs, and the drain on the economy eventually would lead the public to gradually start to question the wisdom of the U.S. strategy in Iraq. Congress, under pressure from the Democrats, began to investigate the exaggeration of data, the abuse of intelligence, and the actual motives for Bush's foreign policy offensive in Iraq. Due to its overreliance on Ahmed Chalabi, a wealthy and corrupt Iraqi exile,[9] the Bush Administration had embraced excessively optimistic assumptions about post-Saddam Iraq. Absent a realistic understanding of the situation, the Bush Administration thought that the Iraqi army would not resist American forces and that the Iraqi people would rise up in support of the U.S. operation, praise the president's resolve, greet democracy with open arms, and soon be able to take over their own security and governance, thus allowing U.S. troops to return home. This was a major strategic blunder indeed, one that cost the lives of American soldiers and many resources,[10] not to mention the continued suffering and human rights violations of the Iraqi people. Elizabeth Drew argues,

> US officials had failed to anticipate the degree of chaos that followed the war: they didn't have an adequate plan, didn't protect hospitals and other public buildings from looters, or citizens from violent crime, and by early May still hadn't restored many basic services. The leaders of long-repressed Shiite Muslims were taking charge of some neighborhoods and calling for a theocratic state. Iraqis were agitating for the US to leave. (2003)

Because the evidence clearly indicated that Saddam had no involvement in the September 11 attacks on the World Trade Center and the Pentagon, and in fact, harbored an antagonistic relationship with the Taliban and al Qaeda, Bush justified the Iraqi invasion by claiming that Saddam's possession of weapons of mass destruction posed an imminent threat to the United States. Bush further suggested that to bring freedom and democracy to the downtrodden in Iraq was in itself a meaningful justification too. Again, this would provide a democratic example to the rest of the Middle East. Superficially framing foreign incursions and invasions in terms of human rights and democracy helped the president win support for his policies. In his 2003 State of the Union Address, Bush used the language of human rights to condemn the abuses committed by Saddam's vicious regime:

International human rights groups have catalogued other methods used in the torture chambers of Iraq: electric shock, burning with hot irons, dripping acid on the skin, mutilation with electric drills, cutting out tongues, and rape. If this is not evil, then evil has no meaning. (Bush 2003a)

As Mertus has argued, presidents do employ a bait and switch strategy, using human rights language to justify their foreign policy adventures with no actual commitment to human rights (2005). Particularly in Iraq, once it became clear that no WMDs would be found, the administration had to continuously reemphasize its humanitarian efforts and its endeavors to encourage freedom and human rights by liberating hapless Iraqis.

Some critics who are suspicious of Bush's motives in going after Saddam believe that Bush was simply attempting to settle a family score and making up for what George W. Bush thought was his father's mistake in leaving Saddam in power after the Gulf War (1990). Bush's desire to attack Iraq even before the September 11 terrorist attacks was clearly demonstrated when, within a month of taking office, Bush already initiated bombing attacks in the suburbs of Baghdad. Bush justified this early attack as the need to enforce the no-fly zone. Steven Zunes referred to Bush's initial Iraq engagement back in 2001 as "foreign policy by catharsis, an expression of anger and frustration against a recalcitrant dictator which may feel good and help a president's standing in public opinion polls, but actually accomplishes little" (2001, 74). Perhaps this is why the younger Bush chose members of the Project for a New American Century to serve in his administration. As previously stated, the New American Century membership included people like Bolton, Perle, Rumsfeld, and Wolfowitz, who had advocated the removal of Saddam Hussein from power and said as much in a forceful letter to President Clinton in January 1998.[11]

FOREIGN AID

As was indicated in previous chapters, the United States Agency for International Development (USAID) proclaims that the purpose of foreign aid is to fund development projects to assist the poor and spread democracy. Development is today the third pillar of U.S. national security, along with defense and diplomacy. Prosperous countries built on the foundations of democracy and capitalism "would also be a profound affirmation of U.S. values and interests" because "life, liberty and the pursuit of happiness are universal" (USAID 2002, 2). After years of decline, support for foreign assistance increased again under George W. Bush, as did the number of foreign aid programs. Mary Cooper reports that even

> the Defense Department is now seeking authority to set up its own foreign-assistance account. As part of a $14 billion request in supplemental spending for 2002, the Pentagon asked for $130 million to create an autonomous account to fund military assistance to foreign governments without going through normal State Department channels. (2002, 382)

Today, foreign aid has clearly been recognized as an effective tool of U.S. foreign policy. It can be used to either contain threats to U.S. security or tackle the root causes of foreign threats. There is also a school of thought that claims that foreign aid can reduce the likelihood of terrorist attacks by averting the causes of terrorism—hopelessness and resentment caused by extreme poverty, illiteracy, and hunger.

The George W. Bush Administration declared that the rationale for granting economic aid was to ease the frustrating poverty suffered by the world's desperate inhabitants. Bush stated that "we can fight evil with military might and weapons devised by [the] high-tech world. As significantly, we can fight evil by doing acts of kindness and decency" (Bush 2002c). With that outlook, the Bush Administration initiated two new foreign aid programs: the Millennium Challenge Account (MCA), and the Global AIDS Initiative. However, foreign aid is a policy tool designed to serve the United States' own interests. By helping poor countries increase their standard of living, these countries' citizens would not fall prey to the ideological underpinning of fanatical fundamentalists and thus would not support anti-American terrorist groups. Bush's human rights rhetoric also linked economic and human development to defense and security issues. Richard Haass, director of the Policy Planning Staff of the State Department, announced, "Today's humanitarian problem can all too easily become tomorrow's strategic threat. . . . [T]hat is why President Bush announced last month his bold initiative to dramatically increase American foreign assistance by 50% over the next three years" (2002). Moreover, under Bush's leadership, a greater amount of the aid, both military and economic, would be given in the form of outright grants rather than low-interest loans, since many recipient governments had difficulty paying back the loans. Of course, the American taxpayer was not given the same consideration.[12]

With the tragedy of 9/11, support for foreign aid increased. Democrats, who have long supported the granting of foreign assistance, were now joined by Republicans in support for higher levels of foreign aid. Of course, as Mary Cooper illustrates, Republican calls for increased foreign aid were for national security goals and not for humanitarian concerns (2002). Included in the foreign aid budget was a request for additional military assistance. After 9/11, Congress deferred to the president on questions of arms exports and security aid allocations.

The Millennium Challenge Account (MCA) was announced just days before the UN International Conference on Financing for Development summit in Monterrey, Mexico (2002). The post-September 11 thinking determined that poverty was linked to violence, and the Bush Administration pledged an increase in U.S. economic aid from its current $10 billion to $15 billion by the year 2006. Poverty and repression are often causes of social instability and civil unrest, which in turn can produce flows of refugees and acts of terrorism. The MCA included a stipulation that the additional funds would be granted only to poor countries that were actively reforming their economies (that is, accepting the neoliberal capitalist model of privatization and free trade) and fighting corruption. In order to be eligible for the Millennium Challenge Account, developing countries would have to eradicate corruption and uphold human rights, adhering to what is commonly referred to as "good governance." But critics believe that the Bush Administration's concern for human rights and development was disingenuous and in fact simply a matter of political expediency. The inclusion of this stipulation was merely an attempt to ensure that the American public would support additional funding, giving the impression that U.S. tax dollars were not being wasted. In the past, foreign aid had been stolen by unscrupulous leaders of foreign countries living extravagant lifestyles at U.S. taxpayers' expense. Unfortunately, this stipulation eliminated any hope that the poor living in undemocratic or inefficient states would receive any additional help.

Bush's 2003 State of the Union Address (Bush 2003a) proposed new funding, a total of $15 billion over five years, to combat HIV/AIDS in Africa. This new program was hailed as the Emergency Plan for AIDS Relief, or the Global AIDS Initiative. The president's supporters believed that the administration realized that poverty and inequality generated hostility and resentment toward the United States, and, for that reason, Washington had to use foreign aid to secure U.S. national interests. Again, the timing of Bush's revelation that human justice and welfare could be related to the United States' long-term security interests was revealing. The administration's sudden attention to HIV/AIDS provided a "wow factor," a compelling proclamation for the State of the Union Address that Bush needed to offset growing criticism of his Iraq policy.[13]

The events of 9/11 changed both the public's and Congress' attitude toward requiring human rights standards when supplying repressive governments with military aid. After September 11, antiterrorism replaced anticommunism as the primary motivation for granting U.S. bilateral foreign aid. Tamar Gabelnick (2002) reports that George W. Bush significantly increased U.S. military aid and contributed funding to an even greater number of states. In a candid statement, Richard Boucher, spokesperson for the Department of State, revealed, "If governments are willing to cooperate against terrorism, that will result in a change in the level of our ability to cooperate with them" (2001b). Bush's desire to mount a global war on terror and expand the global reach of democracy forced him to ally the United States with undemocratic, brutal, human rights-abusing states. States that were once denied aid due to their human rights violations, such as Indonesia, Pakistan, and the Philippines, were now targeted for new military aid packages. Many countries were now asking for and receiving aid packages on the basis of their claims to be fighting terrorism within their borders. Russia, China, and Colombia, the Bush Administration believed, were all countering terrorist insurgents and not simply attempting to eradicate ethnic or political oppositions. Bush routinely provided waivers for states that abused the human rights of their citizens, justified by the abuser's pledge to support the United States' war on terrorism. Armenia, Azerbaijan, India, Pakistan, and Tajikistan all presented security issues that outweighed the consistent pattern of human rights abuses that had formally prevented them from being security aid recipients. However, to provide aid to the United States' "frontline" allies in the fight against terrorism, legislative mandates often had to be dismissed. Gabelnick writes, "Often these allocations of new security assistance can only be made after legal restrictions are brushed aside. Sanctions against both Pakistan and India—imposed because of their nuclear tests in 1998—were dropped immediately after September 11" (2002, 10).

Pakistan's importance for U.S. foreign policy intensified due to its geographical proximity to Afghanistan. Geography alone guaranteed Pakistan ample amounts of U.S. economic and military aid. The citizens of Pakistan still suffer horrific human rights abuses. Yet, Pakistan became a major recipient of U.S. military aid. Pakistan was one country whose human rights abuses would have risen to the level of gross systematic violations, thus disqualifying it for U.S. military aid. The U.S. policy of befriending Pakistan, in the opinion of Paula Newberg, actually exacerbated human rights abuses in Pakistan (2004). Furthermore, the United States' war on terrorism naturally favored autocratic military regimes since these regimes did not need to answer to their citizens but only to the United States' demands.[14] These nondemocratic regimes could more easily be bought off with large grants of technologically advanced military hardware. The price to be paid to secure U.S. geopolitical interests was paid by the local populations in the restrictions on democratic ideals and human rights practices. Human rights legislation that should have prevented Pakistan from receiving military aid was now waived by the president with congressional consent.

Another frontline ally in the war against terrorism, Turkey, also provides a telling example of the Bush Administration's calculated sacrifice of human rights to the benefit of the global war on terrorism. No matter how bad Turkey's human rights record is, the Bush Administration's continuing struggle in the war against terrorism not only assured Ankara's continued access to military arms, but also guaranteed additional economic and military funding. In Washington, there was a new "realization" that Turkey was actually fighting Islamic terrorists within its own territory. Turkey's protracted conflict with the Kurdistan Workers Party (PKK) was now described as a fight against terrorist fundamentalist Islamists, guaranteeing Washington's understanding of and sympathy for Turkey's human rights abuses. Overlooking Turkey's egregious human rights violations, George W. Bush "was constantly showcasing Turkey as a role model for Islamic nations" (Barkey 2004, 394). Unfortunately for the Bush Administration's war against Saddam Hussein, the Turkish Parliament, opting for future European Union acceptance over U.S. friendship, refused to allow U.S. troops to be based in Turkey for the invasion of Iraq. Although the U.S. government, particularly the Department of Defense, felt betrayed by an unfaithful ally, Turkey's strategic location, bordering Iran and Iraq, and its NATO membership ensured that it would continue to receive U.S. military equipment even if that equipment was used to mistreat the Kurdish population and eradicate political dissent. As a reward for Turkey's support in the war against terror, notwithstanding the denial of basic rights, the United States provided Turkey's foreign assistance in the form of a direct cash grant. Since this form of aid is not tied to purchases of U.S.-made commodities and services, Turkey could use the cash on anything it wanted. Direct cash transfers are an exception to the normal aid allocation process and, in the past, were generally limited to the assistance given to Israel and Egypt.

Egypt, a longtime ally and aid recipient, became increasingly important in the U.S. foreign policy. Egypt was still an authoritarian, secular, and centralized state that ruthlessly controlled the population and the growth of Islamic militancy. Denis Sullivan interviewed a State Department bureaucrat who commented that, once the human rights facts were collected for the *Country Reports*, the facts often had to be "massaged" in order to certify to Congress that the country in question was not a gross human rights abuser. Since the inception of Bush's war on terrorism, the U.S. *Country Reports* exposing Egypt's human rights abuses "eased up on Egypt after several years of criticism" (Sullivan 2004, 404). Specifically, as Sullivan reports (2004), the United States stopped censuring Egypt's use of military courts to try civilians. After Bush's decision to also use military courts in the war on terrorism, the State Department moved from condemning the use of military courts to simply critiquing Egypt's inclination to bring inappropriate cases to these courts. The human rights violations in Egypt, similar to many others perpetrated in the pro-American countries of the Middle East, were no longer an important issue when the U.S. foreign policy of Middle Eastern friendship and stability was concerned.

Human rights violations could now be justified by the global fight against terrorism, particularly if the institution of democracy and the respect for human rights would bring to power a political party that did not support U.S. hegemony and influence in the region.

A STAIN ON OUR COUNTRY'S HONOR

Past presidential administrations have been correctly criticized for supporting regimes that brutalize their citizens. But never before had the United States been responsible for violating human rights as a matter of government policy. The United States has signed and ratified international laws that prohibit the use of torture, specifically the United Nations Convention against Torture and Other Cruel, Inhuman, or Degrading Treatment or Punishment; the International Covenant on Civil and Political Rights; and the Geneva Conventions. Furthermore, U.S. domestic law outlaws the use of torture as specified in Title 18 of the federal penal code (18 U.S.C. § 2340A).[15] The ban against torture is a nonderogative protection.

The Bush Administration, directly or indirectly, intentionally or unintentionally, allowed prisoners to be held incommunicato, to be tortured or degraded for the purpose of gaining intelligence, and to be deprived of food and sanitary conditions in violation of American values, fundamental freedoms, basic rights, international law, and essential human decencies. However, the weight of the evidence, given the recently disclosed memos from the Department of Justice (August 1, 2002), indicate that the Bush Administration made torture and cruel, inhuman, and degrading treatment U.S. state policy in the war on terrorism. The Department of Justice Office of Legal Counsel's August 1, 2002, memorandum concluded that the United States could develop legal defenses for the use of "harsh interrogations" of suspected terrorists. Moreover, Bush's presidential finding (Bush 2002b) that the Geneva Conventions' protections did not apply in a war on terrorism further eroded the United States' historic moral and legal protection of foreign soldiers captured during times of conflict. Further evidence to indicate that torture had become state policy was the fact that Major General George Miller was sent from Guantánamo to Iraq to improve intelligence gathering from prisoners. Torture became an acceptable method to protect the United States from further harm by fanatical terrorists.

Alberto Gonzales, as White House counsel and later as attorney general, issued a memorandum stating that, by reclassifying detainees, the United States would have greater "flexibility" in the war against terrorism. Gonzales was of the opinion that this new type of war "renders obsolete Geneva's strict limitations on questioning of enemy prisoners" (Gonzales 2002). The methods used in Copper Green (see below), if the Geneva Conventions were applicable, might have required U.S. officials to be tried for war crimes under U.S. law. Consequently, Attorney General Ashcroft advised the White House to claim an exemption from the Geneva Conventions in order to provide U.S. officials with a defense against charges of torture or other actions in violation of the conventions (Ashcroft 2002). In addition, the Department of Defense determined, in contradiction to 200 years of constitutional history, that the president as commander in chief was not bound by principles of law, treaties, or the Constitution regarding the treatment of detainees. The Pentagon maintained this assertion because it claimed that the president had the power to set aside laws during wartime under the guise of military necessity or self-defense (United States, Department of Defense 2003).

By devising a new classification of detainees, "unlawful combatants," the Bush Administration was able to deny individuals their rights under the Geneva Conventions and in U.S. law. Rumsfeld claimed that "unlawful combatants do not have any rights under the Geneva Conventions" (as reported in Whitlock 2003). By denying the detainees the claim of prisoner of war (POW) status, the protections offered to POWs under the Geneva Convention simply did not come into play. Furthermore, by classifying detainees, either foreign or U.S. citizens, as unlawful combatants, the government denied them rights afforded by U.S. law, such as the right to counsel and the right to a speedy trial. Nevertheless, the Bush Administration was claiming a state's right under the Geneva Conventions. Since the detainees were still referred to as "combatants," they could be held until the "cessation of active hostilities," as the Geneva Conventions stipulated. At the same time, the Bush Administration admitted that the war against terrorism would be a long-enduring effort.

According to investigative reporter Seymour Hersh, the policy of using torture and inhuman treatment to soften up prisoners for more efficient interrogation was given the code name Copper Green. "Copper Green," Hersh writes, "encouraged physical coercion and sexual humiliation of Iraqi prisoners in an effort to generate more intelligence about the growing insurgency in Iraq" (Hersh 2004). Hersh goes on to say that, because the war was going badly and insurgent activity was increasing, further causing U.S. and Iraqi deaths, the American public's support for the war was beginning to fade. Then, "the solution, endorsed by Rumsfeld and carried out by Undersecretary of Defense for Intelligence Stephen Cambone, was to get tough with those Iraqis in the army prison system who were suspected of being insurgents" by using interrogation methods already in place in Guantánamo, such as sleep deprivation, exposure to extremes of cold and heat, and shackling prisoners in uncomfortable "stress positions" for long durations of time (Hersh 2004). Regrettably, the executive branch believed that the pain inflicted by these methods did not constitute torture because the pain was not severe or acute enough to cause death, organ failure, or permanent injury. The administration claimed that mental pain and suffering did not amount to torture unless it "results in significant psychological harm of significant duration, e.g. lasting for months or even years" (United States, Department of Justice 2002). However, the memo also stated that mind-altering drugs could be used. The claims that these methods did not constitute torture were refuted by the human rights nongovernmental organization (NGO) Physicians for Human Rights. Physicians for Human Rights reported that sleep deprivation can result in psychosis, while deprivation of sensory stimulation can produce severe anxiety and hallucinations as well as other psychotic reactions (2004). These interrogation methods, even if not legally defined as torture, certainly constitute cruel, inhuman, and degrading treatment.

By declaring not only that the Geneva Conventions are obsolete in a war against terror but also that the president as commander in chief is not bound by the rules of war or even by U.S. law, and by inventing a new classification of detainees, that of unlawful enemy combatants, the Bush Administration created an environment where soldiers and interrogators believed they were outside the law or beyond the confines of human decency. The horrifying pictures of misconduct and brutality inflicted on the prisoners of Abu Ghraib in Iraq bear witness to this. It was reported that "the abuses took place, the files show, in a chaotic and dangerous environment made even more so by the constant pressure from Washington to squeeze intelligence from detainees" (Pound and Roane 2004).

These methods of torture or cruel and inhumane treatment were made possible by the shroud of secrecy that the administration claimed was vital in the war against terror. But the Bush Administration is accused of an equally repellent practice, that of renditions to countries known for or suspected of using torture. Suspected terrorists were sent to third countries to undergo interrogation methods that were not allowed or acceptable by U.S. courts and the American population. The United States transferred captured suspected terrorists, without extradition proceedings, to a third country (particularly Yemen, Syria, or Egypt), where they were tortured for information. Legislation for the outsourcing of torture was introduced by the speaker of the House of Representatives, Dennis Hastert (R-IL), in the 9/11 Recommendations Implementation Act of 2004 (H.R. 10). Initially, Section 3032 of this legislation was to authorize the use of extraordinary rendition, the transfer of suspected terrorists to countries known to practice torture as a method of interrogation, unless the proposed deportee could show clear and convincing evidence that she or he would be tortured. Furthermore, the legislation would require the Secretary of Homeland Security to modify the terms of the UN Convention Against Torture and Other Forms of Cruel, Inhuman, or Degrading Treatment or Punishment to exclude suspected terrorists from the treaty's protections. Section 3032 was ultimately removed from the legislation.[16]

Still, evidence recently came to light that the CIA also used "phantom" prisons to incarcerate and interrogate "ghost" prisoners in Eastern Europe.[17] The nameless, faceless prisoners held in the secret detention facilities are believed to be senior leaders in the al Qaeda terrorist movement. The *Washington Post* reported that the location of these "black sites," set up following the September 11 terrorist attacks, were known only to a small number of top U.S. government officials (Whitlock 2005).[18] Concerns for the treatment of these prisoners intensified because Vice President Dick Cheney and CIA Director Porter Goss petitioned the U.S. Senate to exempt CIA employees from Senator John McCain's (R-AZ) amendment barring torture and other cruel, inhuman, and degrading treatment of any detainee in U.S. custody or control anywhere in the world.[19] The CIA was already implicated in the abuses resulting in the deaths at Abu Ghraib and at the Bagram Air Base in Afghanistan.

The use of offshore prisons, the failure to name detainees, the holding of prisoners in undisclosed locations, and the additional refusal of Red Cross access to prisons permitted the United States to conceal its illegal and immoral treatment of the detainees in the war on terror. Unknown persons in unknown locations cannot be monitored by human rights organizations. Furthermore, as indicated above, any alleged terrorist was refused judicial protections. The U.S. government believed that judicial review of its activities of renditions and refouling (the forceful repatriation) of terrorists would "jeopardize the intelligence, foreign policy, and national security interests of the United States" (quoted in Human Rights Watch 2005, 35).

CONCLUSION

Regrettably, the Bush Administration's claim to extend democracy globally, and particularly to the Middle East, resulted in discarding or circumventing the U.S. Constitution, the Geneva Conventions, and human rights treaties and obligations that, at one time, protected Americans and foreign citizens from governmental abuses of power. Bush was and still is committed to a military solution to the problem of terrorism. Not only did Bush violate international law, but he also made a mockery of U.S. law in his failure to provide legal protections to terrorist suspects and in his refusal to involve the judicial branch in their lawful prosecution. With the use of indefinite detentions, claims of "special" legal status for prisoners, the holding of prisoners in undisclosed locations,[20] the creation of military tribunals, and the use of "stress and duress" interrogating techniques, Bush eliminated any hope of incorporating a principle of morality and human rights in U.S. foreign policy.

Bush's actions in the aftermath of 9/11 belied his faint attempt of deploying a rhetoric of human rights and fundamental freedoms. President George W. Bush's 2002 State of the Union Address had claimed,

America will lead by defending liberty and justice because they are right and true and unchanging for all people everywhere. . . . America will always stand firm for the non-negotiable demands of human dignity: the rule of law; limits on the power of the state; respect for women; private property; free speech; equal justice; and religious tolerance. (Bush 2002a)

However, by concentrating the governmental power in the executive branch, the Bush Administration could reign freely without judicial review, congressional interference, or public oversight. Free speech, dissent, and peaceful protest were labeled unpatriotic and treacherous. Americans availing themselves of their civil liberties, as a group of scholars and academics have carefully documented, could be surveilled, arrested, and jailed (Brown 2003).

Thus, in the early years of the twenty-first century, the paradoxes that had shaped and given meaning to the United States' human rights policy in the previous decades were now callously resolved. Bush's global crusade against an amorphous evil eliminated the rule of law in the United States, restricted human rights protections for the American people, authorized the torture of foreign citizens, allied the United States with undemocratic regimes, and openly ignored U.S. legislation banning the disbursement of foreign aid to human rights-abusing regimes. Sadly, U.S. human rights policy was now the calculated victim of George W. Bush's war against terror. The victimization of U.S. human rights policy was accomplished with little or no opposition from, and at times with the genuine support of, Congress, the American public, and the media.

CHAPTER 8

Conclusion: Paradox Lost?

The evolution of the United States' human rights policy can best be understood as a succession of paradoxes and not as a simple linear advancement. Yet, far from immobilizing the progression of a functioning human rights policy, these paradoxes have actually shaped human rights foreign policy into what it is today. As the result of several defining paradoxes since its inception in the 1970s, U.S. human rights policy today is a largely inconsistent body of policies, legislations, actions, and rhetorics characterized by failures in certain domains and successes in others. At least, this is what it was, for better or worse, until it was effectively stopped by George W. Bush's forceful erasure of the working paradoxes in the aftermath of 9/11.

Throughout most of the history of U.S. human rights policy, presidents have been restrained by the Constitution, an active Congress, an entrenched bureaucracy, and a vocal civil society. As we have seen, each of these foreign policy actors has been important in the making of U.S. human rights policy. Yet, Congress perhaps holds a more significant role, as it was thanks to Congress that the crucial legislations that allowed human rights policy to exist in words, if not in deeds, appeared during the Nixon Administration. Until the post-September 11 era, Congress often continued to act as the main impetus for U.S. human rights policy by passing additional legislations and earmarking foreign assistance programs. When the president sought to circumvent the law (for example, Sections 116 and 502B of the Foreign Assistance Act), Congress chose to enact country-specific legislation to deny military aid and arms sales on human rights grounds, or it decided to earmark entire foreign aid packages.

During the Nixon Administration, Congress passed legislation that placed restrictions on the allocation of foreign aid to countries that consistently violated the human rights of their citizens. Thus, Congress under Nixon laid the foundation for the United States' human rights policy and, in a sense, for all the successive paradoxes. As we saw, Congress jumpstarted the first paradox by developing a human rights policy at a time when the Nixon Administration's imperial policies made it look like human rights could never be part of U.S. foreign policy. At the same time, though, Congress also failed to fully or determinedly implement its bequest to humanity over the years. Consequently, despite its initially crucial role, Congress' stimulus for human rights protection would remain erratic and inconsistent. Congress would pass legislation forbidding foreign aid to countries that systematically violate human rights, while at the same time it would accept, often without question, a presidential finding or waiver allowing foreign aid to be granted to those same human rights-abusing countries.

On the executive side, presidential inconsistency and inability were often the key components of a wavering human rights policy over the years. Even when a president appeared to honestly attempt to implement the congressionally imposed pro-human rights policies (for example, the Carter Administration), the policies could still end up being disappointments, often as a result of opposing ideologies or differing foreign policy goals among bureaucratic actors, or simply because of bureaucratic conflict. On the part of the Executive, a coherent and effective human rights policy would often become the casualty of the foreign policy bureaucracy backbiting between various presidential advisors, within the Department of State, or between departments. Thus, human rights foreign policy outcomes (when there were any) were often the result of rather haphazard bureaucratic cooperation and rivalries rather than the direct product of a clear coordination between congressional legislations and presidential directives. Effective and successful human rights policies over the years have sometimes depended on cooperation between Congress and the executive branch, with the support of nongovernmental organizations (NGOs) and the American public. Yet, more often than not, they have been the result of the existing and perhaps inherent tensions between these main foreign policy-making protagonists.

An overview of the last thirty years of U.S. foreign policy making reveals that a president cannot simply dispose of congressional mandates that he disagrees with, particularly if the mandate is supported by the public. This explains that, despite some presidents' overt dislike or neglect for human rights constraints (Nixon and Reagan, in particular), human rights remained a core moral value because, at least in the abstract, the American public was still highly committed to the idea of the United

States as a protector and promoter of human rights. Moreover, beginning in the 1980s, NGOs, interest groups, and public opinion started to play an important role in foreign policy decision making. These groups often pressured the Executive and Congress through lobbying, voting, and funding in order to attain their objectives. Thus, despite some of the presidents' personal agendas and Congress' own motivations vis-à-vis the presidency, the issue of human rights still had to be a part of foreign policy strategies and rhetorics.

As discussed in chapter 1, foreign policy is traditionally conducted by an elite group of congressional leaders, the president and his advisors, and the bureaucracy, but with little public input. However, with the reduction in classical foreign policy threats associated with the post-Cold War era and the emergence of NGOs, this framework for foreign policy making was altered. Since the end of the Cold War, human rights advocates have increasingly found themselves pitted against more powerful economic and business interests groups for control over U.S. foreign policy. In this context, as was seen during the Clinton Administration in particular, more tensions would arise, often relegating human rights to a secondary place, particularly if civil society was split on the direction of U.S. foreign policy.

With the terrorist attacks of September 11, 2001, the long-established and time-honored adversarial system (Congress versus the Executive) of foreign policy making that led to many of the defining paradoxes for human rights in U.S. foreign policy broke down. As was shown, U.S. human rights policy became the casualty of yet another imperialist president who chose to run U.S. foreign policy by executive fiat. But, unlike Nixon who had to contend with a Congress that was unwilling to give up on human rights, George W. Bush's own imperial presidency was without any apparent tension within the foreign policy-making process. Bush's grab of power was made possible by a fearful public, a surrendering Congress, an obedient bureaucracy, and a hesitant judiciary. As was argued in chapter 7, the global crusade of good versus evil developed by Bush was used to justify all U.S. actions undertaken to exterminate terrorists and their sympathizers, even if the direct costs of such actions were the negation of the Constitution and the sacrifice of both domestic and international human rights to imperialist politics.

Balancing human rights and national security is a complicated and challenging matter. Advocates of power politics have often claimed that, in order to secure U.S. national interests in an increasingly unstable world, the United States has to abandon human rights considerations to pursue more urgent goals. On the other hand, human rights supporters have continued to believe that the use or abuse of U.S. foreign aid is central to the security interests of the United States. As Human Rights Watch has concluded with regard to recent U.S. foreign policy actions,

[W]hen the United States disregards human rights, it undermines that human rights culture and thus sabotages one of the most important tools for dissuading potential terrorists. Instead, U.S. abuses have provided a new rallying cry for terrorist recruiters, and the pictures from Abu Ghraib have become the recruiting posters for Terrorism, Inc. (Human Rights Watch 2005)

The reinstatement of U.S. human rights policy after the George W. Bush Administration's destruction of it (and of its paradoxical development over the past thirty years) will be a difficult and complex endeavor. To reestablish a U.S. human rights policy abandoned in the war on terror will require the combined efforts of a renewed Congress and a reinvigorated civil society. Congress and the American public must once again become concerned over the rampant violations of human rights directly or indirectly associated with U.S. foreign policy. The American tradition of human rights and morality as foundations for U.S. foreign policy is as important today, if not more, as it was during Nixon's imperial presidency.

Once again, with the war on terror, the George W. Bush Administration appears to have resolved the paradoxes inherent in U.S. human rights policy since its creation in the 1970s. But this forceful resolution of the paradoxes and tensions that make U.S. human rights foreign policy is disheartening. The United States has now become, by many accounts, a blatant human rights abuser.[1] It is morally difficult for the United States to lead a crusade against evil while it detains over 50,000 people, many of them held incognito and without judicial review or human rights protections.

Just as disturbingly, the United States' human rights violations have been used as a justification by many governments throughout the world to repress their own citizens. The United States' moral global leadership, which at one time was used to promote and protect human rights, has taken a gloomy turn. Recently, the Lawyers Committee for Human Rights has reported that "in lowering its own human rights standards, the United States has encouraged other governments, though often inadvertently, to lower the standards of human rights around the world" (2003). A case in point was in 2002, when Liberian President Charles Taylor, an infamously repressive dictator, immediately declared that his opponents were "illegal combatants" against his regime and that they would be tried in military courts for terrorism (Human Rights Watch 2002a).

Yet, there may be one more paradox on the horizon. Perhaps the most vital paradox today is to be found in both local and global anti-American imperialism movements. Bush's overt rejection of human rights norms may ironically reinvigorate a global acceptance and protection of human rights, particularly if opposition to human rights violations starts to be perceived as a way of opposing the United States' global power. The revelations of torture and ill treatment in the Abu Ghraib prison not only fueled anti-American sentiments throughout the world, but also publicized notions of internationally protected human rights and of the illegality of torture and cruel and inhuman treatment. There is now extensive international condemnation of the U.S. government's use of torture and other abusive techniques. In effect, the world has started to rally against the United States in condemnation of human rights abuses. Paradoxically, the United States' blatant violation of human rights norms today may be creating a human rights culture in some foreign countries that do not subscribe to U.S. policies. Even in countries where human rights generally are not respected, there is a new awareness and understanding of human rights.[2] An emergent human rights culture, as a "vehicle through which a particular set of shared beliefs and understandings— human rights norms—take root in and influence a population" (Mertus 2004, 212), can be used by people to demand better, fairer, and more equal treatment from their governments. The contemporary evidence, since the beginning of the war in Iraq, of the use of human rights language and of the growing acceptance of universal human rights norms could lead to a credible global human rights culture with genuine human rights protections.

Unfortunately, there has yet to be a strong domestic response to the Bush Administration's war on human rights. The emerging human rights culture has not, as of 2005, had a large impact on the general American public. As witnessed in the 2004 presidential electoral campaign, for example, criticism of Bush's human rights policy by his opposition has wavered between mild rebukes and timid supportive critiques. With the immediate post-Iraq invasion polls of Bush's foreign policy performance indicating a favorable opinion, it is not surprising to understand how the American public believed that America's war on terror was a fight for human rights and freedom. In 2004, over half of Americans still believed that Saddam Hussein had close ties with the terrorists that destroyed the towers at the World Trade Center, and still trusted that further searching would uncover Iraq's weapons of mass destruction (WMDs). According to the Pew Charitable Trusts' survey, 53 percent of Americans polled said that going to war in Iraq was the right thing to do, and 52 percent continued to think that the mission was going well (Pew Charitable Trusts 2004). Even in the face of visual media evidence that the United States had tortured and ill treated the prisoners (held without trial or other judicial proceedings) at Abu Ghraib, the American public could not be dissuaded from the belief that Bush was indeed to be "identified as a guardian of these sacred American values [human rights and freedom]" (White and Zogby 2004, 84) and was making the world safer. As of April 2006, though, the tide appears to be turning. Sixty-two percent of Americans surveyed by a *Washington Post-ABC News* poll indicated that they disapproved of the situation in Iraq and six out of ten were unhappy with Bush's performance on the job (*Washington Post*, 2006). It seems that the American public is tiring of the costs, both in blood and in treasury, of Bush's failed, militarily imposed democracy in Iraq.

However, and perhaps fortunately, U.S. human rights policy is sheltered by an unwieldy bureaucracy with cumbersome procedures and inertia. Entrenched bureaucratic interests may actively resist modification of both the human rights laws themselves and the implemental structure the laws created (such as the Bureau of Democracy, Human Rights, and Labor). This means that, even today under Bush, there are still laws, and there are still Foreign Service officers with a vested interest in respecting those laws and maintaining a human rights culture within the U.S. government. The slow, obdurate, immovable bureaucracy of the Department of State, as indicated by its performance under the Reagan Administration, may ironically be the best caretaker of U.S. human rights policy.

Far from making America and the world safer, today's repudiation of human rights in U.S. foreign policy has paradoxically made America's strategic position weaker by alienating its allies and generating new enemies. The United States' human rights abuses in Guantánamo and Abu Ghraib have sadly become recruiting billboards for those who wish to harm America. The crucial question left for contemporary U.S. government bureaucrats, NGOs, the media, the U.S. Congress, and the American public to answer is how to reestablish a moral foundation for U.S. foreign policy.

NOTES

INTRODUCTION

1. American exceptionalism is the belief that the United States is a uniquely great nation with a divine mission to lead the world to democracy and freedom. Therefore, due to America's exceptional calling, it is not necessarily bound by international norms and is often required to undertake unilateral missions.

2. During the Cold War, the United States' foreign policy was dominated by a strategy of containment. To block Soviet expansion, it was argued, required a policy of "long-term, patient but firm and vigilant containment of Russian expansive tendencies" (Mr. X 1947).

CHAPTER 1

1. For example, in 1778, the United States signed the Treaty of Alliance with the French government binding the two countries in mutual aid against the British "from the present time and forever" (Article 11). As a result, the United States secured an ally in their fight for independence. Nevertheless, in 1793, with the outbreak of yet another conflict between France and Great Britain, the United States quickly issued a Neutrality Proclamation, averting the possibility that the French government would require the United States to honor the terms of the Treaty of Alliance. In Machiavellian fashion, if treachery, breaches of faith, and breaches of fair dealings are required to further the goals of the state, so be it.

2. The Federalist Papers were a series of eighty-five articles written by Alexander Hamilton, James Madison and John Jay. These articles were published in several leading journals and newspapers of the day in an effort to garner support for the proposed U.S. Constitution. The historical documents are archived at the Library of Congress but can be found in any number of law libraries or Web sites.

3. In 1998, the name "MFN" was changed to "Normal Trade Relations" (NTR). The new name better reflects current trading practices since most states have most favored trade status. Only a few "rogue states" have been refused this normal trade relationship. Countries with MFN or NTR status are subject to the lowest tariff rates for products entering into the United States.

4. The budgetary process for foreign aid is a two-step procedure. First, the authorizing committees of the House Foreign Affairs and the Senate Foreign Relations Committees are responsible for determining the ceiling level of the budget for the next fiscal year. In the meantime, the appropriations committees of the House and the Senate determine the amount each nation, program, and project will receive. The authorization committees of the Senate and the House of Representatives have tended, over the years, to evade their responsibilities for the budgetary procedure concerning foreign aid. For example, during the 1980s, the authorization

committees were able to pass only two authorizing bills (1981 and 1985). Hence, foreign aid authorization, since the 1970s, has often been the result of continuing resolutions, where foreign aid is consolidated with other federal programs into one large sum. Normally, the second step in the budgetary process, after authorization, is the move to appropriate the funds to different countries and programs. Since foreign aid is the consequence of a continuing resolution, the amount that was authorized previously is still authorized. The appropriation committees have become powerful participants in the foreign policy process as they determine how much each nation will receive in U.S. foreign aid.

5. With the general decline in U.S. foreign aid (until the George W. Bush Administration, at least, when U.S. foreign aid jumped to well over $30 billion to fund Iraq's reconstruction and the Millennium Account), the State Department has attempted to gain greater control over these resources to further its foreign policy objectives. The State Department has spearheaded efforts to merge USAID with the State Department. USAID has opposed these efforts, believing that a merger would weaken its development mission. To date, USAID has remained a semiautonomous agency, but USAID's administrator has been placed "under the direct authority and foreign policy guidance of the secretary of state" (quoted in Lancaster 2000, 39).

6. The Defense Security Cooperation Agency (DSCA) is a subordinate unit under International Security Affairs of the Department of Defense (DOD). The director of DSCA is appointed by the undersecretary of defense for policy, and he or she reports to the assistant secretary of defense for international security affairs. Prior to 1998, DSCA was called the Defense Security Assistance Agency (DSAA). The name change reflects the additional responsibilities assumed by the unit. DSCA also manages DOD's Humanitarian Assistance and Demining programs.

7. The U.S. Department of the Treasury reports that, in fiscal year 2001, the United States provided $1.1 billion in new funding to the Multilateral Development Banks, while U.S. bilateral economic assistance for that same year totaled $7.8 billion (United States, Department of the Treasury 2003).

8. Today, nearly all foreign aid, both economic and military aid, is in the form of outright grants. In 2004, less than 1 percent of U.S. foreign assistance was in the form of loans that would need to be paid back to the U.S. government (Tarnoff and Nowels 2004).

9. The Peace Corps is provided under economic aid, but the amount is relatively small: only $244 million worldwide in 2000.

10. The three types of Economic Support Fund (ESF) are as follows:

1. Commodity Import Program (CIP): for the importation of U.S. commodities (half of which must be shipped via U.S. flagged vessels);
2. development aid for specific political/economic programs; and
3. balance of payments support (in the form of cash payments—this is the largest component of ESF): the majority of cash aid goes to Israel, less to Egypt. Although recipients are not supposed to use the cash for direct military purposes, there is an exception for Israel.

11. This funding is listed as "economic aid" since its purpose is to promote political and economic stability in recipient countries to further U.S. political and security interests. ESF is aid given for diplomatic, security, or political purposes, and includes the sale or grant of military arms and equipment.

12. In the year 1994, ESF included $1.4 billion in cash payments ($1.2 billion of which went to Israel), $200,000 in Commodity Import Program funds, and $547,000 in project aid (totaling just over $2.1 billion). Presidents like ESF because of its great flexibility and lack of accountability. ESF can be more easily given to human rights–abusing regimes since it is considered economic assistance and, therefore, it is less likely to be examined by Congress. Furthermore, as economic assistance it suffers fewer congressional earmarks, restrictions, or conditionalities.

13. Foreign Military Financing (FMF), previously known as the Foreign Military Sales (FMS), was once classified under the Military Assistance Program (MAP).

14. Freedom House has regularly given Pakistan's political freedoms a score of 7, the worst possible ranking (2006). Even the U.S. State Department's *Country Report on Human Rights*

Practices, 1999 for Pakistan acknowledges that "the police committed extrajudicial killings. The extrajudicial killing of criminal suspects, often in the form of deaths in police custody or staged encounters in which police shoot and kill the suspects, is common" (United States, Department of State 1999).

15. Aung San Suu Kyi, 1991 recipient of the Nobel Peace Prize, believes that the justifications of culture and development simply "serve as pretexts for resisting calls for democracy and human rights" (1995, 11). The culture, community, and value systems of the poor and the politically disenfranchised, in her opinion, are different from those of people who have access to power and wealth. The elites' call for cultural relativism is an attempt to "block the aspirations of peoples for democratic institutions and human rights" (1995, 11).

CHAPTER 2

1. The term "imperial presidency" refers to a presidential administration where the president has overstepped his constitutional authority and powers by seizing the rights and prerogatives of the other branches of government. The delicate balance of shared power between the Executive and Congress envisioned by the Founding Fathers was not toppled by a series of power-mad presidents. Congress willingly relinquished its power to the president. Presidential historian Arthur Schlesinger writes, "The Presidency had not stolen its power; rather Congress had surrendered it out of fear of responsibility and recognition of incapacity" (1973, 253).

2. The War Powers Act ended the president's ability to wage secret wars or covert security operations without any congressional consent. Prior to the Budget Reform Act of 1974, presidents had refused to spend money appropriated by Congress for programs they did not approve of, thereby thwarting the clear will of Congress. The Budget Reform Act still allows the president to impound the funds, but he has to notify Congress of his actions. Congress then has the power to pass a resolution forcing the president to spend the money Congress allocated for the program. The Case Act was the legislative response to secret executive agreements. The Case Act requires the secretary of state to give Congress a copy of the text of an executive agreement within sixty days. Because Nixon and Ford failed to comply with the terms of the Case Act, Congress passed additional legislation in 1977 to require any department or agency of the U.S. government affected by or having knowledge of the executive agreement to transmit the text of the agreement to the Department of State within twenty days.

3. Lars Schoultz (1981) pioneered the use of statistical measures in the field of human rights and foreign aid. To judge the human rights situation in a country, Schoultz relied on the expert testimony of human rights specialists who chose to answer his survey. Later studies eliminate the arbitrary nature of using a transitory group of experts who would undoubtedly vary in level of experience and training. For a critique and appraisal of the quantitative studies on human rights and foreign aid, see Poe (1990).

4. El Salvador is a prime example of the danger of providing military aid to an ineffectual civilian government. The Reagan Administration supplied the Salvadoran military with billions of dollars' worth of security assistance in its attempt to suppress a left-wing insurgency that threatened the brutal, military-controlled dictatorship. The result was the deaths of over 80,000 Salvadorans during the eight years of Reagan's presidency.

5. Consequently, these items could be legally sent to the Contras even after Congress cut off all military aid to the Nicaraguan rebels.

6. Although economic assistance is believed by the American public to be development aid to help the poor, the majority of economic aid is actually Economic Support Funds (ESFs). As explained in chapter 1, ESF, which accounts for one-half of economic assistance, is financial assistance for budget support. This is done to encourage recipient countries to use their own resources to build up their defense infrastructures. It is given for political and strategic reasons, not humanitarian ones. Development assistance—aid intended to improve the quality of life of the poor—accounts for only about a third of all economic assistance.

7. The system of "usual market requirements" (UMR) requires recipient countries to maintain previous levels of commercial imports of food before food aid is provided by the United

States. UMRs are calculated by averaging a country's commercial food imports for the past five years while considering the following conditions:

1. a substantial change in production in relation to consumption of the commodity concerned in the recipient country;
2. evidence of a significant trend during the reference period in the commercial imports of the commodity concerned by the recipient country;
3. a substantial trend in the balance of payments or general economic position;
4. any exceptional features affecting the representativeness of the reference period;
5. any other consideration that the government may raise in its request. (As quoted from Singer, Wood and Jennings 1987, 58–59)

Although the UMR system is used to protect the interests of the donor state, it is flexible enough to prevent donors from dumping surplus agricultural products onto foreign markets. The flooding of developing countries' markets with cheap U.S. foodstuffs reduces domestic producers' prices and thereby lowers indigenous farmers' profits (Singer, Wood, and Jennings 1987, 40).

8. The Ford Administration opposed the Jackson-Vanik Amendment (402, 19 U.S.C. &2432, Supp.V. 1975), claiming that more could be achieved through quiet diplomacy. In the immediate aftermath of the Nixon Administration, Congress greeted any executive appeal to quiet diplomacy as disingenuous. Quiet diplomacy, by its very nature, is difficult to monitor and cannot be verified. Regrettably, during the Kissinger era, quiet diplomacy was a code word for neglecting or overlooking human rights considerations.

9. The State Department is basically divided into two types of bureaus: regional bureaus and functional bureaus. Regional bureaus have a geographical focus, while functional bureaus are concerned with specific issues on a worldwide basis. Many believe that the real power in the State Department lies within the regional bureaus of the Foreign Service since they have more accurate detailed information on specific countries or regions. Functional bureaus simply lack access to country information and therefore cannot compete with the regional bureaus for political clout. See chapter 1 for a more detailed description of the organization of the State Department.

10. Prior to that time, there was a single human rights officer in the executive bureaucracy. This officer was banished to an obscure office in the State Department and deprived of operating resources or access to the president (Cohen 1979).

11. The bureau's name would change to the Bureau of Democracy, Human Rights and Labor during the Clinton Administration, thus indicating a refocus or redirection from human rights to democratic enlargement and labor rights.

CHAPTER 3

1. The understanding that supporting repressive dictators could prove disadvantageous to the United States' long-term interests was well understood by human rights scholars. For example, in 1979, prior to the Iran Hostage Crisis, Roberta Cohen wrote,

In the case of Iran, planners should seriously question whether U.S. security interests will be served by the provision of massive weapons to a 'one-bullet' dictatorship in which domestic opposition is growing. Short-run gains arising from association with repressive regimes should be appraised constantly in light of long-term losses from such association. (1979, 229)

2. There could be many reasons for approving security aid, such as the fact that the country is not a gross violator of human rights, that it is experiencing improving human rights conditions, or that it is vital to U.S. national interests. Likewise, there are several reasons why security assistance can be denied: the country could be a gross violator of human rights, or the country requested aid that the United States viewed as inappropriate.

3. Not only did Indonesia's President Suharto share the United States' fear of the spread of communism, but Indonesia was an exporter of petroleum. Indonesia did not participate in the OPEC oil embargo during the 1970s, thus cementing its friendship to the Carter

Administration. Indonesian oil exports are important for both the United States and Indonesia. As a matter of fact, "the United States accounts for the bulk of Indonesia oil investment (about 86%) and an increasing amount (about 11%) of our crude oil imports are from Indonesia" (Burr and Evans 2001).

4. Portugal colonized East Timor several hundred years prior to East Timor's subjection to Indonesia. In 1974, a military coup deposed Portugal's authoritarian regime. The new government in Lisbon decided to dismantle Portugal's colonial empire. The Indonesian government attempted to negotiate for control over the population and territory of East Timor, annexing it as Indonesia's twenty-seventh province. The 600,000 people of East Timor, on the other hand, preferred independence. East Timor collapsed into a protracted war for independence and self-determination. It is believed that from the December 1975 invasion and subjugation of East Timor to its ultimate independence, over 200,000 people have died and several hundreds of thousands more have been unlawfully jailed.

5. Section 116 of the Foreign Assistance Act allows U.S. economic aid to be given to even the worst human rights–abusing governments if the aid is used to directly benefit the poor and needy. It becomes a loophole because USAID depicts virtually all of its programs as benefiting the underprivileged. Very few USAID programs fail to be funded, and many are not even scrutinized to determine their human rights consequences.

6. Many scholars and political analysts believe that the voluntary withdrawal of loan consideration is as effective as a negative U.S. vote. The country in question understands that its human rights situation is internationally known and has significant consequences.

7. As a functional bureau, HA is headed by an assistant secretary of state who is assisted by a senior deputy assistant secretary and a deputy assistant secretary, along with several administrative assistants and advisors.

8. The consequences of opposing human rights' dominance of foreign relations were exemplified by the Todman case. After delivering a speech criticizing the overriding focus on human rights in U.S. international relations, Terence Todman, assistant secretary for inter-American affairs, was removed from office and named ambassador to Spain. The dismissal of Todman was not lost on other bureaucrats.

9. S. Cohen (1982) recounts that the Bureau for East Asia claimed that the reports of thousands of Indonesian deaths were highly exaggerated. The bureau admitted that there were, unfortunately, a few cases of abuse committed by the Indonesian Army. It is well established, by multiple independent and reputable sources, that by 1982 more than 100,000 Timorese were murdered by the Indonesian Army. The Bureau for East Asia did not simply miscount or misinterpret the information. In a classic case of clientism, the Bureau for East Asia lied to the American people, the president, and Congress.

10. S. Cohen (1982) provides an instructive example of the State Department's tendency to exaggerate claims of human rights improvements. The Bureau of the Near East reported that the human rights abuses in Iran were improving and that it ought to be granted security assistance. The shah was considering ending his regime's use of torture and political imprisonment, and granting power to a civilian, democratically elected parliament. While the shah was contemplating this new plan, he continued torturing and imprisoning political dissidents. In addition, the elections were rigged. Needless to say, the Iranian Revolution came as a complete surprise to the American people, the president, and Congress.

11. Carter's decision to use Afghanistan as the line in the sand that the Soviets may not cross was curious. Afghanistan was not considered strategically significant and was already a Soviet client state prior to the Soviet invasion. Skidmore (1993) believes that the Carter Doctrine was merely an attempt by a beleaguered president to save his presidency.

12. With the overwhelming political and financial power of the Western democracies, the intent of this provision is to ensure that all needy countries can have access to funding to develop economically and thus to improve the welfare of their citizens, without any regard to a state's political or ideological leanings.

13. 22 U.S.C. 2304(a)(2) and (e).

14. Although Mower (1987) does report that, in these "opposed" votes, the United States opposed 34 percent of the loans under consideration for leftist countries and 31 percent of

those for rightist countries, he believes that this one example may indicate some consistency of opposition for human rights violators.

15. Carter was frequently criticized for being an "amateur" in foreign policy, with no understanding of the national interest, geopolitical realities, and military strategy. Newmann believes that the failure of Carter's foreign policy can be partially attributed to "the clash between Vance's idealism and Brzezinski's realism" (2001, fn. 9). Brzezinski's power in the foreign policy decision-making process took place at the expense of Vance's authority.

CHAPTER 4

1. A Gallup poll asked a group of U.S. citizens to indicate how important they believed promoting and defending human rights in other countries was as a U.S. foreign policy goal. In 1978, 79 percent of those responding declared that promoting and defending human rights in other countries was somewhat to very important. By 1986, this number reached 87 percent (Geyer and Shapiro 1988).

2. Paul Kowert explains that Reagan's decision making involved a small group of "ideologically and politically homogeneous staff" (2002, 53). Reagan chose his staff based on their loyalty and anticommunist posture. These advisors, ideologically attuned to Reagan's anticommunist crusade, would implement the policy and formulate the particulars, often without disturbing the president.

3. Farer (2004) reports that soon after Reagan's inauguration, the State Department's ambassadorial corps was purged of pro–human rights diplomats by General Alexander Haig, Reagan's first secretary of state.

4. The Reagan Administration explained that

> the idea of economic and social rights is easily abused by repressive governments which claim that they promote human rights even though they deny their citizens the basic rights to the integrity of the person as well as civil and political rights. (United States, Department of State 1982, 6)

5. Abuses that violate the integrity of the person include nonjudicial execution, torture, forced disappearance, arbitrary imprisonment, or discrimination based on political or religious beliefs. Crelinsten and Schmid (1995) refer to the violation of physical integrity rights as the politics of pain for social control.

6. Even using the redefined concept of human rights, that is, democracy, Reagan's pet countries in Central America still fell short of this human right. Many were military dictatorships or civilian governments controlled by the military. Additionally, in Nicaragua, the Contras did not have a democratic history, and therefore no level of funding or rhetorical hyperbole could restore Nicaraguan democracy.

7. Several joint publications from Americas Watch, Helsinki Watch, and the Lawyers Committee for Human Rights reported that, after monitoring and analyzing the Reagan Administration's compliance with human rights law, Reagan "openly disregarded many of the laws governing human rights policy" (1982, 6); was found to "ignore, redefine, veto or defy, U.S. laws governing human rights policy" (1984, 6); and "continued to flaunt, circumvent, or bend the meaning of a number of human rights laws to serve its political objectives" (1986, 8).

8. The reality in Central America disproves Kirkpatrick's theory. Although not free of human rights abuses, the left-leaning Sandinista government was far less brutal than what the United States claimed. Human Rights Watch declares that "U.S. pronouncements on human rights exaggerated and distorted the real human rights violations of the Sandinista regime, and exculpated those of the U.S.-supported insurgents, known as the *contras*" (Human Rights Watch 1989). The Sandinistas imposed emergency laws, banned dissent and free speech, imposed censorship, and prevented political opposition. In contrast, the right-wing authoritarian military government of El Salvador was culpable for the deaths of at least 70,000 citizens, the creation of nearly three-quarters of a million refugees, and more than 30,000 disappeared persons (McWilliams and Piotrowski 1997; Gibb 2002). The Reagan Administration, in its

fight against communism, approved the United States' military aid and training used to kill these people.

9. "Quiet diplomacy" is defined as "behind-the-scenes" diplomacy, using friendly persuasion rather than public condemnation or the cutting of aid allocations.

10. The Committee of Santa Fe was composed of L. Francis Bouchey, Roger W. Fontaine, David C. Jordan, Gordon Sumner, and Lewis Tambs. Under Reagan, Fontaine became a National Security Council advisor for Latin American affairs, Sumner became a special advisor to the assistant secretary of state for inter-American affairs, and Tambs became ambassador to Colombia.

11. The Monroe Doctrine (1823) essentially declared that the Western Hemisphere was within the sphere of influence of the United States. Furthermore, the United States would use unilateral military force, if necessary, to safeguard its vital interests in this hemisphere.

12. The Sandinista Front for National Liberation (FSLN) was formed in the 1960s to overthrow the brutal, antidemocratic, and corrupt Somoza dynasty. After years of armed opposition, Somoza was dethroned. In 1979, Somoza escaped to Miami after emptying the Nicaraguan national treasury (Somoza was later assassinated in Paraguay). McWilliams and Piotrowski (1997) describe post-Somoza Nicaragua as "a devastated country." In Nicaragua, the death toll was between 40,000 and 50,000, 20 percent of the population was homeless, and 40,000 children were orphaned. The industrial base was in ruins. The Somocistas had plundered the country, leaving behind a foreign debt of $1.5 billion" (McWilliams and Piotrowski 1997, 328). This was nonetheless the anticommunist, pro-American Nicaragua that Reagan wished to see restored.

13. As a result, Nicaragua became more dependent on the foreign assistance offered by Cuba and the Soviet Union.

14. Forsythe (2004) poses an interesting rhetorical question when he asks whether the Reagan Administration's creation, organization, and funding of the Contras against the sovereign nation-state of Nicaragua provides an example of state-sponsored terrorism.

15. Reagan gauged democracy by the holding of elections, whether or not the candidates and political parties involved were dominated by the military or were closely associated with death squads. In the 1984 Salvadoran elections, the ARENA party ran Major Roberto D'Aubuisson as their presidential candidate. D'Aubuisson was characterized by U.S. Ambassador to El Salvador Robert White as a "psychopathic killer," responsible for, among other atrocities, the assassination of Archbishop Oscar Romero. Arnson provides the testimony of Ambassador Robert White to a House subcommittee hearing: "from the first days in office the Reagan White House knew—beyond any reasonable doubt—that Roberto D'Aubuisson planned and ordered the assassination of Archbishop Romero" (1989, 143).

16. Donnelly quips that the Reagan team defined democracy as anticommunism plus elections. However, "elections [were] not even necessary for friendly regimes with strong anti-communist credentials" (Donnelly 2004, 100).

17. When asked by Gallup pollsters, in 1983, what they thought was the cause of the civil unrest in Central American, 50 percent of the respondents replied that they believed the cause was poverty and the lack of rights, while only 29 percent believed it was subversion from Cuba, Nicaragua, or the Soviet Union. By 1987, only 19 percent of the respondents indicated that they believed the cause of violence in Central America was communist subversion (Geyer and Shapiro 1988).

18. H.R. 2577, approved on August 15, 1985, was assigned Public Law No. 99-88.

19. Section 502B of the Foreign Assistance Act prohibits the allocation of security assistance to any government that engages in a consistent pattern of gross violations of human rights unless the president certifies extraordinary circumstances making it in the national interests to continue providing military aid.

20. Hilde Hey (1995) observes that the Lucas Garcia regime (1978–1982) was the most repressive of the Guatemalan governments. Amnesty International, the Comite Pro Justicia Y Paz, the UN Working Group on Enforced and Involuntary Disappearances, and the Grupo de Apoyo Mutuo por el Aparecimiento Con Vida de Nuestros Familiares (GAM) all documented over 3,000 cases of torture, disappearance, and extrajudicial executions during Garcia's

regime, twice as many as during the Montt (1982–1983), Victores (1983–1985), and Cerezo (1986–1990) Administrations combined.

21. Public Law No. 99-177. This provision was found unconstitutional in 1987, and a reworked version of the bill passed. However, it failed to prevent large budget deficits. In 1990, the act was again reworked and renamed as the Budget Enforcement Act.

22. In 1983, the Reagan Administration appointed the Commission on Security and Economic Assistance (also called the Carlucci Commission) to explore ways in which the foreign assistance program could be made more efficient and effective in furthering U.S. foreign policy goals. The commission recommended the coordination of economic and security assistance. This provided the Reagan Administration with the rationale to use economic aid for strategic purposes by increasing ESF allocations at the expense of development assistance funding.

23. During the Reagan Administration, U.S. financial and military support began to flow in earnest, providing Savimbi with the edge he needed to push out rival forces. By the late 1980s, the U.S.-backed União Nacional para a Independência Total de Angola (UNITA) controlled nearly half the country.

24. A few examples ought to suffice: Abrams referred to Neier's human rights work as "garbage" (Dobbs 2003), and he called Patricia Derian "romantic, sentimental, and silly" (as quoted in Brown 1985, 10).

25. Reagan declared that El Salvador was a democratic government under threat from communist Nicaragua (itself a tool of Cuban aggression).

26. The U.S. ambassador to Guatemala, Frederick Chapin, absurdly declared, "The killings have stopped. . . . The Guatemalan government has come out of the darkness and into the light" (as quoted in Carothers 1991, 62).

27. Specifically by the testimony of Bob Edgar (D-PA), Barbara Mikulski (D-MD), and Gerry Studds (D-MA).

28. However, following the 1980 report of the murder of Archbishop Oscar Arnulfo Romero while conducting mass, and also later that year of four American churchwomen attributable to the Salvadoran military, Reagan understood that public information of the atrocities of the Salvadoran military would hinder his ability to obtain funding from Congress and the support of the American public. Therefore, in 1981, Reagan appointed Deane Hinton as ambassador to El Salvador. Ruttan writes that Hinton "saw his mission more as limiting the negative publicity generated by the Salvadoran government's repressive policies than as changing the policies themselves" (1996, 319). By October 1982, faced with the irrefutable violence and brutality of the Salvadoran military regime, Hinton became publicly critical of the behavior of the Salvadoran government. Hinton then impugned the Salvadoran government with 30,000 murders in a three-year span. Hinton reported in a speech to the American Chamber of Commerce, "Since 1979 perhaps as many as 30,000 Salvadorans have been MURDERED, not killed in battle, MURDERED" (as quoted in Arnson 1989, 99). Those directly responsible, in Hinton's opinion, were members of the military-controlled Salvadoran government. The number of murdered Salvadorans, as estimated by Reagan's own ambassador to El Salvador, was over 30,000 from 1979 to 1982. One has to wonder what was the limit set before Congress would act.

29. CIA Director William Casey did mention the mining. Casey included a short, single-sentence notification concealed in a eighty-four-page briefing document that he provided to the Senate on March 8, 1984. However, even that veiled remark did not mention that the CIA was involved.

30. Congress would make clear that no government entity may provide any type of aid, either directly or indirectly, to the Contras. The more strongly and carefully worded second Boland Amendment stated,

> No funds available to the Central Intelligence Agency, the Department of Defense, or any other agency or entity of the United States involved in intelligence activities may be obligated or expended for the purpose of which would have the effect of supporting, directly or indirectly, military or paramilitary operations in Nicaragua by any nation, group, organization, movement or individual.

31. Abrams moved from the Bureau of Human Rights and Humanitarian Affairs to the position of assistant secretary of state for inter-American affairs.

32. The Brunei government mistakenly wired the money to the wrong Swiss bank account, and the Brunei donation of $10 million never made it to Abrams's Contra fund.

33. The Iran-Contra scandal involved the sale of weapons to the Iranian government (a government listed by the State Department as a terrorism-supporting state) and the diverting of the profits to the Contras. It is worth noting that the majority of the profits for the arms deals never made it to the Contras. The arms sales are estimated to have generated $16 to $25 million, of which only $3.8 million actually made it to the Contras. Millions of dollars made in the illegal and secretive scam were skimmed off by unknown persons. In 1992, the outgoing president George Bush Sr. pardoned six Iran-Contra defendants: Caspar Weinberger (secretary of defense), Robert McFarlane (national security advisor), Elliot Abrams (assistant secretary of state), and three CIA officials, Alan Fiers, Clair George, and Duane Clarridge. Although Oliver North was indicted on 16 felony counts, in 1989 he was found guilty of only three charges: accepting an illegal gratuity, aiding and abetting in the obstruction of a congressional inquiry, and destruction of documents. On appeal, North's conviction was vacated in 1990. North then became a conservative talk show host.

34. Section 701 requires that U.S. representatives to IFI use their "voice and vote" to encourage human rights conditions by channeling assistance to countries that exhibit good human rights policy.

35. Reagan supported the South African regime, regardless of the apartheid system, because it was staunchly anticommunist in a region experiencing Marxist-inspired civil conflict (Angola). Reagan believed a policy of "constructive engagement" would encourage the powerful white elite class to give up power. Constructive engagement is a policy of engaging the rights-abusing country in cooperative and beneficial relationships (economic, military, or diplomatic) in order to modify this country's offending behavior. The Reagan Administration believed that, by engaging Pretoria in mutually beneficial business relationships, the United States could lure South Africa into the rights-loving and rights-guaranteeing community of states. A policy of constructive engagement necessarily precluded the use of public condemnation of South Africa's human rights abuses. Congress overrode Reagan's veto of the Comprehensive Anti-Apartheid Act by 313 to 83 in the House of Representatives, and 78 to 21 in the Senate.

36. To rescind these economic sanctions, the South African government would have to release Nelson Mandela from prison, repeal the state of emergency, permit the organization of political parties, repeal apartheid laws, and negotiate with black representatives.

37. For example, in order to justify his demand for democratic elections in Nicaragua, Reagan had to promote democratic elections in Chile and El Salvador too.

38. Occasionally, there is disagreement over reporting of a particular country. But, overall, the *Country Reports* are believed to be accurate and factual indications of the human rights situation within a country. The controversy no longer revolves around the accuracy of the reports, but around the relationship between the reports and U.S. foreign policy.

CHAPTER 5

1. The George H. W. Bush White House exemplified the foreign policy–making style known as "muddling through," that is, policy making by small, incremental steps. This style is exemplified by the policy maker's attempt to maintain the status quo by using procedures that proved functional in the past, but once the international environment changes and past policies become inefficient, only the smallest, least risky change in policy is made to fix the new foreign policy problem.

2. Leogrande believes that, instead of helping Bush, Aronson's appointment actually "annoyed liberals and conservatives alike" (1990, 597). Aronson, Leogrande believes, was viewed as a collaborator by the liberals and a liberal by conservatives. Aronson helped Reagan to persuade swing Democrat Congress members to vote for Contra aid.

3. The U.S. State Department, on the twelfth anniversary of the atrocity, stated that Saddam Hussein's chemical weapons attack on Halabja was not an isolated incident. It was part of a systematic campaign ordered by Saddam Hussein and led by his lieutenant, Ali Hassan al-Majid, the infamous "Chemical Ali," against Iraqi Kurdish civilians. International observers estimate Iraqi forces killed 50,000 to 100,000 people during the 1988 campaign known as "Anfal." (Boucher 2001a)

4. But, of course, the argument can easily be made that the main culprits in the elimination of the freedom of the press were the media themselves, who prostrated themselves to the White House. One wonders what happened to the great American tradition of investigative reporting or to the role of the heroic war correspondent.

5. In addition to signing the Slavery Convention in the 1950s, both China and the U.S. signed the Supplementary Convention on the Abolition of Slavery, the Slave Trade, and Institutions and Practices Similar to Slavery in 1959 and 1967 respectively.

6. During the Cold War, the Soviets supported Somalia as a client state because Ethiopia (its historic rival) was a Western client. But when a coup established a Marxist government in Ethiopia, the Soviets backed Ethiopia instead (it was larger and had better access to the Gulf). Somalia then looked to the United States for support, and the United States was only too happy to provide Somalia with weapons and foreign aid.

7. "Pipeline" refers to the weapons, spare parts, and weapons systems that have already been approved by Congress and are in the process of being built, manufactured, assembled, or delivered. Generally, even if Congress chooses to suspend aid due to human rights abuses or other restrictions found in U.S. legislation, aid already in the pipeline is not affected.

CHAPTER 6

1. The Clinton Administration claimed that it adopted a global crusade to spread democracy despite this policy's failure during the Reagan Administration. Although democracy would not be used to counter communism, as it was for the Reagan Administration, it would now be used as a tool to directly serve U.S. economic interests. This belief was clearly exposed in a statement made by John Shattuck, assistant secretary of state for democracy, human rights, and labor, and J. Brian Atwood, administrator of the U.S. Agency for International Development. They stated, "U.S. democracy-promotion policy is based on the realistic premise that in today's global market, open societies with democratic governance have the best chance to produce stable and equitable economic development" (Shattuck and Atwood 1998, 168).

2. The Inter-Agency Group on Human Rights and Foreign Assistance, known as the Christopher Committee, was formed to coordinate U.S. human rights policy and examine foreign aid proposals in the context of a recipient country's human rights practices.

3. The special assistant to the secretary and coordinator of international labor affairs was consolidated with the Bureau of Human Rights and Humanitarian Affairs to form the Bureau of Democracy, Human Rights and Labor. Patricia Derian, assistant secretary for human rights and humanitarian affairs under the Carter Administration, was reported to believe that the Clinton Administration's renaming of the bureau in charge of human rights was actually a calculated attempt to downplay the issue of human rights (Hartmann 2001, 403). Democracy and labor rights negotiations often require a conciliatory and compromising attitude, while human rights issues tend to be more confrontational, resulting in the propensity for State Department officials to overlook human rights concerns in order to further the policy of democratic and market economy enlargement. Jack Donnelly, on the other hand, believes that the name change reveals a deeper understanding that human rights protections, in the wake of the fall of Soviet communism, require the building of democratic institutions and sustaining of the democratization process (2004).

4. Clinton's inclusion of respected human rights advocates into the administration did lead to one intriguing trend: human rights NGOs now challenged and criticized their former colleagues who moved into government service.

5. Clinton, in a November 4, 1992, interview with *Nightline: ABC News*, promised to focus on the domestic economy "like a laser beam."

6. President William Howard Taft (1909–1913) first pursued a foreign policy strategy characterized as "dollar diplomacy." From the perspective of dollar diplomacy, the goal of foreign policy and the role of the State Department are to create stability in order to promote and protect American commercial interests and open foreign markets for U.S. investment. The use of economic power rather than military power is to "substitute dollars for bullets" and to influence foreign governments for the benefit of commercial interests.

7. It has been widely argued that Clinton won the presidency as a result of his focus on the nation's economy. His slogan, "It's the economy, stupid," resonated with the American public, who appeared to have little concern for foreign policy and diplomacy at the time. Still, foreign issues did surface that required a response by Clinton.

8. Heilbrunn (1998) reports that Clinton's undersecretary of state, Stuart Eizenstat, was heavily and directly involved in the creation of USA*Engage. This is a charge Eizenstat has denied.

9. Unocal withdrew from the proposed Central Asian gas pipeline project in December of 1998 due to unrelenting pressure from human rights and feminist NGOs and the growing international militancy of the Taliban (Talbot 2002).

10. The goals of the Clinton Administration's conventional arms transfer policy were as follows:

1. Ensuring that our military forces can continue to enjoy technological advantages over potential adversaries.
2. Helping allies and friends deter, or defend against, aggression while promoting interoperability with U.S. forces when combined operations are called for.
3. Ensuring regional stability in areas critical to U.S. interests while preventing the proliferation of weapons of mass destruction and their missile delivery systems.
4. Promoting peaceful conflict resolution and arms control, supporting regional stability, avoiding human rights violations, and promoting other U.S. foreign policy objectives such as the growth of democratic states.
5. Supporting the ability of the U.S. defense industrial base to meet U.S. defense requirements and maintain long-term military technological superiority at lower costs (Newsom 1995).

10. The Helms-Burton Act (officially known as the Cuban Liberty and Democracy Solidarity Act of 1996) is named after its sponsors, Senator Jesse Helms (R-NC) and Representative Dan Burton (R-IN). This law violates international trade law by penalizing foreign companies that do business with Cuba. The Iran-Libya Sanctions Act of 1996 punishes foreign businesses or individuals who do business, by exporting certain goods and technologies or by purchasing more than $40 million in oil or gas, with either country.

11. Russia's brutal military campaign against Chechnyan separatist insurgents—often involving the targeting of the civilian population—was ignored by the Clinton Administration.

12. Among the most significant modifications for UN peacekeeping operations was the determination that U.S. troops would only participate in UN peacekeeping operations if they served under U.S. commanders. PDD-25 restricted U.S. participation unless the peacekeeping operation met the following guidelines:

There is minimal risk to U.S. soldiers.
There are identifiable U.S. interests at stake.
There is a clearly defined mandate with a specified duration.
There are sufficient resources and political will to undertake a successful operation.
There is an exit strategy.

The National Security Restoration Act, a component of the 104th Congress' Contract with America, further restricted the use of U.S. troops in military operations, specifically UN peacekeeping operations, which place these troops directly under foreign command.

13. Des Forges (2004) reports that, by 1998, the Europeans alleged that 200,000 people were missing or killed in Rwanda, while the United States would only acknowledge the murder of 50,000 people, mainly civilians.

14. The Peace, Prosperity and Democracy Act (H.R. 3765) sought to provide a new direction for foreign aid by reorganizing foreign aid around five foreign policy topics:

Title I: Sustainable development.

Title II: Building democracy—this would provide military and economic aid to countries, particularly newly independent states (NIS) and Eastern European countries, in their transition to democracy.

Title III: Promoting peace—this would be used in regional conflicts to resolve those conflicts, to counter security threats, and to promote collective security arrangements.

Title IV: Humanitarian and crisis aid.

Title V: Trade and investment.

15. The Trafficking Victims Protection Act reduces presidential options by requiring the imposition of sanctions. The TVPA states,

SEC. 110. Actions Against Governments Failing To Meet Minimum Standards.
(a) Statement of Policy—It is the policy of the United States not to provide nonhumanitarian, nontrade-related foreign assistance to any government that—
(1) does not comply with minimum standards for the elimination of trafficking;
(2) is not making significant efforts to bring itself into compliance with such standards.
(b) Reports to Congress.—
(1) Annual Report.—No later than June 1 of each year, the Secretary of State shall submit to the appropriate congressional committees a report with respect to the status of severe forms of trafficking in persons that shall include—
(A) a list of those countries, if any, to which the minimum standards for the elimination of trafficking are applicable and whose governments fully comply with such standards;
(B) a list of those countries, if any, to which the minimum standards for the elimination of trafficking are applicable and whose governments do not yet fully comply with such standards but are making significant efforts to bring themselves into compliance; and
(C) a list of those countries, if any, to which the minimum standards for the elimination of trafficking are applicable and whose governments do not fully comply with such standards and are not making significant efforts to bring themselves into compliance.

16. Later, in 1999, it was extended to include training programs authorized under the Defense Department Appropriations bill. The Leahy Amendment in the Defense Appropriations Act (Sec. 8092 of P.L. 106-259) covers only training.

CHAPTER 7

1. Gerald Ford was the first United States president who was not elected to the office of either the president or the vice president. Gerald Ford became the vice president of the United States in 1973, when Spiro Agnew resigned from office after being charged with tax evasion, bribery, and extortion. Ford would later assume the presidency after the resignation of Richard Nixon in 1974.

2. The only other president with a lower honeymoon public approval rating was the nonelected president, Gerald Ford. Ford suffered public disapproval and censure due to his pardon of Richard Nixon.

3. Bush's use of the concept of "evil" and his global crusade against it were reminiscent of Reagan's rhetoric. Bush, like Reagan before him, combined religious fervor with a duty to protect and spread America's values abroad.

4. Neoconservatives were able to influence U.S. foreign policy because, in the words of Elizabeth Drew, "the neoconservatives are powerful because they are cohesive, determined, ideologically driven, and clever (even if their judgment can be questionable), and some high administration officials, including the vice-president, are sympathetic to them" (2003).

5. A few of examples will suffice: Executive Order 13224 (September 23, 2001) froze assets of alleged terrorist groups, businesses, charitable organizations, and individuals; Executive Order 13290 (March 20, 2003) confiscated Iraqi property to be used to assist in the reconstruction of Iraq; and Executive Order 13338 (May 11, 2003) placed economic sanctions against Syria for its support of terrorist groups.

6. The Geneva Conventions are a series of treaties that set the standard for the treatment of prisoners during war or during a humanitarian crisis. The Geneva Conventions include the First Geneva Convention (1864), concerning the treatment of battlefield casualties; the Second Geneva Convention (1906), extending the principles from the first convention to apply to war at sea; the Third Geneva Convention (1929), involving the treatment of prisoners of war; and the Fourth Geneva Convention (1949), relating to the treatment of civilians during wartime by enemies. In addition, there are two additional protocols to the Geneva Convention: Protocol I (1977), concerning the protection of victims in international war; and Protocol II (1977), relating to the protection of victims in noninternational wars.

7. Ashcroft explained that his notion of American liberty was fashioned on the concept of ordered liberty, which Ashcroft credited to either Edmund Burke or George Washington, depending on which speech you read. The

concept [of ordered liberty] embraces liberty and security as complementary, mutually reinforcing values. Without security, there is no liberty; without liberty, no security . . . the concept of ordered liberty acknowledges that for liberty to thrive in America, America must be secure. (Ashcroft 2003)

A big, all-powerful government bureaucracy connotes security that imparts liberty—a big brother to protect you, in other words.

8. Although the Bush Administration refused to admit that the Iraqi resistance was in fact a guerrilla war, General John Abizaid, commander of U.S. Central Command, was quoted as saying that the resistance to the U.S. occupation of Iraq had all the attributes of "a classic guerrilla-type campaign" (quoted in Gordon 2003).

9. Chalabi was convicted, in absentia, of fraud and embezzlement in the collapse of the Jordanian Petra Bank. Chalabi transferred depositors' money into his own accounts. In addition, the State Department, suspecting mismanagement of the $97 million grant they provided to Chalabi's exile organization, the Iraqi National Congress, conducted an audit and suspended funding due to accounting irregularities. There are lingering, but unsubstantiated, suspicions that Chalabi spied for the Iran government. The Bush Administration's belated disapproval of Chalabi increased his credentials among the Iraqi people. Chalabi was Iraq's deputy prime minister and interim oil minister serving under Ibrahim al Jaafari, Prime Minister under the Iraqi Transitional Authority.

10. The cost of the military occupation only of Iraq, and not including the economic reconstruction, has been estimated to be over $1 billion a week (or $60 billion a year; Magstadt 2004).

11. The members of the Project for a New American Century wrote a letter to Clinton warning that his policies of military spending reductions and inattention to Iraq were threatening U.S. national security. In the letter, they wrote,

The only acceptable strategy is one that eliminates the possibility that Iraq will be able to use or threaten to use weapons of mass destruction. In the near term, this means a willingness to undertake military action as diplomacy is clearly failing. In the long term, it means removing Saddam Hussein and his regime from power. That now needs to become the aim of American foreign policy. (New American Century 1998)

This letter was signed by Donald Rumsfeld, Paul Wolfowitz, and Richard Perle, among others.

12. The nation-building exercises in Afghanistan and Iraq, along with the massive counter-terrorism funding, have put the United States' economy and social systems at risk. According to the General Accounting Office, the budget for combating terrorism was $52 billion for the year 2004 alone. Of this amount, the Department of Defense (DOD) received $15 billion (or 29 percent) of the total, while the Department of Homeland Security was allocated nearly $24 billion, or 45 percent of the funding (United States General Accounting Office 2004). In addition, defense spending increased by approximately $155 billion, a 55 percent increase during Bush's first term.

13. The administration's commitment to MCA proved difficult to translate into a working policy. The program's country selection process and funding were not implemented until the end of 2003. The AIDS program suffered from ideological clashes over the appropriate funding levels for abstinence programs and over whether the program ought to even include issues of prostitution and gay sex. Both programs lost much of their political popularity and had a difficult time actually being funded at the proposed levels.

14. Pakistan has been governed under a sham civilian regime with the election of a national assembly and senate. The real power, however, continues to be wielded by the brutal General Pervez Musharraf as president, chief of army staff, and defense minister.

15. Section 2340A of Title 18, U.S. Code, reads,

(1) "torture" means an act committed by a person acting under the color of law specifically intended to inflict severe physical or mental pain or suffering (other than pain or suffering incidental to lawful sanctions) upon another person within his custody or physical control;

(2) "severe mental pain or suffering" means the prolonged mental harm caused by or resulting from—

(A) the intentional infliction or threatened infliction of severe physical pain or suffering;

(B) the administration or application, or threatened administration or application, of mind-altering substances or other procedures calculated to disrupt profoundly the senses or the personality;

(C) the threat of imminent death; or

(D) the threat that another person will imminently be subjected to death, severe physical pain or suffering, or the administration or application of mind-altering substances or other procedures calculated to disrupt profoundly the senses or personality; and

(3) "United States" includes all areas under the jurisdiction of the United States including any of the places described in sections 5 and 7 of this title and section 46501(2) of title 49.

16. Later, an attachment to the supplemental appropriation for military activity in Afghanistan and Iraq (May 10, 2005) banned the use of funds to render any detainee to a country known to use torture.

17. Richard Clarke, former national coordinator for counterterrorism under George W. Bush, is of the opinion that the CIA is the source of the leak concerning its secret prisons. Clarke maintains that the CIA is disgruntled with the task of jail warden because the CIA understands that the use of torture generally produces unreliable information. Either the captured prisoner is trained to withhold genuine information by disclosing unverifiable false information or the suffering prisoner will say anything he thinks the torturer wants to hear (Clarke 2005).

18. Congress' intelligence committees are charged with overseeing CIA activities. The White House's neglect to inform Congress of CIA covert operations defies U.S. law.

19. The White House has aggressively attempted to prevent congressionally imposed restrictions on its interrogation methods. After the U.S. Senate passed the McCain Amendment, 90 to 9, prohibiting cruel, inhuman, or degrading treatment of detainees while in U.S.

custody, Bush threatened to veto the legislation. After intense negotiations, Bush has accepted a modified version of Senator McCain's amendment.

20. Priti Patel (2005) estimates that the Bush Administration has detained at least 50,000 people in Afghanistan, Iraq, and Guantánamo Bay, Cuba. However, this number does not include the unknown and unnamed detainees, referred to as "ghost detainees," held incognito around the world (Patel 2005).

CHAPTER 8

1. See, for example, Hersh (2004), Human Rights Watch (2005), Patel (2005); Physicians for Human Rights (2004), or Pound and Roane (2004).

2. For example, Philip Bergstroms's UNESCO study on women's human rights notes that regardless of gender the college aged youth of Asia-Pacific are more openly involved in the demand for human rights because of the growing attention of the media on the topic of universal human rights standards (2004). Patrick Bond recognizes the fusing of issues on ending the occupations of Iraq and Palestine, with local demands for human rights (2005).

REFERENCES

Abrams, Elliot. July 30, 1983. Statement before the Subcommittee for the House Banking Committee. Washington, DC: Government Printing Office.

Acharya, Amitav. 1987. The Reagan Doctrine and International Security. *Monthly Review* 38:28–36.

Albright, Madeleine. June 28, 1999. *Remarks by Secretary of State Madeleine K. Albright to the Council on Foreign Relations.* New York: Council on Foreign Relations.

Ambrose, Stephen. 1991. *Nixon: Ruin and Recovery, 1973–1990.* New York: Simon & Schuster.

Americas Watch, Helsinki Watch, and Lawyers Committee for International Human Rights. 1982. *The Reagan Administration's Human Rights Policy: A Midterm Review.* New York: Americas Watch.

————. 1984. The Reagan Administration's Record on Human Rights in 1983. New York: Americas Watch.

————. 1986. The Reagan Administration's Record on Human Rights in 1985. New York: Americas Watch.

Amirahmadi, Hooshang, and Weiping Wu. 1994. Foreign Direct Investment in Developing Countries. *Journal of Developing Areas* 28 (2): 167–190.

Amnesty International. 1980. Amnesty International Report 1979. London: Amnesty International.

Apodaca, Clair. 2001. Global Economic Patterns and Human Rights after the Cold War. *International Studies Quarterly* 45 (4): 587–602.

Arnson, Cynthia. 1989. *Crossroads: Congress, the Reagan Administration, and Central America.* New York: Pantheon.

Ashcroft, John. February 1, 2002. Letter from U.S. Attorney General John Ashcroft to President Bush. http://news.findlaw.com/wp/docs/torture/jash20102ltr.html (accessed April 14, 2006).

————. March 4, 2003. War against Terrorism. Testimony of John Ashcroft before the Senate Judiciary Committee. Washington, DC: Federal Document Clearinghouse.

Aung San, Suu Kyi. 1995. Freedom, Development and Human Worth. *Journal of Democracy* 6 (2): 11–19.

Baker, James, III. January 17, 1989. Statement of Secretary of State-Designate James A. Baker III at Senate Confirmation Hearing before the Foreign Relations Committee. *Current Policy* 1146. Washington, DC: U.S. Department of State.

Ballinger, Jeff. February 13, 1998. Oral Testimony of Jeff Ballinger, Director of Press for Change. Presented to International Child Labor Program, Bureau of International Labor Affairs, U.S. Department of Labor. Washington, DC: U.S. Department of Labor, Bureau of International Labor Affairs.

Bandow, Doug. 1996. Shaping a New Foreign Aid Policy for Today's World. *USA Today* 124 (May): 16–17.

Barilleaux, Ryan, and Mark Rozell. 2004. *Power and Prudence: The Presidency of George H. W. Bush*. College Station: Texas A&M University Press.

Barkey, Henri. 2004. United States, Turkey and Human Rights Policy. In *Implementing U.S. Human Rights Policy*, ed. Debra Liang-Fenton, 363–400. Washington, DC: United States Institute of Peace Press.

BBC. July 2, 1998. World: Asia-Pacific, Clinton Upbeat on China's Human Rights. BBC Online Network. http://news.bbc.co.uk (accessed September 3, 2005).

Bennett, William. 2003. *Why We Fight: Moral Clarity and the War on Terrorism*. Washington, DC: Regnery Publishing Inc.

Berger, Sandy. September 8, 1999. White House Press Briefing by National Security Advisor Sandy Berger and National Economic Advisor Gene Sperling. http://hongkong.usconsulate.gov/uscn/wh/db/1999/0908.htm (accessed September 3, 2005).

Bergstrom, Philip. 2004. *Women's/Gender Studies in Asia–Pacific*. Bangkok: UNESCO.

Bloomfield, Lincoln. January 11, 1981. The Carter Human Rights Policy: A Provisional Appraisal. Donated Historical Material, box 34. Jimmy Carter Library, Atlanta, GA.

Bolton, John R. 1994. Wrong Turn in Somalia. *Foreign Affairs* 73 (January–February): 56–66.

Bond, Patrick. 2005. A New War? On Wolfowitz' World Bank. www.counterpunch.org/bond03232005.html (accessed April 12, 2006).

Borowiec, Andrew. 1994. U.S. Called Partner in Colombian Murders. *Washington Times*, March 16, A1.

Bosworth, Stephen. 1981. Statement before the Subcommittee for the House Foreign Affairs Committee. *AFP* 1981 (July 30): 1333.

Boettcher, Robert. 1980. *Gifts of Deceit: Sun Myung Moon, Tonsun Park, and the Korean Scandal*. New York: Holt, Rinehart and Winston.

Boucher, Richard. 2001. Anniversary of the Halabja Massacre. U.S. Department of State Press Statement. www.state.gov/r/pa/prs/ps2001/1322.htm. March 16. (accessed April 14, 2006).

———. 2001b. U.S. Department of State Daily Press Briefing. The Department of State Foreign Affairs Network. www.state.gov/DOSFAN. October 2.

Bozorgmehr, Najmeh, and Guy Dinmore. 2003. Blair warns Tehran Not to Hinder Iraq's Rebuilding or Mideast Peace. *Financial Times*, April 29, A1.

Brennan, Tom. 1987. *Uprooted Angolans: From Crisis to Catastrophe*. Washington, DC: U.S. Committee for Refugees.

Brinkley, Douglas. 1997. Democratic Enlargement: The Clinton Doctrine. *Foreign Policy* 106 (Spring): 110–127.

Brown, Cynthia. 1985. *With Friends Like These: The Americas Watch Report on Human Rights and U.S. Foreign Policy in Latin America*. New York: Pantheon Books.

———. 2003. *Lost Liberties: Ashcroft and the Assault on Personal Freedom*. New York: New Press.

Brzezinski, Zbigniew. 1983. *Power and Principle: Memoirs of the National Security Advisor, 1977–1981*. New York: Farrar, Straus & Giroux.

Buncher, Judith. 1977. *Human Rights and American Diplomacy, 1975–1977*. New York: Facts on File.

Burgermann, Susan. 2004. First Do No Harm: U.S. Foreign Policy and Respect for Human Rights in El Salvador and Guatemala, 1980–96. In *Implementing U.S. Human Rights Policy*, ed. Debra Liang-Fenton, 267–298. Washington, DC: United States Institute of Peace Press.

Burkhalter, Holly. 1994–1995. The Question of Genocide: The Clinton Administration and Rwanda. *World Policy Journal* 11 (4): 44–54.

Burr, William, and Michael Evans. December 6, 2001. Ford, Kissinger and the Indonesia Invasion, 1975–76. National Security Archives, George Washington University. www.gwu.edu/~narchives/ (accessed February 26, 2004).

Bush, George H. W. December 14, 1983. Vice President Bush's Meeting with Salvadorian Officials (11530). U.S. Embassy San Salvador/Secretary of State cable.

———. June 5, 1989. News Conference on the Tiananmen Square Massacre. Archived Presidential Documents. www.presidency.ucsb.edu/ws/index.php?pid=17103.

———. August 25, 1989. Statement on U.S. Emergency Antidrug Assistance for Colombia. http://bushlibrary.tamu.edu/research/papers/1989/89082500.html (accessed March 23, 2006).

———. November 21, 1990. Statement on Signing the International Narcotics Control Act, 1990. PL 101-623. http://bushlibrary.tamu.edu/research/papers/1990/90112106.html (accessed March 23, 2006).

———. January 29, 1991. State of the Union Address. www.c-span.org/executive/transcript.asp?cat=current_event&code=bush_admin&year=1991 (accessed March 23, 2006).

———. March 12, 1992. Statement on Signing the Torture Victim Protection Act of 1991. PL 102-25. http://bushlibrary.tamu.edu/research/papers/1992/92031205.html (accessed March 23, 2006).

Bush, George W. November 19, 1999. A Distinctly American Internationalism. Remarks at the Reagan Library, Simi Valley, CA. www.mtholyoke.edu/acad/intrel/bush/wspeech.htm (accessed March 23, 2006).

———. 2001a. Address to a Joint Session of Congress and the American People. www.whitehouse.gov/news/releases/2001/09/200110920-8.html (accessed April 14, 2006).

———. 2001b. Detention, Treatment, and Trial of Certain Non-Citizens in the War Against Terrorism. President Issues Military Order. www.whitehouse.gov/news/releases/2001/11/20011113-27.html (accessed April 14, 2006).

———. January 29, 2002. State of the Union Address. www.c-span.org/executive/transcript.asp?cat=current_event&code=bush_admin&year=2002 (accessed March 23, 2006).

———. February 2002b. Humane Treatment of al Qaeda and Taliban Detainees. www.washingtonpost.com/wpsrv/nation/documents/020702bush.pdf (accessed April 14, 2006).

———. June 1, 2002. Bush: West Point Grads Answer History's Call to Duty. www.usma.edu/publicaffairs/pv/020607.calltoduty.htm (accessed July 19, 2005).

———. June 12, 2002. President Discusses the Future Technology at White House Forum. www.whitehouse.gov/news/releases/2002/06/20020613-11.html (accessed March 23, 2006).

———. June 24, 2002. President Bush Calls for a New Palestinian Leadership. www.whitehouse.gov/new/releases/2002/06/20020624-3.html (accessed October 2, 2005).

———. October 3, 2002. President Reiterates Need for Terrorism Insurance Agreement. Eisenhower Executive Office Building. www.whitehouse.gov/news/releases/2002/10/20021003-6.html (accessed March 23, 2006).

———. February 26, 2003a. President Discusses the Future of Iraq. Washington Hilton Hotel, Washington, DC. www.whitehouse.gov/new/releases/2003/02/iraq/20030226-11.html (accessed October 2, 2005).

———. March 20, 2003b. Bush Informs Congress of U.S. Efforts in Global War on Terrorism. http://usinfo.state.gov/dhr/Archive/2003/Oct/09-168062.html (accessed April 9, 2006).

Callinicos, Alex. 2003. The New Mandarins of American Power: The Bush Administration's Plans for the World. Cambridge, MA: Polity Press.

Carleton, David, and Michael Stohl. 1985. The Foreign Policy of Human Rights: Rhetoric and Reality from Jimmy Carter to Ronald Reagan. Human Rights Quarterly 7 (2): 205–229.

Carothers, Thomas. 1991. In the Name of Democracy: U.S. Policy toward Latin America in the Reagan Years. Berkeley: University of California Press.

Carr, Edward Hallett. 1939. The Twenty Years' Crisis, 1919–1939. New York: Harper & Row.

Carter, Jimmy. 1975. Why Not the Best? New York: Bantam Books.

———. January 20, 1977. Inaugural Address. Weekly Compendium of Presidential Documents 13:87–88.

—————. May 22, 1977. A Foreign Policy Based on America's Essential Character. Commencement Address at Notre Dame University. *Public Papers of the President of the United States*. Washington, DC: Government Printing Office.

Christopher, Warren. 1979. Testimony. Human Rights and U.S. Foreign Assistance: Experiences and Issues in Policy Implementation (1977–1978). Senate Committee on Foreign Relations. Report by the Foreign Affairs and National Defense Division, C.R.S. Library of Congress, November 1979.

—————. February 14, 1995. Statement before the Senate Foreign Relations Committee. *US Department of State Dispatch* 6:111–17. http://dosfan.lib.uic.edu/ERC/briefing/dossec/1995/9502/950214dossec.html (accessed April 10, 2006).

Cingranelli, David. 1993. *Ethics, American Foreign Policy and the Third World*. New York: St. Martin's.

Clarke, Duncan. 1998. Why State Can't Lead. In *Readings in the Politics of United States Foreign Policy*, ed. Jerel Rosati, 104-14. Fort Worth, TX: Harcourt Brace.

Clarke, Duncan, Daniel O'Conner, and Jason Ellis. 1997. *Send Guns and Money: Security Assistance and U.S. Foreign Policy*. Westport, CT: Praeger.

Clarke, Richard. December 2, 2005. Interview by Charlie Rose. *The Charlie Rose Show*. Television broadcast, PBS.

Clinton, William. December 12, 1991. A New Covenant for American Security. Remarks to Students at Georgetown University. www.dlc.org/ndol_ci.cfm?kaid=128&subid=174&contentid=2783 (accessed March 23, 2006).

—————. November 4, 1992. Interview. *Nightline*. Television broadcast, ABC.

—————. September 27, 1993. Remarks of President Clinton to the 48th Session of the United Nations General Assembly in New York City. *Weekly Compilation of Presidential Documents* (October 4): 1901–08, www.findarticles.com/p/articles/mi_m2889/is_n39_v29/ai_14576028 (accessed March 23, 2006).

—————. March 17, 1994. While America Watched: The Bosnia Tragedy. *Peter Jennings Reporting*, ABC News.

—————. June 22, 1999. Remarks by the president to the KFOR Troops. Skoje, Macedonia. www.clintonfoundation.org/legacy/062299-speech-by-president-to-kfor-troops-in-macedonia.htm (accessed April 14, 2006).

Cohen, Roberta. 1979. Human Rights Decision-Making in the Executive Branch: Some Proposals for a Coordinated Strategy. In *Human Rights and American Foreign Policy*, ed. Donald Kommers and Gil Loescher, 216–246. Notre Dame, IN: University of Notre Dame Press.

—————. 1982. Human Rights Diplomacy: The Carter Administration and the Southern Cone. *Human Rights Quarterly* 4 (2): 212–242.

Cohen, Stephen B. 1982. Conditioning U.S. Security Assistance on Human Rights Practices. *American Journal of International Law* 76 (2): 246–279.

Committee of Santa Fe. 1980. *A New Inter-American Policy for the Eighties*. Washington, DC: Council for Inter-American Security.

Cooper, Mary. 2002. Foreign Aid after Sept. 11. *CQ Researcher* 12 (16): 361–392.

Corwin, Edward. 1957. *The President: Office and Powers, 1787–1957*. New York: New York University Press.

Crabb, Cecil. 1982. *The Doctrines of American Foreign Policy*. Baton Rouge: Louisiana State University Press.

Crabb, Cecil, and Pat Holt. 1980. *Invitation to Struggle: Congress, the President and Foreign Policy*. Washington, DC: Congressional Quarterly Press.

Crabb, Cecil, and Kevin Mulcahy. 1995. George Bush's Management Style and Operation Desert Storm. *Presidential Studies Quarterly* 25 (Spring): 251–267.

Crelinsten, Ronald, and Alex Schmid. 1995. *The Politics of Pain: Torturers and Their Masters*. Boulder, CO: Westview Press.

Des Forges, Alison. 2004. Learning from Disaster: U.S. Human Rights Policy in Rwanda. In *Implementing U.S. Human Rights Policy*, ed. Debra Liang-Fenton, 29–50. Washington, DC: United States Institute of Peace Press.

Dietrich, John. 1999. Interest Groups and Foreign Policy: Clinton and the China MFN Debates. *Presidential Studies Quarterly* 29 (2): 280–296.

Dobbs, Michael. 2003. Back in Political Forefront: Iran-Contra Figure Plays Key Role on Mideast. *Washington Post*, May 27, A1.

Donnelly, Jack. 1993. *International Human Rights*. Boulder, CO: Westview Press.

———. 1995. Post–Cold War Reflections on the Study of International Human Rights. In *Ethics and International Affairs: A Reader*, ed. Joseph Rosenthal, 242–70. Washington, DC: Georgetown University Press.

———. 2004. International Human Rights: Unintended Consequences of the War on Terrorism. In *Wars on Terrorism and Iraq*, ed. Thomas Weiss, Margaret Crahan, and John Goering, 98–112. New York: Routledge.

Donnelly, Jack, and Debra Liang-Fenton. 2004. Introduction. In *Implementing U.S. Human Rights Policy*, ed. Debra Liang-Fenton, 3–28. Washington, DC: United States Institute of Peace Press.

Doyle, Kate. May 11, 2003. Human Rights and the Dirty War in Mexico. National Security Archives. George Washington University. www.gwu.edu/~narchives/ (accessed October 2, 2005).

Drew, Elizabeth. 1977. *American Journal: The Events of 1976*. New York: Random House.

———. 1994. *The Clinton Presidency*. New York: Simon & Schuster.

———. 2003. The Neocons in Power. *The New York Review of Books* 50 (10): www.nybooks.com (accessed September 3, 2005).

Drezner, Daniel. 2000. Ideas, Bureaucratic Politics, and the Crafting of Foreign Policy. *American Journal of Political Science* 44 (4): 733–750.

Dueck, Colin. 2003–2004. Hegemony on the Cheap: Liberal Internationalism from Wilson to Bush. *World Policy Journal* 20 (4): 1–11.

Dumbrell, John. 1997. *American Foreign Policy: Carter to Clinton*. New York: St. Martin's.

Eizenstat, Stuart. September 8, 1998. Testimony of Under Secretary Eizenstat. Bipartisan Senate Task Force on Sanctions. Washington, DC. http://canberra.usembassy.gov/hyper/WF980909/epf306.htm (accessed March 23, 2006).

Elving, Ronald. 1996. *Congress and the Great Issues: 1945–1995*. Washington, DC: Congressional Quarterly Press.

Farer, Tom. 2004. The Interplay of Domestic Politics, Human Rights, and U.S. Foreign Policy. In *Wars on Terrorism and Iraq*, ed. Thomas Weiss, Margaret Crahan, and John Goering, 29–60. New York: Routledge.

Fisher, Louis. 1998. *The Politics of Shared Power: Congress and the Executive*. College Station: Texas A&M University.

Fiske, Robert. 1991. Free to Report What We're Told. In *Gulf War Reader: History, Documents, Opinions*, ed. Micah Sifry and Christopher Cerf, 376-80. New York: Random House.

Fleck, Robert, and Christopher Kilby. 2001. Foreign Aid and Domestic Politics: Voting in Congress and the Allocation of USAID. *Southern Economic Journal* 67 (3): 598–630.

Forsythe, David. 1987. Congress and Human Rights in US Foreign Policy: The Fate of General Legislation. *Human Rights Quarterly* 9 (3): 382–404.

———. 1988. *Human Rights and U.S. Foreign Policy: Congress Reconsidered*. Gainesville: University of Florida Press.

———. 1990. Human Rights in U.S. Foreign Policy: Retrospect and Prospect. *Political Science Quarterly* 105 (3): 435–454.

———. 1995. Human Rights and US Foreign Policy: Two Levels, Two Worlds. *Political Studies* 43:111–130.

———. 2000. *Human Rights in International Relations*. Cambridge: Cambridge University Press.

———. 2004. U.S. Foreign Policy and Human Rights in an Era of Insecurity: The Bush Administration and Human Rights after September 11. In *Wars on Terrorism and Iraq*, ed. Thomas Weiss, Margaret Crahan, and John Goering, 77–97. New York: Routledge.

Franck, Thomas, and Edward Weisband. 1979. *Foreign Policy by Congress*. New York: Oxford University Press.

Fraser, Donald. 1977. Freedom and Foreign Policy. *Foreign Policy* 26:140–156.

————. 1979. Congress' Role in the Making of International Human Rights Policy. In *Human Rights and American Foreign Policy*, ed. Donald Kommers and Gil Loescher, 247–54. Notre Dame, IN: University of Notre Dame Press.

Freedom House. 2006. Freedom in the World Comparative Ranking 1973-2005. www. freedomhouse.org/template.cfm?page=15&year=2005.

Frum, David. 2003. *The Right Man*. New York: Random House.

Gabelnick, Tamar. 2002. Security Assistance after September 11. *Foreign Policy in Focus* 7 (4): 10.

Galey, Margaret. 1985. Congress, Foreign Policy and Human Rights Ten Years after Helsinki. *Human Rights Quarterly* 7 (3): 334–372.

Gardner, Richard. 1992. Practical Internationalism. In *Rethinking America's Security: Beyond Cold War to New World Order*, ed. G. Allison and G. F. Treverton, 267–278. New York: Norton.

Garfinkle, Adam. 2001. Strategy and Preventative Diplomacy: US Foreign Policy and Preventive Intervention. *Orbis* 45 (4): 503–517.

Garten, Jeffrey. 2002. A Foreign Policy Harmful to Business. *Business Week Online*, October 14. www.businessweek.com/magazine/content/02_41/b3803085.htm (accessed March 23, 2006).

Gellman, Barton. 2005. The FBI's Secret Scrutiny. *Washington Post*, November 6, A1.

Genova, Jim. 1995. Peace Elusive in Angola. *People's Weekly World,* January 28. www. hartford-hwp.com/archives/37/005.html (accessed January 29, 2005).

Geyer, Anne, and Robert Shapiro. 1988. A Report: Human Rights. *Public Opinion Quarterly* 52 (3): 386–398.

Gibb, Tom. 2002. US Role in Salvador's Brutal War. *BBC News*. March 24. http://news.bbc. co.uk/2/hi/americas/1891145.stm (accessed March 23, 2006).

Gonzales, Alberto. January 25, 2002. Decision Re-application of the Geneva Convention on Prisoners of War to the Conflict with Al-Qaeda and the Taliban. Memorandum to the President. http://msnbc.msn.com/id/4999148/site/newsweek/ (accessed April 10, 2006).

Gordon, Craig. 2003. Iraqi Conflict a "Guerrilla" War. Newsday.com, July 17. www.Newsday.com/news/ (accessed July 19, 2005).

Goshko, John, and Daniel Williams. 1994. U.S. Policy Faces Review by Helms. *Washington Post*, November 13, A1.

Greenberger, Robert. 1995. Dateline Capitol Hill: The New Majority's Foreign Policy. *Foreign Policy* 101 (Winter): 159–170.

Gwertzam, Bernard. 1977. Security Links Cited. *New York Times,* February 25, 1-2.

Haass, Richard. 2002. Defining U.S. Foreign Policy in a Post–Cold War World. April 22. www.state.gov/s/p/9632.htm (accessed July 19, 2005).

Hartmann, Hauke. 2001. US Human Rights Policy under Carter and Reagan, 1977–1981. *Human Rights Quarterly* 23 (2): 402–430.

Hastedt, Glenn. 1997. *American Foreign Policy*. Upper Saddle River, NJ: Prentice Hall.

Heaps, David. 1984. *Human Rights and U.S. Foreign Policy*. New York: American Association for the International Commission of Jurists.

Heilbrunn, Jacob. 1998. The Sanctions Sellout: The Corporate Takeover of Foreign Policy. *New Republic* 218 (21): 21–26.

Hersh, Seymour. May 24, 2004. The Gray Zone. *New Yorker*. www.newyorker.com/fact/content/?040524fa_fact (accessed March 23, 2006).

Hertzke, Allen, and Daniel Philpott. 2000. Defending the Faiths. *National Interest* 61 (Fall): 74–81.

Hey, Hilde. 1995. *Gross Human Rights Violations: A Search for Causes*. Amsterdam: Martinus Nijhoff.

Hook, Steven, and John Spanier. 2002. *American Foreign Policy since World War II*. Washington, DC: Congressional Quarterly Press.

House Foreign Affairs Committee. 1989. *Report of the Task Force on Foreign Assistance.* Washington, DC: House of Representatives.

Hoy, Paula. 1998. *Players and Issues in International Aid.* West Hartford, CT: Kumarian Press.

Human Rights: A Suitable Target for Foreign Policy? 1997. *Economist,* April 12, 15–20.

Human Rights Watch. 1989. Nicaragua. www.hrw.org/reports/1989/WR89/Nicaragu.htm (accessed March 23, 2006).

———. 1992. World Report 1992. www.hrw.org/reports/1992.wr92 (accessed March 5, 2005).

———. 1993. *State of War: Political Violence and Counterinsurgency in Colombia.* New York: Human Rights Watch.

———. 2000. World Report 2000. www.hrw.org/wr2k/wrd.htm (accessed April 10, 2006).

———. 2002. Leading Liberian Journalist Re-arrested: Facing Possible "Terrorist" Charges. www.hrw.org/press/2002/07/liberia0704.htm (accessed December 10, 2004).

———. 2005. *Still at Risk: Diplomatic Assurances No Safeguard against Torture.* http://hrw.org/reports/2005/eca0405/ (accessed April 10, 2006).

Hutchison, Kay Bailey. July 9, 1999. *A Foreign Policy Vision for the Next American Century.* Heritage Lecture no. 639. Washington, DC: Heritage Foundation.

Hyland, William. 1999. *Clinton's World: Remaking American Foreign Policy.* Westport, CT: Praeger.

Ingersoll, Robert. June 1974. Testimony. Fiscal Year 1975 Foreign Assistance Request: Hearing before the House Committee on Foreign Affairs, 93rd Congress, 2nd Session, 280–281. Washington, DC: U.S. Government Printing Office.

Jacoby, Tamar. 1986. Did Carter Fail on Human Rights? *Washington Monthly* 18 (6): 1–57.

———. 1986. The Reagan Turnaround on Human Rights. *Foreign Affairs* 64 (Summer): 1066–1086.

Jewett, Aubrey, and Marc Turetzky. 1998. Stability and Change in President Clinton's Foreign Policy Beliefs, 1993–96. *Presidential Studies Quarterly* 28 (3): 638–665.

Kagan, Robert. 1988. Losing in Latin America. *Commentary.* 86 (5): www.commentarymagazine.com.

———. 2001. Clinton Legacy Abroad: His Sins of Omission in Foreign and Defense Policy. *Weekly Standard,* January 15, 25–28.

Kane, John. 2003. American Values or Human Rights? U.S. Foreign Policy and the Fractured Myth of Virtuous Power. *Presidential Studies Quarterly* 33 (4): 722–800.

Kaplan, Lawrence, and Sarah Wildman. 2000. Would W.'s Israel Policy Be as Bad as His Father's? *The New Republic,* November 6, 24-26.

Kaufman, Victor. 1998. The Bureau of Human Rights during the Carter Administration. *Historian* 61(1): 51–66.

Kegley, Charles, Jr. 1989. The Bush Administration and the Future of American Foreign Policy: Pragmatism, or Procrastination? *Presidential Studies Quarterly* 19 (4): 717–732.

Kennan, George. 1985–1986. Morality and Foreign Policy. *Foreign Affairs* 64 (Winter): 205–18.

Kennedy, John F. March 22, 1961. Special Message to the Congress on Foreign Aid. www.jfklink.com/speeches/jfk/publicpapers/1961/jfk90_61.html (accessed March 23, 2006).

Kinzer, Stephen. 1983. Human Rights Aide Defends U.S. Policy. *New York Times,* January 20, A3.

Kirkpatrick, Jeane. 1979. Dictatorships and Double Standards. *Commentary* 68:34–45.

Kissinger, Henry A. 1973. Statement of Secretary of State-Designate Henry A. Kissinger at Senate Confirmation Hearing before the Foreign Relations Committee. *Current Policy* 503. Washington, DC: U.S. Department of State.

Klare, Michael. 2001. U.S. Aid to Colombia's Military: The Oil Connection. *North American Congress on Latin America (NACLA) Report on the Americas* 34 (4): 20–21.

Klinghoffer, Arthur Jay. 1998. *The International Dimension of Genocide in Rwanda.* New York: New York University Press.

Korey, William. 1983. *Human Rights and the Helsinki Accord.* Foreign Policy Association no. 264. New York: Foreign Policy Association.

————. 1990. The Helsinki Accord: A Growth Industry. *Ethics and International Affairs* 4:53–70.

————. 2001. Human Rights NGOs: The Power of Persuasion. *Ethics and International Affairs* 13:151–175.

Kowert, Paul. 2002. *Groupthink or Deadlock: When Do Leaders Learn from Their Advisors?* Albany: State University Press of New York.

Lancaster, Carol. 2000. *Transforming Foreign Aid: U.S. Assistance in the 21st Century.* Washington, D.C.: Institute for International Economics.

Lawyers Committee for Human Rights. 1989. *Human Rights and US Foreign Policy: Linking Security Assistance and Human Rights.* New York: LCHR.

————. March 2003. *Imbalance of Powers.* New York: LCHR. www.lchr.org/us_law/loss/imbalance/powers.pdf (accessed October 2, 2005).

Leogrande, William. 1990. From Reagan to Bush: The Transition in US Policy towards Central America. *Journal of Latinamerican Studies* 22 (3): 595–621.

Levy, Leonard. 1997. Foreign Policy and War Powers: The Presidency and the Framers. *American Scholar* 66 (2): 271–275.

Liang-Fenton, Debra. 2004. *Implementing U.S. Human Rights Policy.* Washington, DC: United States Institute of Peace Press.

Lindsay, James. 2003. Deference and Defiance: The Shifting Rhythms of Executive-Legislative Relations in Foreign Policy. *Presidential Studies Quarterly* 33 (3): 530–547.

Lippman, Thomas. 1997. State Department Seeks Gain for Women. *Washington Post,* March 25, A01.

Lumsdaine, David. 1993. *Moral Vision in International Politics: The Foreign Aid Regime, 1949–1989.* Princeton, NJ: Princeton University Press.

Maechling, Charles. 1983. Human Rights Dehumanized. *Foreign Policy* 52 (Fall): 118–135.

Magstadt, Thomas. 2004. *An Empire if You Can Keep It.* Washington, DC: Congressional Quarterly Press.

Matlock, Jack, Jr. 2004. U.S. Policy on Human Rights in Relations with the USSR, 1961–1991. In *Implementing U.S. Human Rights Policy,* ed. Debra Liang-Fenton, 245–65. Washington, DC: United States Institute of Peace Press.

Maw, Carlyle. 1976. Testimony. International Security Assistance Act of 1976: Hearing before the House Committee on International Relations, 94th Congress, 1st and 2nd Sessions, 207–8. Washington, DC: U.S. Government Printing Office.

Maxfield, Sylvia. 1998. Understanding the Political Implications of Financial Internationalization in Emerging Market Countries. *World Development* 26 (7): 1201–1219.

Maynard, Edwin. 1989. The Bureaucracy and Implementation of US Human Rights Policy. *Human Rights Quarterly* 11 (2): 175–248.

McDougall, Walter. 1997. Back to Bedrock: The Eight Traditions of American Statecraft. *Foreign Affairs* 76 (2): 134–146.

McNamara, Thomas. 1991. *Clear and Present Dangers: The U.S. Military and the War on Drugs in the Andes.* Washington, DC: Washington Office on Latin America.

McWilliams, Wayne, and Harry Piotrowski. 1997. *The World Since 1945: A History of International Relations.* Boulder, CO: Lynne Rienner.

Mead, Walter. 2002. *Special Providence: American Foreign Policy and How It Changed the World.* New York: Routledge.

Mertus, Julie. 2004. *Bait and Switch: Human Rights and U.S. Foreign Policy.* New York: Routledge.

Meyer, Karl. 1999. Enforcing Human Rights. *World Policy Journal* 16 (3): 45–50.

Meyer, William. 1998. *Human Rights and International Political Economy in Third World Nations.* Westport, CT: Praeger.

Milbank, Dana. 2002. In War, It's Power to the President. *Washington Post,* November 20, A1.

Moens, Alexander. 1990. *Foreign Policy under Carter.* Boulder, CO: Westview Press.

Morgenthau, Hans. 1949. *Politics among Nations: The Struggle for Power and Peace.* New York: Knopf.

Morrison, Kevin M., and David Weiner. 2000. Declining Aid Spending Harms U.S. Interests. Overseas Development Council. www.odc.org/commentary/cbpprpt.html (accessed December 10, 2004).

Mower, Glenn, Jr. 1987. *Human Rights and American Foreign Policy.* New York: Greenwood Press.

Mr. X [George F. Kennan]. 1947. The Sources of Soviet Conduct. *Foreign Affairs,* July, 89–106.

Muravchik, Joshua. 1986. *The Uncertain Crusade: Jimmy Carter and the Dilemmas of Human Rights Policy.* Lanham, MD: Hamilton Press.

Murchland, Bernard. 2002. Rethinking the New World Order. *Civic Arts Review* 15 (2): www.car.owu.edu (accessed September 8, 2005).

Nathan, James, and James Oliver. 1994. *Foreign Policy Making and the American Political System.* Baltimore: Johns Hopkins University Press.

Natsios, Andrew. 1997. Humanitarian Relief Intervention in Somalia. In *Learning from Somalia,* ed. Walters Clarke and Jeffrey Herbst, 77–95. Boulder, CO: Westview Press.

Neier, Aryeh. January 24, 1994. Watching Rights. *The Nation* 258 (3): 79.

————. 1996–1997. The New Double Standard. *Foreign Policy* 105:91–101.

New American Century. January 26, 1998. Letter to President Clinton. www.newamericancentury.org/iraqclintonletter.htm (accessed April 14, 2006).

Newberg, Paula. 2004. Missing the Point: Human Rights in U.S.-Pakistan Relations. In *Implementing U.S. Human Rights Policy,* ed. Debra Liang-Fenton, 147–166. Washington, DC: United States Institute of Peace Press.

Newmann, William. 2001. Causes of Change in National Security Processes: Carter, Reagan, and Bush Decision Making on Arms Control. *Presidential Studies Quarterly* 31 (1): 69–103.

Newsom, Eric. 1995. U.S. Conventional Arms Transfer Policy: Press Briefing. *DISAM* 17 (Spring): 40-43, also at www.dsca.mil/PressReleases/ARMSTRAN95.htm (accessed March 23, 2006).

Nixon, Richard M. 1973. *New York Times,* December 23, A01.

Ogata, Sadako. 1995. *The World's Refugees: In Search of Solutions.* UNHCR. Oxford: Oxford University Press.

Oliver, James. 2004. The Foreign Policy Architecture of the Clinton and Bush Administrations. White House Studies 4(1):47-69.

Pastor, Robert. 1991. The Bush Administration and Latin America: The Pragmatic Style and the Regionalist Option. *Journal of Interamerican Studies and World Affairs* 33 (3): 1–34.

Patel, Priti. Winter 2005. Ensuring Accountability: International Law and Post 9/11 U.S. Detention Policy. *Human Rights Brief* 12 (2): 5–8.

Payaslian, Simon. 1996. *US Foreign Economic and Military Aid.* Lanham, MD: University Press of America.

Pew Charitable Trusts. 2004. American Public Opinions Polls. www.pewtrusts.com/pfd/PRC_Sept04_Iraq.pdf (accessed March 5, 2005).

Physicians for Human Rights. 2004. Interrogations, Torture and Ill Treatment: Legal Requirements and Health Consequences. www.phrusa.org/reserach/pdf/iraq_medical_consequences.pdf (accessed March 5, 2005).

Poe, Steven. 1990. Human Rights and US Foreign Aid: A Review of Quantitative Studies and Suggestions for Future Research. *Human Rights Quarterly* 12 (4): 499–512.

Pound, Edward, and Kit Roane. 2004. Hell on Earth. *U.S. News & World Report* 137 (2): 10–18.

Reagan, Ronald. March 10, 1983. Remarks on Central America and El Salvador at the Annual Meeting of the National Association of Manufacturers. www.reagan.utexas.edu/archives/speeches/1983/31083a.htm (accessed December 10, 2004).

————. August 8, 1985. Statement on Signing the International Security and Development Cooperation Act of 1985 Public Law 99-83. www.reagan.utexas.edu/archives/speeches/1985/80885d.htm. (accessed April 14, 2006).

Rosati, Jerel. 1981. Developing a Systematic Decision-Making Framework: Bureaucratic Politics in Perspective. *World Politics* 33:234–252.

————. 1993a. *The Politics of United States Foreign Policy.* Fort Worth, TX: HBJ.

————. 1993b. Jimmy Carter, a Man before His Time? The Emergency and Collapse of the First Post–Cold War Presidency. *Presidential Studies Quarterly* 23 (Summer): 459–476.

Rosner, Jeremy. 1995. *The New Tug-of-War: Congress, the Executive Branch and National Security.* Washington, DC: Carnegie Endowment.

Ross, Jeffrey. 1992. Religion, Human Rights and Foreign Policy: An Interpretive Essay. In *The New World Order: Rethinking America's Global Role,* ed. Carol Rae Hansen. Flagstaff: Arizona Honors Academy Press.

Rossiter, Caleb. 1984. *Human Rights: The Carter Record, the Reagan Reaction.* Washington, DC: Center for International Policy.

Roth, Kenneth. September 9, 1998. Testimony for Human Rights Watch before the U.S. Senate Task Force on Economic Sanctions. Washington, DC: Bipartisan Senate Task Force on Sanctions.

Rubin, Barry. 1987. *Secrets of State: The State Department and the Struggle over U.S. Foreign Policy.* New York: Oxford University Press.

Rumsfeld, Donald. 2001. Secretary Rumsfeld Interview. *New York Times,* October 12, 2001, A1.

Ruttan, Vernon. 1996. *United States Development Assistance Policy: The Domestic Politics of Foreign Economic Aid.* Baltimore: Johns Hopkins University Press.

Salzberg, John, and Donald Young. 1977. The Parliamentary Role in Implementing International Human Rights: A U.S. Example. *Texas International Law Journal* 12:251–278.

Schaefer, Donald. 1998. U.S. Foreign Policies of Presidents Bush and Clinton: The Influence of China's Most Favored Nation Status upon Human Rights Issues. *The Social Science Journal* 35 (3): 407–421.

Schlesinger, Arthur, Jr. 1973. *The Imperial Presidency.* Boston: Houghton Mifflin.

————. 1979. Human Rights and the American Tradition. *Foreign Affairs* 57 (3): 503–524.

————. 1994. The Diplomats, 1939–1979. *Foreign Affairs* 73 (4): 146–51.

Schoultz, Lars. 1981. *Human Rights and United States Policy toward Latin America.* Princeton, NJ: Princeton University Press.

Schulz, William. 2001. *In Our Own Best Interest.* Boston: Beacon.

Sciolino, Elaine. 1998. On Sanctions, Clinton Details Threat to Truth. *New York Times,* April 29, A1.

Shattuck, John. April 1, 1998. Human Rights and Democracy. Statement before the House Committee on Appropriations, Subcommittee on Foreign Operations. Washington, DC: House Committee on Appropriations, Subcommittee on Foreign Operations.

————. 1999. Human Rights and Democracy in Practice: The Challenge of Accountability. In *Deliberative Democracy and Human Rights,* ed. Harold Hongju Koh and Ronald C. Slye, 301–306. New Haven, CT: Yale University Press.

Shattuck, John, and J. Brian Atwood. March–April 1998. Defending Democracy: Why Democrats Trump Autocrats. *Foreign Affairs* 77 (2): 167–170.

Shifter, Michael, and Jennifer Stillerman. 2004. U.S. Human Rights Policy and Colombia. In *Implementing U.S. Human Rights Policy,* ed. Debra Liang-Fenton, 331–361. Washington, DC: United States Institute of Peace Press.

Silberman, Laurence. 1979. Toward Presidential Control of the State Department. *Foreign Affairs* 57 (4): 872–893.

Singer, Hans, John Wood, and Tony Jennings. 1987. *Food Aid.* Oxford: Clarendon.

Skidmore, David. 1993. Carter and the Failure of Foreign Policy Reform. *Political Science Quarterly* 108 (4): 699–730.

Spanier, John, and Steven Hook. 1998. *American Foreign Policy since World War II.* Washington, DC: Congressional Quarterly Press.

Steel, Ronald. 1977. Foreign Affairs: So Far, So So. *Politicks and Other Human Interests* 1(1): 20.

Stephens, Beth. 2004. Upsetting Checks and Balances: The Bush Administration's Efforts to Limit Human Rights Litigation. *Harvard Human Rights Journal* 17 (Spring): 169–205.

Stohl, Michael, David Carleton, and Steve Johnson. 1984. Human Rights and US Foreign Assistance from Nixon to Carter. *Journal of Peace Research* 21 (2): 215–233.

Sullivan, Denis. 2004. U.S.-Egypt Partnership. In *Implementing U.S. Human Rights Policy*, ed. Debra Liang-Fenton, 401–431. Washington, DC: United States Institute of Peace Press.

Sweeny, John. 1999. *Tread Cautiously in Colombia's Civil War*. Background paper #1264. Washington, DC: Heritage Foundation.

Talabot, Karen. 2002. Afghanistan, Central Asia, Georgia: Key to Oil Profits. International Council for Peace and Justice. http://icpj.org/afghanistan.html (accessed April 10, 2006).

Tarnoff, Curt, and Larry Nowels. 2004. *Foreign Aid: An Introductory Overview of U.S. Programs and Policy*. Washington, DC: Congressional Research Service Report for Congress.

Thornton, William. 2000. Back to Basics: Human Rights and Poer Politics in the New Moral Realism. *International Journal of Politics, Culture and Society* 14(2):315-332.

Trimble, Phillip. 2002. *International Law: United States Foreign Relations Law*. New York: Foundation Press.

Tucker, Robert, and David Hendrickson. Spring 1990. Thomas Jefferson and Foreign Policy. *Foreign Affairs* 69:135–156.

Turley, Jonathan. 2003. Presidential Papers and Popular Government: The Convergence of Constitutional and Property Theory in Claims of Ownership and Control of Presidential Records. *Cornell Law Review* 88 (3): 651–732.

UNICEF. September 24, 1998. *Committee on Rights of Child Concludes Review of Situation of Children's Rights in Iraq*. HR/CRC/98/45. New York: UNICEF.

USAID. March 1994. U.S. *Strategies for Sustainable Development*. Washington, DC: USAID.

———. 2002. *Foreign Aid in the National Interest: Freedom Security and Opportunity*. www.usaid.gov/fani/overview/index.htm (accessed March 23, 2006).

———. About USAID. http://www.usaid.gov/about_usaid (accessed April 2, 2006a).

———. USAID History. http://www.usaid.gov/about_usaid/usaidhist.html (accessed April 2, 2006b).

United States Congress. 1973. International Protection of Human Rights: The Work of International Organizations and the Role of US Foreign Policy. Hearing before the Subcommittee on International Organizations and Movements of the Committee on Foreign Affairs, House of Representatives, 93rd Congress, 1st Session. Washington, DC: U.S. Government Printing Office.

———. 1974. *Human Rights in the World Community: A Call for U.S. Leadership*. A report of the Subcommittee on International Organizations and Movements of the Committee on Foreign Affairs, House of Representatives, 93rd Congress, 2nd Session. Washington, DC: U.S. Government Printing Office.

———. 1979. *Senate Report No. 95-841*. A report of the Senate Committee on Foreign Relations, 95th Congress, 2nd Session. Washington, DC: U.S. Government Printing Office.

———. 1981. Foreign Assistance and Related Programs Appropriations for 1982, Hearings, Part 1, 97th Congress, 1st Session. Washington, DC: U.S. Government Printing Office.

———. 1989. New Reports of Human Rights Violations in the Angolan Civil War. Hearing before the House Subcommittee on Africa of the Committee of Foreign Affairs, House of Representatives, 101st Congress, 1st Session. Washington, DC: U.S. Government Printing Office.

United States, Department of Defense. 2003. *Working Group Report on Detainee Interrogations in the Global War on Terrorism: Assessment of Legal, Historical, Policy, and Operational Considerations*. www.washingtonpost.com/wp-srv/nation/documents/040403dod.pdf. (accessed April 14, 2006).

United States, Department of Justice. 2002. *Memorandum for Alberto R. Gonzales, Counsel to the President. RE: Standards of Conduct for Interrogation Under 18 U.S.C.§§ 2340-2340A.* www.washingtonpost.com/wp-srv/nation/documents/dojinterrogationmemo20020801. pdf. (accessed April 14, 2006).

United States, Department of State. 1981. *Country Reports on Human Rights Practices, 1981.* Washington, DC: U.S. Government Printing Office.

——. 1982. *Country Reports on Human Rights Practices, 1982.* Washington, DC: U.S. Government Printing Office.

——. December 1987. *Bulletin.* Washington, DC: U.S. Government Printing Office.

——. 1988. *Country Reports on Human Rights Practices, 1988.* Washington, DC: U.S. Government Printing Office.

——. 1990. *Country Reports on Human Rights Practices, 1990.* Washington, DC: U.S. Government Printing Office.

——. 1994. *Somalia Human Rights Practices*, 1993. http://dosfan.lib.uic.edu/ERC/democracy/1993_hrp_report/93hrp_report_africa/Somalia.html (accessed March 23, 2006).

——. 1999. *Country Reports on Human Rights Practices, 1999.* www.state.gov/g/drl/rls/hrrpt/1999/ (accessed March 23, 2006).

——. Department Organization. http://www.state.gov/r/pa/ei/rls/dos/436.htm (accessed April 2, 2006).

United States, Department of the Treasury. 2003. *Summary: The Multilateral Development Banks.* www.ustreas.gov/offices/interntional-affairs/intl/fy2003/tab/0_multilateral_development_banks.pdf. (accessed April 14, 2006).

United States General Accounting Office. 1993. *The Drug War: Colombia Is Undertaking Antidrug Programs, but Impact Is Uncertain.* Washington, DC: General Accounting Office.

——. March 29, 2004. *Budget of the United States Government: Historical Tables Fiscal Year 2005.* www.gpoaccess.gov/usbudget/fy05/hist.html (accessed March 23, 2006).

Vance, Cyrus. April 30, 1977. Human Rights and Foreign Policy (also known as "Law Day Speech at the University of Georgia"). Reprinted in *The Diplomacy of Human Rights*, ed. David Newsom (Lanham, MD: University Press of America, 1986).

——. 1978. Testimony. Senate Subcommittee on Foreign Operations Appropriations, Foreign Assistance and Related Programs Appropriations for FY 1978. Washington, DC: U.S. Government Printing Office.

Vogelgesang, Sandy. 1980. *American Dream, Global Nightmare.* New York: W. W. Norton.

Washington Post-ABC News Poll. 2006. American Public Opinion Poll. April 10.

——. http://www.washingtonpost.com/wp-srv/politics/polls/postpoll_immigration_041006.htm (accessed April 14, 2006).

Weissbrodt, David. 1977. Human Rights Legislation and United States Foreign Policy. *Georgia Journal of International and Comparative Law* 7:231–284.

Weissbrodt, David. 1981. The Influence of Interest Groups on the Development of United States Human Rights Policies. In *The Dynamics of Human Rights in U.S. Foreign Policy*, ed. Natalie Kaufamn Hevener, 229–78. New Brunswick, NJ: Transaction Books.

Western, Jon. 2004. U.S. Policy and Human Rights in Bosnia. In *Implementing U.S. Human Rights Policy*, ed. Debra Liang-Fenton, 217–244. Washington, DC: United States Institute of Peace Press.

What Foreign Policy? 1991. *The New Republic* 205 (14): 5–7.

White House. May 2001. *Reliable, Affordable and Environmentally Sound Energy for America's Future* [U.S. national energy policy, 2001]. Report of the National Energy Policy Group. www.whitehouse.gov/energy/ (accessed March 23, 2006).

Whitlock, Craig. 2005. U.S. Faces Scrutiny over Secret Prisons. *Washington Post*, November 4, A20.

Wiseberg, Laurie, and Harry Scoble. 1981. Recent Trends in the Expanding Universe of NGOs Dedicated to the Protection of Human Rights. In *Global Human Rights: Public Policies, Comparative Measures, and NGO Strategies*, ed. Ved Nanda, James Scarritt, and George Shepherd, 229–260. Boulder, CO: Westview Press.

White, John, and John Zogby. 2004. The Likeable Partisan: George W. Bush and the Transformation of the American Presidency. In *High Risk and Big Ambition*, ed. Steven Schier, 79–96. Pittsburgh, PA: University of Pittsburg Press.

White, Robert. 1981. Testimony. Foreign Assistance and Related Programs Appropriations for 1982, Hearings, Part 1, 97th Congress, 1st Session. Washington, DC: U.S. Government Printing Office.

Wiarda, Howard. Spring 2000. Beyond the Pale: The Bureaucratic Politics of United States Policy in Mexico. *World Affairs* 162 (4): 174–190.

Wickham, DeWayne. 2000. Ron Brown's Trade-Bill Legacy. *USA Today*, May 30.

Whitlock, Monica. 2003. Legal Limbo of Guantanamo's Prisoners. BBC News/Americas May 16. http://news.bbc.co.uk/1/low/world/americas/3034697.stm (accessed April 10, 2006).

Wolfowitz, Paul. 2000. Statesmanship in a New Century. In *Present Dangers: Crisis and Opportunity in American Foreign and Defense Policy*, ed. Robert Kagan and William Kristol, 307–36. San Francisco: Encounter Books.

Wood, Dan, and Jeffrey Peake. 1998. The Dynamics of Foreign Policy Agenda Setting. *American Political Science Review* 92 (1): 173–184.

World Bank. 2001. *World Development Report 2000/2001: Attacking Poverty*. Oxford: Oxford University Press.

Wright, Robin. 2001. Powell Intends to Curb US Use of Diplomatic Sanctions. *Los Angeles Times*, January 22, A1.

Zimmerman, Robert. 1993. *Dollars, Diplomacy and Dependency: Dilemmas of U.S. Economic Aid*. Boulder, CO: Lynne Rienner.

Zimmerman, Warren. 1999. *Origins of a Catastrophe*. New York: Times Books.

Zunes, Stephen. 2001. Foreign Policy by Catharsis: The Failure of U.S. Policy toward Iraq. *Arab Studies Quarterly* 23 (4): 69–87.

INDEX

Realpolitik, 30–32
Rumsfeld, Donald, 165, 175, 177
Rwanda, 26, 152–154
    Operation Support Hope,
        152–154

S
SALT, *see* Strategic Arms Limitation
    Talks
Salzberg, John, 50–51
Santa Fe Committee, 86–87
Schifter, Richard, 106, 108
Schneider, Mark, 69
Security assistance, *see* Military aid
Shattuck, John, 137, 140
Somalia
    Battle of Mogadishu, 152
    Operation Restore Hope,
        124–125, 151–152
Soviet Union, xvii, 6, 31, 45–46,
    62–64, 73–74, 79, 82–84,
    86–89, 96–98, 112, 116
Strategic Arms Limitation Talks
    (SALT), 62, 64
Subcommittee on Human Rights and
    International Organizations,
    33, 43, 47, 74, 100

T
Taliban, 145, 148, 166, 174–176,
    178, 207
Tiananmen Square, *see* China
Transfers of Excess Defense Articles
    (EDA), 21; *see also* Military
    aid
Turkey, 156, 161–162, 183–184

U
U.S. Agency for International
    Development (USAID),
    14–15, 19–20, 32, 37, 41,
    42, 75, 156, 158, 179, 198,
    201

U.S. Department of Defense (DOD),
    15, 21, 198, 210
U.S. Department of Homeland
    Security, 166, 172, 187, 210
U.S. Department of State, xvii, 10,
    12, 13–14, 20, 46–49, 53,
    75, 97, 108–109, 110, 160,
    198, 200, 201
U.S. Department of the Treasury,
    15–16, 76–78, 104
USA*Engage, 145, 146, 207
USA Patriot Act, 172–173
USAID, *see* U.S. Agency for
    International Development
United States human rights
    legislation; *see also* Human
    rights and foreign aid
    legislation
    International Religious Freedom
        Act, 159–160
    Jackson-Vanik Amendment,
        43
    Leahy Amendment (Foreign
        Operations Appropriation
        Act), 157, 161–162
    Prevention of Genocide Act,
        119
    Torture Victims Protection Act,
        133
    Trafficking Victims Protection
        Act, 160

V
Vance, Cyrus, xvi, 53, 56, 60–63

W
White, Jeremy, 101
Wolfowitz, Paul, 146, 168

Z
Zimmerman, Warren, 126